# Drug Abuse Treatment

by
Robert L. Hubbard
Mary Ellen Marsden
J. Valley Rachal
Henrick J. Harwood
Elizabeth R. Cavanaugh
Harold M. Ginzburg

Foreword by Jerome H. Jaffe

# Drug Abuse Treatment

A National Study of Effectiveness

The University of North Carolina Press
Chapel Hill and London

The paper in this book meets the guidelines for
permanence and durability of the Committee on
Production Guidelines for Book Longevity
of the Council on Library Resources.

93   92   91   90      5   4   3   2

Library of Congress Cataloging-in-Publication Data

Drug abuse treatment : a national study of effectiveness /
by Robert L. Hubbard . . . [et al.].
        p.   cm.
    Bibliography: p.
    Includes index.
    ISBN 0-8078-1864-X (alk. paper)
    ISBN 0-8078-4313-X (pbk.: alk. paper)
    1. Drug abuse—Treatment—United States—Evaluation.
I. Hubbard, Robert L.
    [DNLM: 1. Substance Abuse—therapy.   2. Substance
Dependence—therapy.   WM 270 D793435]
RC564.D774   1989
362.29'0973—dc20                                    89-4937
DNLM/DLC                                                CIP
for Library of Congress

*To the memory of William C. Eckerman,*
*who chaired the advisory committees for the*
*Treatment Outcome Prospective Study, and*
*Milas G. Kirkpatrick, who coordinated*
*and supervised the data collection for the study*

*and*

*To the staff and clients of the programs*
*that participated in the research*

# Contents

# Tables

# Figures

# Foreword

Less than 30 years ago, it was generally accepted that drug addiction was incurable. "Once an addict, always an addict" was the common expression. So widely accepted was this view, even in professional circles, that when in 1958 Synanon, the first "therapeutic community" claimed that former heroin users in Synanon were free of drugs for more than a year it generated national headlines, a full-length movie, and more than a little skepticism. Synanon's confrontational methods, and its rejection of outside professionals, did not help to make it easy to verify its claims or learn from its achievements. From a scientific perspective, there were many reasons to be skeptical. First, there were no control groups. Conceivably, Synanon had found a way to retain the 5 to 10 percent of those heroin addicts who managed to stay abstinent after discharge from other programs such as the Federal Hospital at Lexington. No attempt was made to consider the possible impact of self-selection on the outcomes from Synanon. Second, there was no "objective" verification of abstinence. Even if the results were real and not due to self-selective factors, there were still other important unanswered questions. Would abstinence from opiates be sustained after the addicts left Synanon? Could the process be replicated or did it depend too heavily on the charisma of its founders?

In 1965, before any of these questions could be answered, Vincent Dole and Marie Nyswander announced a very different approach to the treatment of heroin addiction: methadone maintenance. This treatment began from a radically different premise; that heroin dependence reflected a metabolic disease and not, as Synanon proclaimed, fundamental defects in character and maturation. The early success rates claimed for methadone maintenance were as startling as those made by Synanon, but the idea of maintaining heroin users on an opioid drug—even if it was now called a medicine—did not find ready acceptance in many circles and generated bitter hostility in others. There were several major positive points to be made about the early work on methadone maintenance. The reduction in heroin use could be objectively verified with urine tests. The improvements were sustained in the communities where the addicts lived, and it became apparent within two or three years that independent investigators could replicate the results. Yet doubts remained, and for good reason. Control groups were lacking; it was not clear to what degree self-selection influenced the results; and there was no information on when it might prove possible to discontinue methadone.

Variations of these approaches to treatment as well as other distinct modalities such as outpatient drug-free programs soon began to proliferate. It would have been ideal had events permitted a careful evaluation of these approaches to the treatment of addiction, but that was not to be. The mid-1960s found the United States in the grip of an epidemic of illicit drug use, and while the problems involved a range of drugs from marijuana to LSD, amphetamines, and heroin, it was heroin that in the public mind was the drug most clearly associated with overdose deaths and crime in the streets.

Despite the bitter mutual recriminations among proponents of different approaches to the treatment of drug addiction, it was becoming apparent that the old adage about its incurability was wrong. Heroin addicts could recover or at least exhibit significant improvement, less antisocial behavior and more productive activity. The epidemic of addiction and the inability of law enforcement to constrain drug supply left few realistic policy options other than to expand all of those approaches that might reduce the overall cost of drug abuse to society. Yet, even as Richard Nixon's 1971 War on Drugs produced the great expansion of treatment programs across the United States, policymakers recognized that they had no precise or objective measures of which programs produced which changes for which drug users (and for how long, and at what cost). This recognition generated an interest in the development of data bases to provide more definitive and comprehensive information about outcomes.

Several efforts to develop such data were undertaken in the early 1970s (e.g., the Drug Abuse Reporting Program [DARP] at Texas Christian University and the Interdrug Project at Johns Hopkins University). These often suffered from an overreliance on the willingness of new and overburdened treatment programs to provide baseline data and fluctuating support from funding agencies. Despite the problems, DARP and other evaluations were implemented and contributed much needed information. Their results strongly suggested that treatment did have impact, and that for many heroin users the impact was surprisingly strong and long lasting. But there were still almost as many questions left unanswered. Would the successors to the prototypic programs work as well without the initial enthusiasm and leadership of their early innovators? Would they work as well for populations of older drug users? Would they work as well with the clients with the most severe problems who returned again and again, or was their success limited to those most successful clients who went on about their lives? Would they have any impact on the use of drugs other than heroin? Perhaps of central importance for public policy, did the money invested in treatment produce equal or greater benefits than money invested in law enforcement, jails, and other alternative policy actions? It was to answer such questions that in the mid-1970s the National Institute on Drug Abuse initiated additional research to measure the impact of drug abuse treatment.

One goal, a national study of effectiveness, was realized after extensive planning and preparation. The Treatment Outcome Prospective Study (TOPS) was launched in 1976, and the data base continues to be an important resource for the study of treatment effectiveness. This book summarizes the findings of the TOPS, the largest, most comprehensive study of the effectiveness of drug abuse treatment ever undertaken. TOPS was a multi-year study conducted by a team of investigators at the Research Triangle Institute in North Carolina. More than 10,000 drug users who entered treatment in 1979, 1980, or 1981 were interviewed when they first entered 37 selected drug abuse treatment programs in the United States representing three major modalities. These patients were followed at intervals while they were in treatment, and samples of each cohort were reinterviewed at intervals after leaving treatment.

The major finding of this study—that treatment works—may not come as a surprise to those who have been following the literature for the past decade. But this book is a treasure chest of more specific conclusions and insights about which programs work for which patients, about the longer-term impact of treatment, the relative costs and benefits of treatment, the shortcomings of the existing system, the impact of inflation on the ability of these programs to deliver services, and the role that treatment could play in dealing with the current epidemics of cocaine use and AIDS.

This book is likely to stand for many years as the standard in the field, against which other efforts at treatment evaluation will be measured. It will provide valuable information for the discussion of how drug abuse treatment can contribute to reducing the demand for drugs. The book's description of new concepts, refined methods, and detailed findings provides an unparalleled resource for researchers, policymakers, and others who wish to learn more about drug abuse treatment.

Jerome H. Jaffe
Director,
Addiction Research Center of the National Institute on Drug Abuse

# Preface

Despite extensive evidence that treatment of drug abuse does work, questions about its effectiveness continue to be raised. While this book will add to that accumulating evidence, our purpose in writing it is much broader. The problem of drug abuse is complex, and its treatment is difficult. In order to improve the effectiveness of treatment in reducing drug abuse, policy analysts, program directors, and researchers need to understand the factors that contribute to the success of treatment. We need to know more about the clients entering programs, the treatment received, the outcomes during and after treatment, and the returns on public investments in treatment. In order to update and expand current knowledge on these issues, we report on data from a national sample of publicly funded drug abuse treatment programs, the Treatment Outcome Prospective Study (TOPS).

The goal of TOPS was to describe the clients, programs, and outcomes of treatment provided in the period 1979–1981. This study was the second large-scale study of drug abuse treatment. The first was the Drug Abuse Reporting Program (DARP), which examined outcomes for clients entering drug abuse treatment in the years 1969–1974. A third national study, the Drug Abuse Treatment Outcome Study (DATOS), is scheduled to assess outcomes for programs in the 1990s. Each of these studies has built upon the design and findings of previous research. Each also considered the particular problems facing treatment providers at the time the study was implemented. Thus, the results described in this book need to be considered in the context of patterns of drug abuse that have changed as rapidly as the treatment systems designed to reduce them. Although many attempts have been made to control drug abuse over the past century, the problem has persisted, and the nature and extent of abuse has altered dramatically over the past decade. Extensive abuse of multiple drugs and alcohol by young adults in the general population as well as by drug abusers entering treatment has increased.

There have also been far-reaching changes in the drug abuse treatment system. The early treatment system examined in DARP was composed primarily of publicly funded outpatient methadone, residential, and outpatient drug-free programs. The system at the time of the TOPS study was also composed of these three major types of program, but the programs had had time to develop and stabilize. The treatment system which DATOS will study includes a broader array of public and private program types in many settings with various funding sources, including private health insurance and client fees. Further, programs must now allocate resources to educating clients about the risk of transmission of the Human Immunodeficiency Virus (HIV) that causes Acquired Immune Deficiency Syndrome (AIDS) through sharing of contaminated needles and syringes and through sexual intercourse.

Although the data presented in this book were collected from programs operating in the period 1979–1981, the findings remain important for policymakers, program directors, and researchers. This period marked the culmination of a decade of intensive federal, state, and local efforts to design, implement, and sustain a comprehensive system of drug abuse treatment programs throughout the United States. After the Omnibus Reconciliation Act of 1981 established block grant funding of programs through the states, this comprehensive system received less attention and support, resulting in diminishing public expenditures for treatment in the 1980s. This neglect has been recognized and attempts made to rejuvenate the system with increased public funds. How the public treatment system will meet the demands to treat cocaine abuse and prevent AIDS raises many critical questions about treatment effectiveness.

The period covered in the TOPS research, then, is an optimal and critical one for gauging the effectiveness of drug abuse treatment. The publicly funded treatment approaches now available and the basic characteristics of drug abusers appear very similar to those examined in the TOPS research. Although new problems such as AIDS and the cocaine epidemic may change the environment in which programs function, the TOPS data provide fundamental information about clients, treatment, and outcomes in publicly funded programs. Future studies of the effectiveness of publicly funded treatment can use the findings reported in this book as benchmarks to estimate the effectiveness of established, reasonably funded programs and to develop appropriate expectations about returns on increased investment in drug abuse treatment. Further analyses of the Treatment Outcome Prospective Study data are in progress and will result in additional advances in understanding drug abuse treatment effectiveness.

The eight chapters of this book describe the Treatment Outcome Prospective Study, the nature of drug abuse treatment and treatment clients, the reduction of drug abuse and building of productive lives during and after treatment, and the cost effectiveness of drug abuse treatment. Chapter 2 describes the prospective design, methods of data collection and approaches to data analysis for the Treatment Outcome Prospective Study. The types of data collected to examine the nature of drug abuse treatment as well as changes in client behaviors, and types of descriptive and explanatory analyses conducted are delineated. Chapter 3 examines the nature of drug abuse treatment in the three major publicly funded modalities of drug abuse treatment—outpatient methadone, residential, and outpatient drug-free programs. For each modality, information about average size and program structure, therapeutic approaches, available services and financing is presented. This information provides the background for understanding the various treatment settings and their potential impact on drug abuse treatment clients. Chapter 4 describes the sociodemographic characteristics, the nature and severity of drug abuse, and other behaviors of clients entering each of the three major treatment modalities. Changes in client populations over the past decade and within the time period that the Treatment Outcome Prospective Study was conducted are discussed. Because of the distinctiveness of the client populations across the modalities, research findings are presented separately for each population throughout the remainder of the book.

Chapters 5 and 6 examine the major issues by describing, respectively, the nature and extent of drug abuse and the types of behavior that interfere with productive lives before, during, and after treatment. Abstinence and improvement rates for each modality are presented. Factors affecting posttreatment drug abuse and such other behaviors as criminal activity, employment, depression, and alcohol use are examined, focusing on the relationship between these outcomes and the clients' pretreatment characteristics and duration of treatment. Chapter 7 considers the costs and benefits of drug abuse treatment in terms of its impact on crime reduction. Although criminal activity does not account for the total burden of drug abuse to the nation, it constitutes a major portion of the total amount; therefore, changes in criminal activity during and after treatment are a basic measure of treatment impact. Chapter 8 provides an overview of research findings about the major issues and specific problems and discusses unresolved questions about the nature and effectiveness of drug abuse treatment. The conclusions are discussed in terms of confirmation of previous findings and implications for treatment in the future.

Each chapter was based on the extensive data and results produced by the TOPS study, and they summarize and highlight the major findings of a decade of research. Dr. Robert L. Hubbard, senior program director for alcohol and drug abuse research at the Research Triangle Institute, was principal investigator and responsible for overall conduct of the study since its inception. He provided direction for the day-to-day activities, including design of the study, data collection, data analysis, and reporting. Dr. Mary Ellen Marsden, senior research sociologist, played a major role in the analysis of the TOPS data and preparation of research reports and publications. J. Valley Rachal, center director and senior economist, was program director for the study, responsible for project management and timely performance of project tasks. Henrick J. Harwood, a senior economist, developed the cost-benefit analysis summarized in Chapter 7 and examined the effects of treatment on employment. Elizabeth R. Cavanaugh helped coordinate all phases of the study, collaborating in the preparation of questionnaires and study materials and editing major reports and publications. Dr. Harold M. Ginzburg is currently a senior medical consultant in the Health Resources Services Administration responsible for health resources for intravenous drug abusers with AIDS and was project officer for the study when he was at the National Institute on Drug Abuse. He played a major role in developing the study's concept, design, and analysis, and coordinated the management of various phases of the study at the national level.

As we reviewed and summarized findings of the TOPS research, we have confirmed our conviction that treatment can and does work. The findings, however, also show that much needs to be done to improve the publicly funded treatment system as a major means of reducing drug abuse. The system must be strengthened to further meet the new demands placed upon it by the cocaine and AIDS epidemics. We hope this book will help policymakers, administrators, and researchers meet this challenge.

# Acknowledgments

Over the fifteen-year course of the development and implementation of the Treatment Outcome Prospective Study, many organizations and individuals made valuable contributions to the research. We can only cite here some of the major contributors to this effort.

The necessity of a prospective outcome study of drug abuse treatment for the National Institute on Drug Abuse was foreseen by Dr. John C. Scanlon, now at the Addiction Research Center. The support of the succession of NIDA directors, Drs. Robert L. DuPont, William Pollin, Jerome H. Jaffe, and Charles R. Schuster, and the division directors and branch chiefs at NIDA, Drs. Barry S. Brown, Roy W. Pickens, and Marvin Snyder have been essential to the successful development and implementation of the TOPS research. The NIDA has supported this research by a series of contracts (271-75-1016 (WO-01), 271-77-1205, 271-79-3600, and 271-79-3611) and grants (DAO3457, DAO3814, DAO3866). Dr. Frank M. Tims has been the NIDA project director for the grants and has guided and encouraged the broader use of the TOPS data base. Additional funding for the data collection was provided by the National Institute of Justice and a grant (85-IJ-CX-0024) which enabled the detailed study of criminal behavior and the calculation of the cost/benefit ratios described in Chapter 7. Dr. Bernard A. Gropper, the NIJ project officer, helped develop support for these important studies of drug abuse and crime.

Throughout the research, many of the leading experts in the field of evaluation and drug abuse treatment provided valuable guidance and critiques. The advisory committees for TOPS were chaired by the late Dr. William C. Eckerman, Vice President for Social Sciences at RTI, who also provided counsel and institutional support for the RTI research team. Dr. Jay R. Williams coordinated the planning meetings that developed the framework for TOPS, and Marilyn K. Sandorf helped supervise the pretesting of instruments and methods.

The research team for TOPS was assembled from RTI staff having a broad range of expertise. The fundamental task of coordinating and supervising the collection of complete and accurate data was the responsibility of the late Milas G. Kirkpatrick. His intensive and tireless work with programs, interviewers, and the research team was in large part responsible for the success of the study. Others who supervised the data collection in the programs included Beverly Wrenn, Al Williams, and Jeff Hill. The location and interviewing of clients after treatment was directed by Archie T. Purcell and later by Jim Devore with the help of Jeff Hill and Jill Anderson.

The statistical sampling of clients to be followed was directed by the late Dr. Douglas Drummond. Drs. Roy Whitmore, Charles Benrud, and Sara Wheeless developed and implemented the sampling procedures and constructed sampling weights for the follow-up data. Dr. Brenda Cox provided the procedures for imputation of missing data. Data editing and processing was completed by a dedicated staff of editors, coders, and data entry keyers under the supervision of Martha Roberts, Brenda Hair, and Ann Brinkley. The construction of data files and computer analysis involved Linda Quinn, Linda Nixon, Grady Elliott, Tommy Vinson, Danny Allen, Jimmy Knight, Jay Hoge, and Eva Silber.

The authors also benefited greatly from working with a team of investigators who have prepared many of the reports and publications summarized in this book. The Center for Social Research and Policy Analysis at RTI, under the direction of Dr. Alvin M. Cruze, provided an environment which facilitated the collegial interaction of researchers from many backgrounds and disciplines. Dr. James J. Collins has extensively analyzed the criminal behavior of drug abusers and the role of criminal justice system referral reported in Chapter 6. Dr. Robert M. Bray generated approaches to summarizing patterns of drug abuse. Dr. William E. Schlenger assessed the role of alcohol abuse among drug abuse treatment clients and contributed to the development of assessment of patterns of drug abuse. Margaret Allison had a major role in analyses of treatment process and depressive symptoms. Dr. George H. Dunteman provided consultation on the statistical aspects of the analysis. In addition to writing a report on drug abuse before and during treatment, S. Gail Craddock directed the preparation of data files and coordinated the processing for data analysis. Susan Bailey has contributed to a number of the TOPS publications, especially papers on retention, treatment history, and intravenous drug abuse. Terry Crotts worked on the construction of analysis files and later assumed the responsibility for conducting the computer processing. For ten years Donna Albrecht, the secretary for TOPS, has diligently processed the volume of reports, proposals and papers generated in the course of this research as well as the numerous drafts of the manuscript for this book. When needed, other secretarial help was provided by Brenda Smith, Lillian Clark, and Nita Blake.

We would also like to recognize others who contributed directly to the preparation of this book. Paul Betz of the University of North Carolina Press has served as editor of this book, providing encouragement and guidance to expedite publication. A professional development award from RTI was made to Dr. Hubbard to support his time required for the preparation of this manuscript. Finally, we would like to thank the staff and clients of the participating programs and local and state agencies. Without their commitment, cooperation, and support, it would not have been possible to conduct the Treatment Outcome Prospective Study.

# Drug Abuse Treatment

# 1. Introduction

Drug abuse costs the United States billions of dollars every year. The last detailed calculation was $60 billion in 1983 (Harwood et al. 1984). Expenditures for prevention and treatment programs, costs incurred by the criminal justice system in confronting drug-related crime, and welfare support paid out to drug abusers and their dependents in part account for this enormous economic toll. But the related loss in human potential, as measured by the lowered productivity and impaired health associated with drug abuse and by the damages suffered by the victims of drug-related crime, also figures into the staggering cost to the nation. The 1983 estimates, however, were made before the magnitude of the epidemic of Acquired Immune Deficiency Syndrome (AIDS) among intravenous drug abusers was fully recognized (Ginzburg 1984; Turner, Miller, and Moses 1989). Revised cost estimates will need to incorporate the health care expenditures for the increasing numbers of intravenous drug abusers developing AIDS each year.

The design of new, and improvement of existing strategies to effectively reduce drug abuse is, therefore, a critical undertaking. This book investigates the role of treatment in reducing drug abuse, its contributions toward improving other aspects of clients' lives, and its effectiveness in terms of reducing societal costs. The focus is on heroin addiction and the abuse of such other drugs as cocaine, prescription psychotherapeutics (tranquilizers, sedatives, amphetamines, and barbiturates), and marijuana.

The major goal of publicly funded treatment programs is to reduce or eliminate drug use among the abusers and addicts who seek treatment each year in programs across the nation. A further aim of many programs is to lessen the criminal activity that supports addiction. Indeed, the reduction of criminal activity has been one of the major justifications for public support of drug abuse treatment (Courtwright 1982; Jaffe 1987; Musto 1987). Many treatment programs also seek to restore drug abusers to productive lives or to develop their capacity to support themselves. For these reasons, federal, state, and local governments have funded drug abuse treatment programs over the past thirty years. Three types of treatment—methadone clinics, therapeutic communities, and outpatient drug-

*1*

free programs—have been the backbone of the publicly funded system. In recent years, other kinds of inpatient and outpatient programs have emerged, which mainly serve abusers covered by private health insurance (Jaffe 1984; Harwood, Rachal, and Cavanaugh 1985).

In contrast to the efforts to stem the availability of illicit drugs such as heroin and cocaine, treatment programs are meant to reduce the demand for addictive drugs. To date, the payoff from the "supply-side" approach to the nation's drug abuse problem is questionable. Despite the enormous public expenditures for prevention programs, border patrols, drug seizures, and law enforcement, these supply restriction strategies have not ameliorated the crisis of substance abuse and addiction (Nathan 1983; Polich et al. 1984; U.S. General Accounting Office 1988). Although recent surveys suggest a leveling off in the percentage of adults and youth who use drugs (NIDA 1988b), cocaine use escalated during the 1980s (Clayton 1985). Population estimates from the most recent national survey conducted by the National Institute on Drug Abuse (NIDA) indicate that during 1985 almost 37 million adults and youth, or about 19 percent of the population, engaged in illicit or nonmedical drug use (NIDA 1987). Of this number, only about one-half million abusers enter publicly funded drug abuse treatment each year (Butynski and Canova 1988). The numbers of abusers who are addicted, dependent, or who may benefit from treatment is a matter of considerable speculation and debate (Reuter 1984; Spencer 1989). Regardless of the accuracy of estimates of the magnitude of the abusing and addicted populations, treatment offers the major hope for recovery for many abusers. After three decades of clinical experience and careful research, it has been demonstrated that treatment programs have succeeded in helping large numbers of abusers and addicts recover from their dependency on drugs. Although treatment alone will not eradicate the drug abuse problem, treatment can make significant contributions.

Interest in the effectiveness of drug abuse treatment has increased because of the recognition that while other strategies have not been notably effective in stemming drug abuse, treatment can reduce drug abuse and lead drug abusers to more productive lives. But perhaps the most compelling reason for increased interest in drug abuse treatment is the emergence of the AIDS epidemic. It is generally agreed that the sharing of contaminated needles and syringes by intravenous drug abusers is one of the primary means of transmitting the human immunodeficiency virus (HIV). Intravenous drug users are second only to homosexual men in running the risk of contracting AIDS (Turner, Miller, and Moses 1989; Watkins et al. 1988) and comprise one-fourth of the reported AIDS cases. They are also responsible for most of the transmission of the disease through heterosexual intercourse and through perinatal contact between infected mother and fetus (Day et al. 1988; DesJarlais and Friedman 1988). Effective treatment programs that reduce intravenous drug use can, therefore, help to slow the spread of AIDS, which is projected to cost the United States $66.5 billion a year by 1990 (Scitovsky and Rice 1987).

## The Drug Abuse Treatment System

The nature of drug abuse treatment has evolved throughout this century in response to changes in the definitions of drug abuse and addiction, changes in the kinds of drugs being abused, and changes in client populations (Jaffe 1987; Musto 1987). Public support and funding for drug abuse treatment has waxed and waned accordingly. The first efforts were directed primarily at opioid abusers and were generally conducted in medical settings. Opioid drugs include such derivatives of opium as morphine and heroin, as well as synthetic compounds such as methadone and codeine. Treatment is now available for nonopioid abusers as well and is provided in a variety of settings in addition to hospitals. Nonopioid drugs include cocaine, barbiturates and other sedatives, amphetamines and other stimulants, tranquilizers, hallucinogens, and marijuana. Largely financed by public funds, the current system treats addiction, dependency, and abuse related to all types of opioid and nonopioid drugs.

At the beginning of the twentieth century, there was a brief period of publicly supported treatment for morphine addiction. However, by the 1920s support for treatment waned in favor of the strategy of controlling the availability of addictive drugs (Courtwright 1982; Jaffe 1987; Musto 1987). Changes in public attitudes toward addiction were reflected in the passage of the Harrison Narcotic Act in 1914, which was meant to control the sale of heroin and other dangerous drugs legally defined as narcotics. The U.S. Supreme Court decisions of 1916 and 1919, restricting physicians' prescriptions of heroin for addicts, reinforced the public opposition to medical treatment of addicts. In 1919 the 44 public maintenance clinics that had been established met with public protest, and by 1923 the last of the clinics had been closed (Musto and Ramos 1981).

The next major attempt to treat addiction medically came about when Public Health Service hospitals were established in Lexington, Kentucky, and Fort Worth, Texas, during the 1930s (Musto 1987). With the growth of heroin addiction in urban areas in the 1950s, there was a resurgence of interest in treatment. During the 1960s, the rise in crime rates was thought to be related to increased numbers of heroin addicts (DuPont 1972). As a result, publicly funded community-based efforts were developed in the 1970s in hopes of controlling the problem, if not actually preventing or remedying it (Jaffe 1979).

The treatment programs started in the 1960s were focused on the client who primarily—and, as a rule, exclusively—used one particular opioid, heroin. Public health officials and policymakers supported these new programs because of evidence indicating the effectiveness of such efforts as the Beth Israel methadone maintenance program (Dole and Nyswander 1965; Dole, Nyswander, and Warner 1968) and such pioneering therapeutic communities as Phoenix House, Gateway, Synanon, and Daytop (Brook and Whitehead 1980; Glaser 1974; Yablonsky 1965). From 1966 to 1971, increasing amounts of private funds and funding from all levels of government were committed to the treatment of drug abusers. With the creation of the Special Action Office for Drug Abuse Prevention (SAODAP) by President Nixon, the determination to deal with the issue of drug abuse had developed into national public policy (Jaffe 1979). By the mid-1970s, as the number and type of treatment strategies proliferated, methadone maintenance, detoxification, and residential therapeutic community treatment became the predominant types of programs (Glasscote et al. 1972).

During the late 1970s, a new federal strategy fostered the provision of treatment for those dependent on drugs other than heroin and on combinations of drugs (Benvenuto and Bourne 1975; Braucht, Kirby, and Berry 1978; Duncan 1975; Wesson et al. 1978). As the evidence grew that abuse of nonopioids could cause dependency and have other detrimental effects, outpatient drug-free treatment programs were developed (Strategy Council on Drug Abuse 1979), the keystone of which is individual counseling (Kleber and Slobetz 1979; Wesson et al. 1974). With the development of outpatient drug-free programs, a broad complement of treatment approaches was established and supported by public funds.

To sum up, the three major "modalities" or types of treatment currently being administered are the outpatient methadone clinics, therapeutic communities, and outpatient drug-free programs. The clients in outpatient methadone programs are opioid abusers, and most of them use or have used heroin intravenously. They receive a variety of services after stabilization with medically prescribed doses of methadone. This treatment is meant to help clients maintain or resume productive lives in the community while they visit the clinics for daily methadone doses and regular counseling sessions. By contrast, therapeutic communities rely heavily on the use of trained program graduates to provide highly structured, round-the-clock efforts to change addicts' lifestyles. Group counseling and the community environment within the residence are key ther-apeutic tools. This comprehensive approach requires long-term stays in residential facilities. Like therapeutic communities, the outpatient drug-free programs treat both opioid and nonopioid users, but they tend to be much more oriented toward the nonopioid user. In outpatient drug-free programs, the emphasis is on the counseling and therapy often provided by psychotherapists and social workers. Among the three modalities, there are great variations in program size and structure, therapeutic approach, services, and funding. Other treatment methods are now being developed, including broad-based programs designed to address a variety of chemical dependencies. These short-term inpatient regimens were originally designed to help guide alcohol abusers through the first phases of the 12 steps of the Alcoholics Anonymous recovery program (Cook 1988; Laundergan 1982).

Although the proportion of treatment programs supported by health insurance and client fees is increasing (Jaffe 1984; Harwood, Rachal, and Cavanaugh 1985; Rosenbaum, Murphy, and Beck 1987), the current treatment system for drug abuse remains largely dependent on public funds. Each year federal, state, and local governments spend over a billion dollars to provide treatment to alcohol and drug abusers (Harwood et al. 1984). The very magnitude of this public expenditure raises critical questions about the efficacy and cost-effectiveness of drug abuse treatment.

## The Effectiveness of Drug Abuse Treatment

A series of studies conducted primarily over the past two decades has demonstrated the effectiveness of the publicly funded methadone maintenance and therapeutic community approaches (Tims 1981; Tims and Ludford 1984). Except for alcohol and marijuana use, which tended to increase rather than decrease with treatment (Simpson and Lloyd 1977), use of most drugs declined during and after treatment (DeLeon 1984; Holland 1982b; Sells 1974; Sells and Simpson 1976; Smart 1976). Researchers have also observed a substantial reduction in criminal activity among program clients, particularly during treatment (Dole and Joseph 1978; Gorsuch, Abbamonte, and Sells 1976; Nash 1976; McGlothlin, Anglin, and Wilson 1977). Less is known, however, about the extent of changes in employment and psychological well-being associated with treatment participation. Moreover, there have been few studies of the cost-effectiveness of drug abuse treatment, and many of the findings concerning the factors associated with positive treatment outcomes have not been replicated.

Although drug abuse treatment has existed in many forms since the beginning of this century, there is only limited information about the client populations and effectiveness of programs administered before 1969. The establishment in 1966 of a treatment system based in federal hospitals under the Narcotic Addict Rehabilitation Act (NARA) provided researchers with the opportunity to collect systematic data on a large population of opioid, cocaine, and marijuana abusers. A number of important studies on the natural history and correlates of drug addiction were generated from this treatment system (Chambers 1974; Chambers and Moffett 1969; Gold and Chatham 1973; O'Donnell 1969; Vaillant 1966; Voss and Stephens 1973). The findings suggest that although some addicts were able to maintain their abstinence, many relapsed to their addiction once they returned to their communities (Maddux 1988). Until 1969 there were few community-based programs to help prevent relapse or to provide additional outpatient treatment.

Two major national data collection efforts have been undertaken to examine the effectiveness of community-based systems inaugurated in the late 1960s. These studies vary in emphasis and scope, but both provide needed information about publicly funded treatment programs in the United States during the 1970s and 1980s. The studies provide in-depth information about the nature of clients and treatment effectiveness, focusing on factors associated with positive outcomes. The first, the Drug Abuse Reporting Program (DARP), studied clients entering treatment from 1969 to 1974 and followed samples of the client population for up to twelve years posttreatment. The second, the Treatment Outcome Prospective Study (TOPS), provided information about a national sample of clients who entered treatment from 1979 to 1981 and then were asked to respond to follow-up questionnaires for up to five years after leaving treatment. Studies of this scope are necessary to answer many of the questions about treatment effectiveness in the broad range of settings across the nation.

*The Drug Abuse Reporting Program*

The Drug Abuse Reporting Program was the first comprehensive, nationally based evaluation of drug abuse treatment effectiveness. Conducted by the Institute for Behavioral Research of Texas Christian University, DARP examined the admission records of over 44,000 clients in 52 NIDA-supported agencies during the early years of community-based treatment, from 1969 to 1974. DARP also included bimonthly status records on each of the clients until they left treatment. Replicated studies of the nature of the treatment administered, the type of client who participated, and their performance during treatment were conducted on successive admission cohorts, and the results were published in five volumes (Sells 1974; Sells and Simpson 1976).

The first series of DARP posttreatment follow-up studies began in 1974. A total of 6,402 clients admitted in three successive years were selected from 34 treatment agencies for follow-up interviews. These interviews were conducted an average of six years after each client's admission to DARP treatment and obtained information on outcomes immediately following treatment (Sells, Demaree, and Hornick 1979; Simpson et al. 1978) as well as long-term outcomes and trends (summarized by Simpson 1984; Simpson and Sells 1982). A sample of 697 opioid addicts was chosen for a second wave of DARP follow-up interviews beginning in 1982, approximately twelve years after admission (Simpson et al. 1986). In addition to those enrolled in one of the three major treatment modalities, participants in detoxification programs and a comparison group composed of persons who registered but never received treatment are represented in these studies.

The body of research emerging from the DARP study provides convincing evidence of the effectiveness of drug abuse treatment in community-based programs. The major findings were briefly summarized by Simpson (1984) and have been presented in numerous publications, monographs, and papers. Positive treatment outcomes, in terms of changes in drug use and criminal activity, were produced in the three major modalities but not in detoxification programs or among those who enrolled but did not return for treatment. However, there were no significant differences in outcomes among the three major modalities, indicating perhaps that all three produced similar, positive outcomes. What distinguished positive outcomes was the length of time spent in treatment. A minimum of three months was necessary to produce positive changes; beyond those first three months, outcomes improved with time spent in treatment. Simpson concludes that it may be the amount of time spent in treatment rather than the specific modality that produces good outcomes, and that duration of treatment and satisfactory completion were more useful predictors than other client characteristics.

The DARP study produced a large body of knowledge about the effectiveness of community-based treatment programs during the early 1970s, a system that was in its formative stages and whose effectiveness was unknown. The study was influential in confirming the efficacy of treatment in reducing drug abuse and criminal activity, as well as other negative behaviors. The scope of the research allowed for the comparison of effectiveness across a variety of treatment settings, and the large, nationally representative sample enabled researchers to draw fairly strong conclusions. However, changes in the treatment system since the early 1970s (Greenberg and Brown 1984; Jaffe 1984) and the shift in the client population from those primarily addicted to opioids to those who abuse nonopioids and/or multiple drugs required updating and elaboration of these findings.

*The Treatment Outcome Prospective Study*

The Treatment Outcome Prospective Study, which provides the basis for the findings reported in this book, is a long-term, large-scale study of the nature of treatment, clients, and client behaviors before, during, and after treatment in publicly funded programs. The study design was built upon the methodology and findings of the earlier DARP study and other existing studies. In contrast to earlier studies, TOPS provides more extensive information about the nature of drug abuse treatment, describes the characteristics and behavior of abusers prior to treatment more comprehensively, and collects data from clients within the first year after leaving treatment. Supported by a series of contracts and grants provided by the National Institute on Drug Abuse, TOPS was conducted by the Research Triangle Institute, located in Research Triangle Park, North Carolina. Over 11,000 drug abusers who entered treatment in 1979, 1980, and 1981 were interviewed upon their admission to 41 selected drug abuse treatment programs across the nation, including the three major modalities as well as detoxification. Three annual admission cohorts were followed one month after their entry into treatment and at three-month intervals during treatment. Samples of each cohort were located and interviewed at specified intervals after leaving treatment—three months, one year, two years, and three to five years. The breadth of the study has enabled researchers to examine a range of clinical, research, and policy questions. Prior to the appearance of the present volume, findings from TOPS were presented in a number of publications and monographs, and the extensive data base is still being used to investigate the issues related to treatment effectiveness. This book provides an overview of those findings.

## Questions about Treatment Effectiveness

The study of drug abuse treatment effectiveness is necessarily complex, involving an assessment of the nature of treatment provided, the problems and characteristics of clients, and the outcomes attributable to interaction between treatments and clients. Because treatment has goals in addition to reducing drug abuse, evaluation of impact must be based on a consideration of multiple treatment outcomes, both behavioral and psychological. Other issues complicating evaluation include the array of programs providing treatment and the variety of clients entering treatment, whose problems differ in degree of severity. The study of effectiveness thus requires consideration of many causal factors and methodological issues, some of which are common to evaluative studies and others specific to the assessment of drug abuse treatment.

Part of the complexity of the study of treatment effectiveness arises from the diversity of approaches and settings in which treatment occurs. Drug abuse treatment is provided in three major modalities by hospitals, community public health agencies, and a variety of independent organizations. The array of therapeutic approaches used ranges from psycho- and biomedical therapy to self-help groups and social services. Treatment varies in outcome goals, planned duration, and degree of management of client activities. The number, type, and intensity of services vary, as do staff experience, training, and qualifications.

The drug abuse treatment population is similarly complex; clients are not characterized by a common set of demographics or problems. They vary in age, social and economic background, number and type of drugs abused, health status, and psychological well-being. Some have lengthy histories of addiction and treatment, while others are entering treatment for the first time in the early stages of dependence. Clients may be highly involved in criminal activity or may not have committed any crime other than drug possession. Clients also tend to have many medical, psychological, economic, family, and legal problems in addition to their addiction.

Changes in client behaviors and psychological states depend on a variety of factors, including motivation to change, the potential for productive lives, effective matching of clients with treatment appropriate to their problems, and availability of quality services. Given a relatively high dropout rate in the first weeks of treatment, a major challenge for treatment providers is keeping the client in treatment long enough to benefit from the available services. The services range from efforts to help rehabilitate clients with skills that have been eroded by drug abuse to basic attempts to habilitate individuals with little education or training. To reduce the probability of relapse, once the basic course of treatment is completed, the client needs to maintain continuing contact with programs or become engaged in a support system for many months or years.

Given the complex interplay of client, treatment, and outcome, questions about effectiveness must go beyond the simple query, "Does treatment work?" Research and personal testimonials demonstrate that treatment has worked for many recovering abusers. Unfortunately, many others drop out of treatment or relapse shortly after completing treatment. Such information on success rates has limited value for the development of public policy and the improvement of treatment. Rather, three basic questions must be asked in order to assess the role of treatment in an overall strategy to combat drug abuse. These questions are general ones, phrased in terms of the impact of drug abuse treatment across the range of settings and for clients with varying degrees of dependence and associated problems.

1. How effective is drug abuse treatment in reducing drug use and restoring clients to productive lives?

2. What is the return on the investment in drug abuse treatment for the individual client and society?

3. How can the effectiveness of drug abuse treatment be increased with prudent allocation of resources?

The first question, that of the overall effectiveness of drug abuse treatment, concerns the extent to which there is change in client behaviors, attitudes, and overall well-being during and after treatment. Changes in these behaviors are indicative of the rehabilitative strength of the treatment. Questions of overall effectiveness can be considered by comparing client behaviors before, during, and after treatment and by looking at short-term results as well as those for longer periods following treatment. Prior research indicates that there are short- and long-term improvements associated with treatment, but that "cures" or "abstinence" are extremely difficult to achieve. The recurrence of drug abuse is common, as is relapse for alcoholism, and many clients have extensive histories of drug abuse treatment episodes. The issue then becomes how to increase effectiveness by maximizing long-term rehabilitation and minimizing the likelihood of relapse and return to treatment.

In this book we examine changes in drug abuse and other key outcomes during and after treatment. Because many clients had long careers of addiction and dependence, improvement as well as abstinence can be a reasonable objective of treatment. We therefore describe both abstinence and improvement for each of the outcome measures. The cessation or decrease of criminal activity and sustained or increased employment are basic measures of the intended changes in behavior expected after treatment. Alcohol abuse and depression are also included as major treatment outcomes because of their interference with the successful completion of treatment and positive treatment outcomes.

Although the question of overall effectiveness may be considered independently of return on investment, both issues must be pursued. Investment in treatment is difficult to justify if the expenditures substantially exceed the return, in this case the reduction in social and economic costs to society among drug abusers who have undergone treatment. We look at the return on investment of drug abuse treatment by considering the effect that treatment may have in reducing crime and by gauging the impact of the reduction of crime on the social and economic costs that drug abuse exacts on the nation. Although our discussion focuses on the crime-related costs of drug abuse and the reduction of those costs through treatment programs, these are only part of the overall costs of drug abuse. For instance, independently of decreases in criminal activity, drug abuse treatment may improve the employability and productivity of clients, thereby reducing the costs of drug abusers to the nation. Another new cost element, the medical care for AIDS provided to intravenous drug abusers, their spouses, and their newborn infants will escalate dramatically over the next decade. The drug abuse treatment system is the major resource available to help contain the spread of AIDS among intravenous drug abusers. However, crime-related costs are a major part of the burden of drug abuse to the nation, and analyses of the effects of drug abuse treatment on crime reduction are indicative of the magnitude of economic returns that can be realized from treatment.

How, then, should drug abuse treatment be structured to ensure that the most positive outcomes are produced in terms of overall effectiveness and comparative return on the resources invested? This final question concerns issues such as the length of stay and the intensity of services that are necessary to produce positive treatment outcomes and thus the relative effectiveness of various approaches. We investigate factors associated with positive treatment outcomes by conducting multivariate analyses that predict the major treatment outcomes, including drug abuse, criminal activity, alcohol use, suicidal symptoms, and employment. Our discussion focuses on how pretreatment behavior and time in treatment can contribute to posttreatment behavior. From these findings we draw conclusions about how the effectiveness of treatment can be improved with reasonable investment of limited resources.

Related to the three major issues examined in this book are specific questions regarding the success of programs in retaining drug abusers in treatment and the effectiveness of the treatment made available to specific client populations, including intravenous drug users and clients referred by the criminal justice system. We consider how clients referred by the criminal justice system fare relative to other clients and the course of intravenous drug use during and after treatment. We also consider the role of the nature and intensity of services received during treatment, the impact of time spent in treatment, and the impediments of alcohol abuse and psychological problems to achieving positive outcomes. These analyses provide more specific information about how effectiveness might be enhanced.

Considerable research has been conducted on these three issues and related questions over the past decades, but thus far the results have not provided the systematic up-to-date information to help formulate national public policy and improve the design of publicly funded treatment programs. Much of the research has been conducted in single sites using specific therapeutic approaches, and the findings cannot be generalized across the broad range of program types and communities. The issues are very complex, requiring careful consideration of a multiplicity of individual characteristics and treatment elements that may contribute to changes in behavior.

The period covered by the TOPS research marked the culmination of a decade of intense federal, state, and local efforts to design, implement, and sustain a comprehensive system of drug abuse treatment programs throughout the United States. After the Omnibus Reconciliation Act of 1981 established block grant funding of programs through the states, this system received less attention and less support. While chemical dependency programs treating clients with private health insurance or the financial resources to pay fees have proliferated during the 1980s, public expenditures for drug abuse treatment diminished (U.S. Government Accounting Office 1985). The period under discussion in this book is therefore an optimal one for establishing a benchmark for the effectiveness of drug abuse treatment. The ultimate aim of this book is to aid policymakers and program administrators in their efforts to design more effective treatment programs, determine the level of public funding for drug abuse treatment, and consider the role of treatment in an overall strategy to reduce drug abuse.

# 2. The Treatment Outcome Prospective Study

The major objective of the Treatment Outcome Prospective Study (TOPS) is to assess the magnitude of treatment effects on key outcomes and to identify factors that contribute to these outcomes. To achieve this objective, a study of broad scope was designed that collected data from a national sample of drug abuse treatment programs and clients within those programs. The result has been a decade of research investigating issues fundamental to the understanding and improvement of treatment. The intent was to provide current descriptive information about the nature of treatment being provided in programs across the nation, the backgrounds and characteristics of clients at entry to treatment, and the magnitude of change in drug abuse and other behaviors and problems during and after treatment. In addition, the study sought to conduct explanatory analyses of the factors related to treatment effectiveness, including such factors as treatment modality, type and intensity of services received, time spent in treatment, and the severity of clients' drug abuse and related problems at entry to treatment. A detailed examination of the costs and benefits of the major modalities was also conducted, and procedures used in this substudy are described in Chapter 7. The study both builds on and expands prior studies of treatment effectiveness and cost-effectiveness.

This research examines and describes how drug abuse treatment brings about behavioral and psychological changes in clients. Because treatment has multiple goals, outcomes are evaluated according to a number of behavioral and psychological measures such as drug use, criminal activity, employment, alcohol use, and depression. Treatment effectiveness is thus viewed along several behavioral and psychological dimensions rather than one single or composite criterion of success. Both short- and longer-term changes in these measures are examined to determine the immediate and sustained effects of treatment.

## Development of the Research Design

The Treatment Outcome Prospective Study has documented the progress of 11,750 clients who entered treatment for drug abuse in 1979,

1980, or 1981 in 41 selected programs across the nation. These three annual admission cohorts were interviewed at intake and again one month after entry to treatment, then at three-month intervals during treatment. Samples of each cohort were located and interviewed at specified intervals after leaving treatment: three months, one year, two years, and three to five years after termination. Clients' clinical/medical records were abstracted to provide comprehensive information about the nature of their treatment. In addition to data provided by or about clients, surveys were also conducted with program directors and counselors. In this book we consider only those approximately 10,000 clients who entered 37 programs representing the three major modalities of drug abuse treatment—outpatient methadone, residential, and outpatient drug-free programs. Detoxification services and participants are excluded from the analyses discussed here because detoxification is more properly viewed as a short-term public health service that provides limited, if any, habilitation and rehabilitation services. Further, only four detoxification programs were included in TOPS, making it difficult to generalize the findings for that type of service.

*Planning and Implementation*

The design of the TOPS research was based on recommendations from a planning meeting held in 1975. A group of experts in the area of drug abuse treatment research and program evaluation recommended a study that would build upon and augment the design of the previous national study, the Drug Abuse Reporting Program (DARP). DARP collected data on clients admitted to drug abuse treatment programs from 1969 to 1974 and followed them for up to 12 years after treatment. After the basic data collection instruments and field procedures were drafted (Williams 1975), a contract to complete additional stages of a longitudinal study was awarded to Research Triangle Institute in 1977. In contrast to earlier studies, TOPS was able to draw upon a developing body of substantive and methodological knowledge about the study of drug abuse treatment effectiveness. The depth of resources and available expertise have contributed to a comprehensive research design based on state-of-the-art approaches.

Before data collection was begun, a six-month study was conducted to field-test and modify collection procedures and forms and to develop, test, and redesign as necessary the data management system procedures. This period also allowed review and consideration of a variety of design and definitional issues fundamental to the research. Approximately 400 clients were interviewed in a pretest conducted at nine programs (four outpatient methadone, three residential, and two outpatient drug-free programs) in four cities in 1978. Director/counselor surveys and clinical/medical review forms were also pretested in one methadone, two residential, and one outpatient drug-free program.

After the pretest and redesign period, the national study was then implemented in two major phases, each with multiple components. The first phase focused on clients at admission and during treatment. This Client/Treatment Study phase included data collections on the nature of treatment (based on surveys of clinic directors and counselors) as well as intake surveys of clients and abstracts of clinical/medical records on each client interviewed. The first 12-month collection of data for clients entering treatment in 1979 was implemented as a pilot study. After feasibility, design, and procedures were assured, the 1980 and 1981 admission cohorts were added. The Follow-up Study phase consisted of interviews with clients, conducted at specified periods after each cohort left treatment. Subsequent grants and contracts have supported more detailed analyses of the data to address a wide range of research issues, including criminal activity, vocational services, treatment careers, employment, patterns of heroin use, and interactions of types of treatment and types of clients.

Advisory committees met several times during the study to review the project and to recommend the implementation of subsequent phases of the research plan. The phased approach to the development and implementation of TOPS has enabled the National Institute on Drug Abuse (NIDA) and the researchers to modify the design and instrumentation to best meet current and future research and policy needs and to focus analyses on research and policy issues.

*The Prospective Cohort Design*

The Treatment Outcome Prospective Study uses a longitudinal, prospective cohort design with client interviews conducted before, during, and after treatment to examine the nature of changes in clients' behaviors associated with treatment. These data are supplemented with information about the nature of treatment and client populations collected from program administrators, counselors, and client records, as well as data collected to validate the client survey responses.

This research design recognizes the need for comprehensive, valid, and reliable information from clients with which to assess treatment effectiveness and the need to control for the potential problems inherent in collecting data from a drug-abusing population. The longitudinal research design makes it possible to assess the effects of multiple factors, including client characteristics, treatment regimen, and factors external to treatment on client behavior. Cross-sectional designs do not allow the separation of these types of effects, particularly the effects of historical societal changes occurring outside treatment. The design is prospective rather than retrospective, to allow the tracing of actual changes in client behaviors as they occur rather than the assessment of the magnitude and direction of changes based on client recall. By following three separate admission cohorts rather than one, the cohort design allows conclusions to be drawn that are not based on a single, possibly anomalous, group of clients.

The prospective cohort design is an approach that has been used in natural life history studies to identify and determine the influence of key variables on outcomes (Baltes 1968; Labouvie 1978; Schaie 1965, 1977). The study also includes a number of naturally occurring, nonequivalent control or comparison groups (Campbell and Stanley 1963; Cook and Campbell 1979). Thus, although a principal goal of the study is to provide descriptive information on the characteristics of clients entering selected drug abuse treatment programs and their behaviors before, during, and after treatment, the design provides strong support for evaluative and causal inferences. Rather than relying on random assignment, which has not proven successful across modalities (Bale et al. 1980; Hall 1984), causal inference is accomplished through extensive measurement of key explanatory variables, quasi-experimental comparison of multiple cohorts with pre- and posttests, and through replication that can rule out alternative hypotheses.

The study continues and expands the use of the methodology of prospective cohort designs, which have contributed greatly to knowledge about treatment effects. Studies using similar methodologies include large-scale, national multisite studies (Armor, Polich, and Stambul 1978; Polich, Armor, and Braiker 1981; Simpson 1984), comparative studies of specific programs (Ball et al. 1987; Finney, Moos, and Mewborn 1980; McLellan et al. 1984), in-depth clinical assessments in single programs (DeLeon 1984; McLellan et al. 1982; Rounsaville and Kleber 1986), and natural history studies of treated populations (McGlothlin and Anglin 1981; McGlothlin, Anglin, and Wilson 1977; Vaillant 1983).

Although clinical trials with random assignment are often purported to be the optimal research design to assess effectiveness, that methodology was deemed inappropriate for the major questions to be addressed about drug abuse treatment. The primary advantage of a clinical trial is use of random assignment to control for differential selection into a particular type of well-specified treatment regimen. Rather than control self-selection and minimize variation in treatment, the purpose of the TOPS research was to assess the naturally occurring variation in treatment and clients. Further, clinical trials are likely to create artificial selection conditions and atypical treatment atmospheres that cannot be generalized confidently to established programs operating in most communities. In previous attempts at random assignment across major modalities, the low compliance with assignment to programs, crossover to nonassigned programs within the trial, and attrition from assigned programs severely compromised the design (Bale et al. 1980). Simple random assignment is inappropriate across modalities or demonstrably different treatment approaches because of the researcher's lack of control and the client's strong disposition toward self-selection (Hall 1984). In addition, a study of the scope of TOPS would not have been feasible with in-depth clinical trials. Singer (1986) suggests that a clinical trial design considering even a small proportion of the possible combinations and interactions between client types and treatment types would require sample sizes larger than the total number of clients admitted to all programs in any one year. Thus, for both theoretical and methodological reasons, an epidemiological approach is preferable for studying the major issues and specific questions about treatment effectiveness faced by clinicians, researchers, and policymakers.

Despite the strengths of the prospective cohort design, it is often argued that changes in client behaviors cannot be unambiguously attributed to the drug abuse treatment episode, owing to the lack of a control group of drug abusers who did not experience treatment. The populations of drug abusers who enter treatment or remain in a program are likely distinctive; they may be more motivated to change or their problems may have a severity that necessitates treatment. Without a randomly assigned comparison, it is difficult to separate a treatment effect from the effect of self-selection and unmeasured factors extraneous to treatment (Berk et al. 1987; Cook and Campbell 1979).

By partitioning on length of time spent in treatment, identifying appropriate comparison groups, and considering key correlates of self-selection with careful statistical analysis, causality can be inferred. The comparison groups that have commonly been used in analyses of the TOPS data include a contact-only group staying less than one week and groups of clients who stayed in treatment for varied periods of time (less than 3 months, 3 to 12 months, and one year or more). We expect to see any treatment effect displayed disproportionately across these and other comparison groups. Other comparison groups that have been examined include the three annual admission cohorts, birth cohorts, and cohorts defined by age at first addiction. The use of multiple admission cohorts and multiple program sites further strengthens the design. Use of three admission cohorts controls for many of the historical and maturational threats to validity. By conducting the same study in several programs in several cities, we build in replications that make it difficult to question consistent evidence about treatment effectiveness. Thus, the design allows us to rule out most historical events, such as changes in the availability of drugs or treatment, as explanations for changes in client behaviors. By replicating the study across sites, we eliminate certain variations that are specific to a population, program, or place. As is the case for any single quasi-experiment, clinical trial, or epidemiological study, however, evidence of causal relationships must be compared and contrasted with other research. The logic of causality requires rejection of alternative explanations. The information available from TOPS, coupled with the evidence of such other epidemiological research as DARP or controlled clinical studies, provides the multiple confirmation of results necessary to confidently attribute client behavioral changes to retention and particular elements of treatment process.

## The Sample

The TOPS sample is not based on a random selection of cities, drug abuse treatment programs, or clients. Rather, cities and programs were purposely chosen for participation in TOPS. Neither the *programs* nor the *clients* are a nationally representative sample in statistical terms. However, comparisons with characteristics of programs in a national directory of drug abuse treatment programs (National Drug and Alcoholism Treatment Utilization Survey [NDATUS] in NIDA 1983) and a national census of clients (Client Oriented Data Acquisition Process [CODAP] in NIDA 1982) confirmed that the programs did reflect adequately the range of treatments available and the different types of clients entering treatment between 1979 and 1981 (Allison, Hubbard, and Rachal 1985; Hubbard, Bray, Cavanaugh, et al. 1986). Within these cities and programs, a complete census of drug abuse treatment clients entering treatment in 1979, 1980, and 1981 was contacted for participation in the Client/Treatment Study. Participating clients were interviewed at intake as well as after one month, three months, and each subsequent three months the client remained in treatment. During the Follow-up Study, samples of clients in each admission cohort and each modality were selected to be located and interviewed after termination of treatment. Clients from the 1979 admission cohort were interviewed one year and two years after treatment;

clients from the 1980 admission cohort were interviewed three months and one year after treatment; and clients from the 1981 admission cohort were interviewed three to five years after leaving treatment. The number of clients admitted to each modality each year and the number of those clients selected for follow-up is shown in Appendix Table A-1.

*Cities and Programs*

Programs in 10 cities across the nation were identified to reflect the nature of drug abuse treatment in large- and medium-sized urban areas with certain types of drug problems and with programs that were believed to have effective approaches to treatment. The cities were: Chicago, Des Moines, Detroit, Miami, New Orleans, New York, Philadelphia, Phoenix, Portland (Oregon), and San Francisco. In these cities, 37 stable, established programs representing the three major modalities were recruited to permit an assessment of the effect of drug abuse treatment conducted under optimal conditions. An attempt was made to include at least one methadone, residential, and outpatient drug-free program in each city, but large outpatient drug-free programs appropriate for the TOPS research could not be recruited in Chicago and Detroit.

Seventeen programs in five cities (Chicago, New Orleans, New York, Phoenix, and Portland) were involved in TOPS for all three admission cohorts. The other 20 programs participated for only one or two years. In 1979 the programs included eight outpatient methadone programs, seven residential programs, and seven outpatient drug-free programs in Chicago, Des Moines, New Orleans, New York, Phoenix, and Portland. Programs in Miami and San Francisco were added in January 1980, and in Detroit and Philadelphia in January 1981.

Using information from the National Drug and Alcoholism Treatment Utilization Survey data on staffing and budgets, comparisons of the TOPS programs with programs across the country indicate general similarities. Any difference in size and organization reported in the NDATUS and TOPS research may be related to the selection criteria for programs participating in the TOPS research. The programs for TOPS were in urban areas, had at least 100 admissions per year, and were chosen because they were stable, functioning programs representing the optimal type of treatment being delivered.

According to NDATUS, about one-half of the 516 reporting methadone maintenance treatment units in 1982 were free-standing facilities; only 15 percent were in general hospitals, and the remainder were in a variety of other settings (NIDA 1983). In TOPS, over half were affiliated with hospitals. NDATUS clinics had an average enrollment of about 200 clients. In contrast, 14 of the 17 methadone clinics included in the TOPS study had over 200 clients. The ratio of hours worked by medical staff to hours worked by counselors and other professional staff in the TOPS methadone programs is similar to that for NDATUS. The 17 TOPS methadone clinics had an average budget of $1,945 per client, somewhat less than the $2,174 for the typical client in methadone programs reporting to NDATUS. Only three small TOPS clinics had per client budgets higher than the NDATUS average.

The average capacity of TOPS residential facilities was 64 clients, compared to only 31 for the 361 single modality units reporting to NDATUS in 1982 (NIDA 1983). Staffing patterns were comparable in TOPS and NDATUS facilities. The average cost per bed for the 12 residences providing budget data for TOPS in 1980 was $6,135, somewhat under the average cost of $7,329 per bed for residences in 1982 (NIDA 1983). The lower per bed costs of residential facilities in this study may be due to the larger sizes of the facilities in TOPS, because fixed costs such as rent, administrative staff, and utilities are distributed over a larger number of clients.

The typical outpatient drug-free program reporting to NDATUS in 1979 had about 40 clients enrolled. In contrast, the programs participating in TOPS were much larger, with an average of about 160 clients enrolled at any given time. The bias may be due to the inclusion of larger programs in TOPS or to differences in the definition of what constitutes a client. The programs participating in TOPS had a similar distribution across types of hospital, correctional institution, and community mental health center settings. The staffing pattern in the NDATUS census and in the TOPS programs was similar. The average annual cost of treatment per client in the TOPS outpatient drug-free programs was $2,000, 25 percent higher than the national average cost of $1,600. This is in direct contrast to the comparatively lower costs per client found in TOPS versus NDATUS methadone and residential programs. These cost data, combined with information on staff, suggest that the programs chosen for TOPS were more oriented toward intense professional treatment than the typical outpatient drug-free program.

The focus on larger and established programs is not expected to bias or to reduce the generalizability of findings about the delivery of treatment in programs across the nation. The information about the nature of drug abuse treatment discussed in this book must, however, be interpreted as describing treatment in larger programs in urban areas. Treatment process, including staffing, services, and financing, may differ in other newer, smaller, or less stable programs.

*Client Population*

The Client/Treatment Study employed a census rather than a sample of clients in each participating program in the three major modalities. A census permits greater quality control, eliminates sampling error, and permits the observation of the variety of client behaviors occurring in a single treatment program. Including all clients in each of the programs also allowed the study resources to be focused more directly and economically. During this phase a total of 9,989 clients were interviewed at intake to outpatient methadone, residential, and outpatient drug-free programs participating in TOPS in 1979, 1980, and 1981. In 1979, 2,985 clients were interviewed at intake to 22 programs; in 1980, 3,626 clients were interviewed in 28 programs; and in 1981, 3,378 clients were interviewed in 29 programs. Additional intreatment interviews were conducted with these clients after one month, three months, and each subsequent quarter a client remained in treatment. Intreatment data collection was terminated in December 1981. Over the three admission cohorts, 4,184 outpatient methadone, 2,891 residential, and 2,914 outpatient drug-free clients were interviewed at entry to treatment, for a total of 9,989 clients across the three major modalities.

Comparison of the TOPS and CODAP data within each modality indicates that the TOPS clients are comparable to the national population of drug abuse treatment clients and that the results of the TOPS research are generalizable to the national population of such clients (Hubbard, Bray, Cavanaugh, et al. 1986). The sociodemographic composition of the TOPS and CODAP populations was highly similar, according to comparisons of characteristics of age, sex, race, and marital status in both data bases. TOPS had somewhat fewer clients under age 20 and in the older age categories (i.e., 25 or older), especially in the residential and outpatient drug-free modalities. TOPS and CODAP diverged more on race/ethnic composition. In all years there were more whites in TOPS outpatient drug-free programs than in CODAP (80 percent compared to 70 percent). TOPS also had a higher percentage of blacks in residential programs than CODAP (40 percent compared with 28 percent). Probably because of the cities and programs selected for inclusion in TOPS, TOPS had fewer Hispanics in outpatient drug-free programs and more in outpatient methadone than CODAP.

Comparison of the primary drug of abuse among TOPS clients and the national census of clients available from CODAP shows again that the TOPS data provide a good representation of drug abuse patterns across the nation. Information on primary drug of abuse for TOPS and CODAP is not directly comparable because the usage questions and categorization of drugs differed. In CODAP, clinicians and intake workers made the assignment of primary problem drug in completing CODAP forms, but in TOPS, primary drug of abuse was based on client self-reports. Further, in CODAP, only heroin and other opioids were recorded as primary problem drugs for methadone clients. Despite these differences, there is a fair degree of correspondence between CODAP and TOPS as to the primary drug of abuse, excluding those clients who reported no major drug of abuse in the TOPS data.

Among methadone clients, primary abuse of heroin/methadone was reported for 81 percent of CODAP clients and 77 percent of TOPS clients. Among residential clients, heroin/methadone was reported for 30 percent of CODAP clients and 29 percent of TOPS clients; and tranquilizers/barbiturates/sedatives by 12 percent of CODAP clients and 11 percent of TOPS clients. Among outpatient drug-free clients, tranquilizers/barbiturates/sedatives were reported as the primary type of drug abused by 13 percent of CODAP clients and 18 percent of TOPS clients; heroin/methadone by 16 percent of CODAP clients and 11 percent of TOPS clients. Marijuana was reported as the primary drug of abuse by somewhat fewer TOPS clients than CODAP clients; marijuana was the primary drug of abuse for 8 percent of TOPS residential clients and 14 percent of CODAP residential clients and 18 percent of TOPS outpatient drug-free clients and almost 30 percent of CODAP outpatient drug-free clients. Overall, the CODAP and TOPS data appear to correspond fairly well as to the primary drug of abuse, and differences appear to be largely attributable to differences in the reporting requirements of the programs rather than the distinctiveness of the TOPS clients.

*Follow-up Sample*

The Follow-up Study was intended to describe the posttreatment behavior of clients who contacted treatment programs in 1979, 1980, or 1981 and to determine the factors associated with variation in posttreatment behaviors. Together with the Client/Treatment Study data, data from the Follow-up Study allow the assessment of the magnitude and direction of behavioral and psychological changes associated with drug abuse treatment.

The population from which the follow-up samples were selected was composed of all those who completed an intake interview in 1979, 1980, or 1981 at a program participating in this research. Three samples were selected from clients who completed an intake interview, one sample for each admission cohort. Sizes of each of the follow-up samples of the three admission cohorts were determined in order to estimate proportions of clients with particular outcomes, using acceptable levels of statistical precision achievable within budget constraints. The samples also included clients from the Treatment Alternatives to Street Crime (TASC) programs in Chicago, Des Moines, Phoenix, Portland, and Miami who were referred to a treatment program participating in this research. TASC programs identified drug users who came into contact with the criminal justice system, referred eligible clients to treatment, and monitored their progress. Because of the analytical interest in the TASC clients, all who were assigned to one of the outpatient drug-free or residential programs and who completed an intake interview were selected into the follow-up sample.

The design for the Follow-up Study called for first- and second-year posttreatment follow-up interviews with 1,159 clients who applied for admission to a TOPS program in 1979, three-month and first-year posttreatment follow-ups of 2,111 clients who applied to a TOPS program in 1980, and follow-ups of 1,000 clients in the 1981 admission cohort between the third and fifth year posttreatment. Modalities were treated as primary sample selection strata for the sample cohorts. Secondary strata for the 1979 cohort samples were treatment program by time-in-treatment categories (short- and long-term, or less than three months in treatment versus greater than or equal to three months in treatment). Secondary strata for the 1980 and 1981 cohort samples were simply the treatment programs, because the magnitude of interest in time in treatment as an analytic domain could not be determined at the time of sample selection. Across the three major modalities, 1,539 outpatient methadone, 1,282 residential, and 1,449 outpatient drug-free clients who completed an intake interview were selected for participation in the Follow-up Study, for a total of 4,270 clients.

Because of the difficulty of mounting a continuous follow-up of clients over each of the five years after treatment, two major data collections were conducted: the first in 1981 and 1982 for the 1979 and 1980 admission cohorts, and the second in 1985 and 1986 for the 1981 admission cohort. These data collection periods were selected so that the admission cohorts could be contacted at different key periods after treatment. Between 70 and 80 percent of the eligible sample was interviewed in each data collection.

## Data Collection

The two major types of data collected as part of the TOPS study—treatment program data and client interview data—are described here.* Additional types of data, such as urinalysis, FBI arrest records, and information from death certificates, were also collected but are not described here because analyses presented in this book are based primarily on the treatment program and client interview data. Selected analyses of the urinalysis and arrest record data are described later in this chapter.

### Treatment Program Data

Data were collected to describe the nature of treatment available and rendered in a broad range of outpatient methadone, residential, and outpatient drug-free programs across the nation, as well as the nature of changes in drug abuse treatment over the past decade.

The TOPS study used several types of procedures to gather information about the nature of treatment, including information on program structure, therapeutic approaches, treatment services, and financing. Information about program structure includes a description of average clinic size, location, and staffing. Information about therapeutic approaches includes a description of policies and practices, approaches to and goals of treatment, treatment plans, and sanctions and privileges. Treatment services are the range of services offered by programs, including medical, psychological, family, vocational, educational, legal, and financial services. Information about the financing of the programs is based on the average public expenditures for treatment within the three major modalities.

The treatment data were collected at the clinic rather than program level because of the considerable variation in the nature of treatment delivered across locations and directors even within one "program." Treatment services were provided in 54 distinct clinics within the 37 treatment programs included in the TOPS study. Each clinic had a director or supervisor and provided services at a single location. Clinics were chosen for participation in the treatment program substudy if they had at least five clients remaining in treatment for three months or more. Ten clinics closed before records could be obtained, and three clinics did not have the minimum number of clients. The final sample of clinics includes 17 methadone, 14 residential, and 10 outpatient drug-free clinics.

---

*Copies of the program data collection instruments and intake, intreatment, or follow-up questionnaires may be obtained from Dr. Robert L. Hubbard, Research Triangle Institute, Center for Social Research and Policy Analysis, P.O. Box 12194, Research Triangle Park, N.C., 27709.

Questionnaires were obtained from the director, clinical supervisor or head counselor, and more experienced counselors (those with at least one year's experience in the clinic) in 37 of the eligible 41 clinics; this questionnaire is called the Director/Counselor Checklist. Topics covered in the checklist included program policy and philosophy, approach to treatment, emphases and goals for treatment, size of the program, caseload per counselor, services provided at the program or through referral, and criteria for completion of the program or discharge from the program. Clinical/medical records from all 41 clinics were examined; these data were collected on the Clinical/Medical Record Review Form, which was designed to allow TOPS data collectors to gather information from client files on a variety of issues relevant to treatment process. To the extent possible, information on client sociodemographic characteristics, services received, treatment plans, drug use, medications prescribed, treatment history, follow-up services, and criminal activity were obtained. Some of these types of information were also collected with the client surveys.

Both the Director/Counselor Checklist and the Clinical/Medical Record Review Form were pretested in one methadone, one outpatient drug-free, and two residential programs. Some instruments were revised based on the findings of the pretest, and a comprehensive instruction manual was prepared to guide data collection. Data collection supervisors randomly reabstracted 10 percent of the records for each data collector to check data quality.

## Client Survey Data

Client survey data were collected in face-to-face interviews using a structured survey questionnaire. Professional interviewers hired, trained, and supervised by RTI field staff were assigned full time to specific programs to conduct the intake and intreatment interviews. This approach substantially reduced the burden on programs and insured consistency in the quality of interviewing across programs. Follow-up interviews were conducted by trained interviewers with experience in field surveys. The interviews included detailed and comprehensive questions concerning client background, demographic characteristics, lifestyle and life changes, prior treatment experience, and the client's history of drug use, alcohol use, criminal activity, and employment.

### POINTS OF INTERVIEW

The time points chosen for the client survey are critical both conceptually and operationally. The major conceptual issues for selecting the points of interview include identifying key points in the treatment process, identifying points at which major behavioral or psychological changes occur, plotting trends in behavior, and establishing boundaries of time periods by key events or chronological dates. The operational concerns include problems in scheduling interviews, the length of time over which respondents could accurately recall behavior, the effects of repeated testing and respondent burden, and the timely notification of treatment termination.

Both empirical and impressionistic data were used to determine the best points of interview. The retention patterns of a variety of programs clearly show that there is a high rate of dropout in the first month of treatment followed by a leveling off. Discussions with program staffs indicated that major behavioral changes were most likely to occur early in treatment. For the sake of comparison with the results of other studies, consistent follow-up periods, such as one year after leaving treatment, were chosen. However, there is also reason to assess behaviors in the period immediately after clients leave treatment because of the likelihood of relapse.

Interviews at fairly frequent intervals are necessary to obtain more accurate recall of certain behaviors and to assess attitudinal and evaluative data about treatment. Past studies have indicated, for instance, that recall of major events such as arrests or employment is reasonably accurate for up to one year (Hubbard 1976; Hubbard et al. 1978). However, past sporadic behaviors such as drug use, criminal activity, or odd jobs are often forgotten or confused with more recent events. The desirability of closely spaced intreatment and follow-up interviews, though, must be weighed against the effects of closely repeated interviews on response rates, response quality, and study costs.

The points of interview for the intreatment and follow-up studies were thus selected to best assess behavioral changes during and after treatment. Based on both technical and operational considerations, the following schedule was recommended and implemented for TOPS interviewing:

at initial contact with a program
1 month after admission
3 months after admission
6 months after admission
9 months after admission
1 year after admission
3 months after leaving treatment
1 year after leaving treatment

2 years after leaving treatment
3 to 5 years after leaving treatment.

In addition, a small sample of clients remaining in treatment over one year, mainly in methadone maintenance programs, was interviewed quarterly. The three-month follow-up interview provides detailed information about treatment termination. The one-year follow-up interview corresponds to the standard follow-up period used in a variety of evaluation studies. Follow-ups two or more years after treatment termination focus on behavior in the year before the interview but also ask about information on the anniversary dates of treatment termination. For the pretreatment period, data are available for the behaviors three months and one year prior to entering treatment. Analyses have shown that behaviors such as drug use and criminal activity are particularly pronounced in the immediate pretreatment period and less pronounced in the year before, arguing for consideration of behaviors in both time periods as indicators of pretreatment behavior.

These points of interview allow comparisons of client behaviors across program types and across admission cohorts within the same periods of time and allow comparison with the results of related studies using similar time periods. The design with follow-ups beginning immediately after treatment was a major improvement over such studies as DARP. In DARP the first follow-up was delayed until five years after admission and required clients to recall behaviors for a period up to five years.

INTERVIEW CONTENT

The TOPS data are very broad in scope, encompassing social, social-psychological, ecological, and socioeconomic perspectives. A fairly consistent set of questions is included across each of the points of interview, but some supplementary questions are included in some of the interviews. The intake interview, for instance, provides life history information, while the one-month intreatment interview provides information about treatment, and the three-month follow-up interview provides information about social support and community agency contact after treatment. Attempts were made to validate information within and across interviews in the Follow-up Study through program records, through authorized checks of such official records as FBI arrest reports and Social Security Administration employment data, and through urinalysis. More specifically, the client interviews included the following types of information:

• Sociodemographic characteristics, including age, sex, race/ethnicity, marital status and living arrangements, education and training

• Admission characteristics, including source of referral, criminal justice status, and health insurance coverage

• Drug use, including lifetime use, age at first use, age at first regular use, route of administration, and frequency of current use for 12 major drugs or classes of drugs (marijuana, hashish, THC; inhalants; hallucinogens; cocaine; heroin; street or illegal methadone; other opioids; minor tranquilizers; major tranquilizers; barbiturates; sedatives and hypnotics; amphetamines or stimulants). (Nonmedical and medical use of prescription psychotherapeutic drugs were distinguished.)

• Alcohol use, including age at first use, age at first regular use, quantity and frequency of current drinking

• Symptoms of depression, as measured by client acknowledgment of indicators of depression and suicidal thoughts or attempts

• Treatment history, including past treatment for drug-related problems by modality, past treatment for alcohol-related problems, past treatment for mental health or emotional problems, and drug-related problems (medical, psychological, family, legal, employment, and financial) experienced during the past year

• Social and community support, such as participation in self-help groups, contact with social service agencies and interaction with family and friends

• Criminal activity, including self-reports of arrests and offenses committed for 11 classes of offenses (aggravated assault, robbery, burglary, theft, auto theft, forgery/embezzlement, sale of stolen property/fencing, gambling, pimping/prostitution, sales/manufacturing of illegal drugs, driving while intoxicated)

• Employment, including labor force status, weeks worked and hours worked per week, and occupation before program contact

• Income and expenditures, including sources and amounts of income (legal and illegal), and expenditures (food and housing costs and other living expenses, medical bills, and amounts spent on drugs)

Where possible, the interview questions and coding of the data conform to widely used conventions. For example, data on criminal activity followed categories used by the Uniform Crime Reports, and employment data followed reporting conventions on labor force activity of the Department of Labor.

*Data Collection Procedures*

Intake, intreatment, and posttreatment interviews were conducted by interviewers selected, trained, and closely monitored by a staff of Research Triangle Institute survey supervisors assigned full time to the study. Intake and intreatment interviews were conducted at the program sites. Interviewers assigned to specific programs to conduct interviews were called "program researchers." They were responsible for recruiting subjects for intake and subsequent intreatment interviews, scheduling and conducting interviews, completing a clinical/medical form for each client selected for the follow-up study and, in general, keeping RTI staff informed of program operations and changes in program activities. The work of the program researchers was integrated with the operation of the treatment program to minimize disruption and establish a cooperative relationship with each program. Although most program researchers had extensive interviewing experience, they received five days' training in interviewing concepts and techniques, including practice interviewing.

The interview design obtained response rates of 80 percent of all clients entering treatment (Hubbard et al. 1981). Rates were 80 percent for methadone, 88 percent for residential, and 72 percent for outpatient drug-free programs. Because data collection was restricted to the programs, many clients who had minimal contact with programs often could not be located for intake interviews. For clients staying in treatment at least one month, the response rates were 93 percent for methadone, 97 percent for residential, and 87 percent for outpatient drug-free programs. Analysis of characteristics of clients who were not interviewed indicated no substantial bias in age, sex, race, or primary drug of abuse.

Different interviewers were selected for the Follow-up Study. Most had at least two years' experience interviewing populations similar to the client populations and received two days' additional training in interviewing techniques. They were responsible for locating, contacting, and interviewing clients in the communities after termination from a program. Posttreatment interviews were conducted at a variety of sites, including homes, restaurants, treatment programs, and prisons. The interviewers were responsible for obtaining informed consent, conducting the interview, and obtaining releases for information contained in confidential records. The quality of interviewing was closely monitored by a full-time staff of survey supervisors.

The response rates to the follow-up also varied by modality and length of time since leaving treatment (Purcell et al. 1983). Three-month follow-up interviews were completed with 75 percent of methadone, 81 percent of residential, and 84 percent of outpatient drug-free clients. Similar rates were obtained for the 12-month follow-up: 75 percent, 81 percent, and 82 percent, respectively. The rates decreased to 70 percent, 78 percent, and 79 percent for the 24-month follow-up and to about 65 percent for the three-to-five-year follow-up. About 2 percent of the clients in each follow-up data collection refused to participate, and another 2 percent were deceased. The remainder could not be located despite intensive efforts. Multivariate analysis, including demographic characteristics, drug use patterns, time in treatment, illegal activity, depression, and employment before treatment revealed few differences among clients who were interviewed and those who could not be located. There were no significant differences between the two groups on demographic or drug use patterns. Methadone clients who had no prior treatment and reported no criminal behavior were significantly less likely to be interviewed. Clients who left residential programs within one week and those referred to outpatient programs from community agencies were also harder to locate and interview. The bias resulting from the nonresponse to the follow-up appears to be minimal and should not distort the conclusions derived from this study.

A variety of procedures was followed for this study to insure efficient and accurate data processing. All interview forms were mailed directly to the Research Triangle Institute, where they were manually edited for consistency and then converted to machine-readable form using a sophisticated data entry system. The resulting data base was then machine edited, and machine-readable code books were prepared that contained descriptions of all data items. Data collection supervisors randomly re-abstracted 10 percent of the records for each data collection to check data quality. Basic analysis files were prepared that were accessible by SAS and that included selected information from the intake, intreatment, and follow-up interviews. Complete data files for each interview were also readily available.

*Reliability and Validity of Client Survey Data*

A major concern of many who perform or use research on drug abuse is the quality of self-reported data obtained from such populations. Data on client drug use, alcohol use, and criminal behavior, for instance, may be deliberately underreported to mask the severity of the client's problems or overreported in an attempt to comply with survey questions or to seek to justify admission to treatment. These problems may be exacerbated by recall problems or misunderstandings. If these reporting problems are severe, conclusions about the nature and extent of client problems at entry to treatment and the nature and extent of changes associated with treatment may be affected. Reliance on other types of evidence may be warranted, or it may be possible to make certain adjustments to the survey data to partially correct for under- or overreporting of some behaviors.

During the course of the TOPS research, a series of comprehensive examinations were conducted of the reliability and validity of client survey data collected during the study. Taken together, the concepts of reliability and validity address the question of whether survey items accurately assess what they purport to measure. Results of investigations of the reliability and validity of TOPS data are summarized in Hubbard, Marsden, and Allison (1984).

Prior studies of the reliability and validity of survey responses of drug abusers show that addicts do provide generally truthful and accurate information (Bonito, Nurco, and Shaffer 1976). Addicts' reports on sensitive topics such as drug use and criminal activity, as well as answers to more straightforward questions concerning marital status, employment, and the like, have been found to be largely accurate (Ball 1967; Cox and Longwell 1974; Maddux and Desmond 1975; Simpson, Lloyd, and Gent 1976; Stephens 1972). Other studies, such as one of prescription drug use conducted by Parry, Balter, and Cisin (1971), suggest that the degree of accuracy depends on the behavior in question. Although some responses may be dependent on recall problems, O'Donnell (1975) maintains that the veracity of reports of illegal acts varies with the seriousness and time elapsed since the act. Eckerman et al. (1976) found a high degree of correspondence of self-report and urinalysis data for arrestees but that admission of drug use depended on such factors as data collection techniques, recency of drug use, type of drug, and type of arrest charge.

These findings suggest the overall accuracy of self-reports of deviant behavior among drug abuse treatment clients, with some inaccuracy in the reporting of certain types of behavior. These findings are supported by related analyses of the TOPS client survey data. Analyses show that the client data are, on the whole, reliable and valid, as indicated by various approaches to ascertaining the degree of accuracy of survey responses.

The approaches to assessing data quality may be subsumed under three categories: checks on internal validity or reliability, construct validity, and empirical validity. Internal validity was assessed by examination of data collection methods used to assure data quality, interviewer perceptions of the interview situation and the accuracy of responses, the internal consistency of responses, and the extent of nonresponse to certain items. Construct validity was established by comparing TOPS findings on drug use patterns with those from the Client Oriented Data Acquisition Process and the Drug Abuse Reporting Program studies, as well as by comparing the TOPS depression index with several widely used depression inventories. Empirical validity was approached by comparing TOPS responses with several record checks (FBI rap sheets and a Clinical/ Medical Record Review substudy) and the results of urinalysis. These studies are described in more detail in Hubbard, Marsden, and Allison (1984) and Hubbard, Collins, et al. (1982).

TOPS interviewers judged drug use responses to be of low or very low accuracy in only 3 to 5 percent of the cases; nonresponse to the set of drug use items was also extremely low, less than 2 percent. On the basis of these two criteria, the drug use items fared better than some other types of items, such as those regarding criminal activity. The extent of nonresponse to questions concerning drug use in the past three months and past year, however, appeared to show that clients were more likely to be untruthful about recent behavior.

Comparisons of TOPS drug use data with similar data from other drug abuse treatment populations, previous research and clinical records, and/or urinalysis results for the same client support the assessment of accuracy. TOPS clients were remarkably similar to 1979–1981 CODAP clients in primary drug used, although TOPS clients appeared to be more likely to use other opiates and less likely to use marijuana.

Comparisons of client self-reports and clinical/medical records indicate strong evidence of validity (Allison, Hubbard, and Rachal 1985; Hubbard, Marsden, and Allison 1984). Although there is a high degree of agreement of self-reports and clinical/medical records during treatment, the prevalence of heroin was understated in the self-report data. Results of urinalysis revealed a tendency to underreport use of all drugs in the clinical setting, but underreporting by a small group did not appear to affect aggregate results (Hubbard, Marsden, and Allison 1984). Clients were less likely to admit recent use than current use, a tendency toward face-saving that is consistent with prior research (Chick, Kreitman, and Plant 1981; Luetgert and Armstrong 1973).

These varied analyses demonstrate that the TOPS data are on the whole reliable and valid. However, they highlight the need for careful attention to the interview situation as a prime determinant of data quality. Although substantial improvements were made in the quality of self-reported data in TOPS, and its general level of validity has been demonstrated, there is still substantial error. One must accept, however, the fact that a certain amount of error will occur, even with the more carefully constructed and administered instruments. Because the validity criteria are themselves suspect and incomplete (Hubbard, Eckerman, and Rachal 1977), it is impossible to gauge precisely the nature and extent of the deviation of self-reports from the true level of behavior. The important issue is the extent to which error in the data may produce bias or misleading results. Harwood et al. (1988) demonstrated that regardless of the assumption made about missing and unreliable data, a positive cost-benefit ratio of the impact of treatment on crime can still be demonstrated.

## Data Analysis

Both descriptive and explanatory analyses have been conducted to address the major issues and specific questions that are the subject of this book. Basic descriptive analyses have examined the nature of drug abuse treatment and clients and the nature and extent of client behaviors before, during, and after drug abuse treatment. More comprehensive analyses have considered the factors that account for observed behavioral and other changes and the cost-effectiveness of treatment.

*Analysis Framework*

Analyses conducted to date have been based on a general conceptual framework that portrays client behaviors and psychological states in the period after treatment to be a function of four types of factors:

• client background factors, including sociodemographic characteristics, prior treatment history, and criminal justice status
• client behaviors and psychological states in the period before entering drug abuse treatment
• the treatment experience, including modality, length of time spent in treatment, and services received
• other conditions such as community-based services received during and after treatment and drug abuse treatment episodes subsequent to the treatment episode

These variables and their interrelationships are illustrated in Figure 2-1. This general model indicates the time periods for which particular types of variables are available, and arrows indicate the assumed temporal and causal direction of the relationships. Sometimes bidirectional relationships are specified, such as in the case of the relationship between client behaviors and subsequent treatment episodes, where it is assumed that the two sets of variables could influence each other.

The model indicates that client characteristics, behaviors, environ-

Figure 2-1 General Model of Relationships among Client Characteristics, Drug Abuse Treatment, and Outcomes

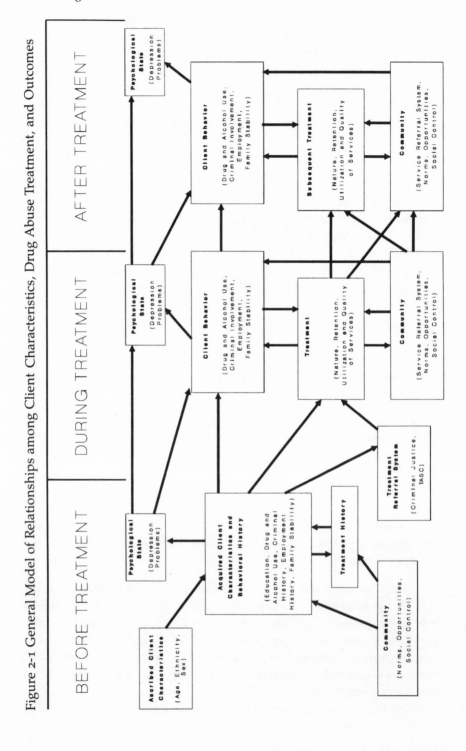

ments, and psychological states have effects that persist throughout and after treatment. They also affect the client's response to treatment and the potential to change behavior. In the model, the role of treatment is to change behaviors and psychological states and to direct clients to community resources during and after treatment. Thus, the effect of particular treatment episodes must be considered in comparison with the effects of the variety of other factors that may contribute to outcomes. It should be noted that no direct effect of treatment on posttreatment behavior is shown. Programs have no direct control on behavior after clients leave treatment. Rather, treatment should influence posttreatment behavior indirectly through changes in psychological states and behavior during treatment. To the extent possible, the basic multivariate analyses described in this book attempt to consider the relative effects of the factors included in this model.

*Measurement*

Several key measures were used in analyses reported in this book to characterize the nature of drug abuse, alcohol abuse, criminal activity, and depression. Construction of these measures is described briefly here, and construction of other measures is described in the text as they are introduced.

Drug abuse patterns may be described in a number of ways, in terms of the specific drugs abused, the number of drugs abused concurrently, the frequency and severity of use, the length of addiction, and drug abuse history. In analyses reported in this book, drug abuse is described primarily in terms of regular (that is, weekly or daily) use of specific drugs during the past year and a drug abuse pattern index that measures the multiple drug abuse of this generation of drug abusers. Drug abuse is also described in terms of the number of drugs abused concurrently and in terms of the primary drug of abuse in the three months before admission. The drug abuse pattern index was developed (Bray et al. 1982; Hubbard, Bray, Craddock, et al. 1986) for this research, based on weekly or daily use of eight drug types. The index is hierarchical, that is, the seven categories describe drug abuse patterns of increasing severity and complexity, from minimal use of any drugs to regular abuse of heroin and other opioids.

Alcohol use is described in terms of a widely used index that captures the quantity and frequency of drinking during the three months before admission or during three-month periods during or after treatment. The measure is based on the drinking level typology developed by Mulford and Miller (1960) and used in most national studies of alcohol use (Clark and Midanik 1982; Rachal et al. 1975, 1980). The typology defines five drinking levels ranging from abstainer to heavy drinker. Because of the pervasiveness of drinking among the drug abuse treatment population and the concern about alcohol abuse among clients, heavy drinkers are emphasized in most analyses in this book.

Criminal activity is assessed in the TOPS research in terms of self-reported involvement in 11 types of crimes, including drug-related crimes, property crimes, and violent crimes. In analyses reported in this book, a measure of involvement in predatory crimes is the primary measure of criminal activity, because of the concern for income-generating crimes among clients and the relationship between drug use and income-generating crime. Predatory crimes include aggravated assault, robbery, burglary, larceny, auto theft, forgery/embezzlement, and dealing in stolen property.

In the TOPS research three items were used to assess symptoms of depression—feeling so depressed that one could not get out of bed in the morning, having thoughts of suicide, or having attempted suicide within the previous year. The prevalence of symptoms of depression according to these three items was compared in a pretest to the Beck, Koss and Butcher, and CES-D depression inventories. The comparisons showed that the three items, although brief, formed an adequate instrument for screening clients for depression (Allison et al. 1986). In many of the analyses described here, we focus only on suicidal indicators.

*Descriptive Analysis*

Many of the descriptive analyses have simply compared client behaviors before, during, and after treatment to ascertain the magnitude of changes. In these cases, prevalence figures or scores on behavioral indexes are compared for entire cohorts or for specific subgroups for the periods before, during, and after treatment. Other descriptive comparisons are made of the direction and extent of change in those indicators, including one-year abstinence rates and improvement rates.

Because of the discontinuity in the funding of the various phases of the TOPS study, behaviors of the same group of clients could not be traced at the same time points during and after treatment. All three admission cohorts were interviewed at intake and periodically during treatment, but the cohorts were interviewed at different intervals after leaving treatment. The 1979 admission cohort was interviewed one and two years after treatment, the 1980 admission cohort three months and one year after treatment, and the 1981 admission cohort three to five years after treatment. Thus, instead of tracing the experience of a single cohort throughout the observation period, we conceptualize the behaviors of different groups of the admission cohorts at the various time points as a synthetic cohort of treatment clients. That is, we assume that the behaviors of the different groups at each time point before, during, and after treatment would approximate the behavior of an actual cohort of clients if we were able to follow that group over the complete time span. The lack of differences in key characteristics among the cohorts reported in Chapter 4 supports this assumption. Sample sizes for each of these time periods are presented in Table A-1 in the Appendix. The descriptive data for behaviors before, during, and after treatment are shown in Tables A-2 and A-3 for the three modalities separately. Percentages for the year before and three months in treatment are based on the 1979 and 1980 cohorts combined; the three-month follow-up, on the 1980 cohort; the one-year follow-up, on the 1979 and 1980 cohorts combined; the two-year follow-up, on the 1979 cohort; and the three- to five-year follow-up, on the 1981 cohort.

*Explanatory Analyses*

Multivariate analyses were also conducted using log-linear regression or least-squares regression techniques to examine factors accounting for posttreatment behaviors. Regression analyses were, in general, conducted separately for each modality because of the differences in client populations across modalities. Independent variables in most of these models included sociodemographic characteristics, referral from the criminal justice system, number of prior treatment admissions, treatment variables such as time in treatment and service intensity, and pretreatment behaviors such as drug or alcohol abuse or the outcome behavior in question.

Dependent variables were often categorized to indicate whether a client reported a level of abuse or concomitant problems. The criteria for abuse and problems include regular use of specific drugs such as heroin or cocaine, any predatory criminal activity, less than full-time employment (working 35 or more hours per week for 40 or more weeks), heavy alcohol use, and suicidal symptoms. These analyses define which client groups have a higher likelihood of positive posttreatment outcomes, controlling for relevant pretreatment and treatment factors.

Considerable attention was given to the specification of the type and structure of the independent variables included in the regression models. Categorical variables were developed that reflected most of the concepts in the general model and met statistical criteria for logistic regression analysis. The basic model employed in most of the analyses reported in this book included the independent variables presented in Table 2-1. Because of the different distribution of these variables in the three modalities, somewhat different categories of each variable were used.

The logistic regression procedure provides log-odds coefficients for

Table 2-1 Independent Variables and Categories Used in Regression
Models

| Independent Variable | Categories |
| --- | --- |
| Sex | • Male<br>• Female |
| Marital status | • Married<br>• Never married<br>• Separated, widowed, or divorced |
| Education | • Less than high school<br>• High school graduate |
| Age | |
|   Methadone | • 25 or less<br>• 26–30<br>• 31 or older |
|   Residential and outpatient<br>    drug-free | • 20 or younger<br>• 21–25<br>• 26–30<br>• 31 or older |
| Race/ethnicity | • White<br>• Black<br>• Hispanic |
| Prior treatment admission | • None<br>• 1–2<br>• 3 or more |
| Source of referral | |
|   Methadone | • Self<br>• Family or friends<br>• Community agency and other sources |
|   Residential and outpatient<br>    drug-free | • Self<br>• Family or friends<br>• Criminal justice system<br>• Community agency and other sources |

*(continued on next page)*

Table 2-1  Independent Variables and Categories Used in Regression Models *(continued)*

| Independent Variable | Categories |
| --- | --- |
| Pretreatment drug abuse pattern | |
|   Methadone | • Heroin |
| | • Heroin and opioids |
| | • Other opioids |
| | • Former daily heroin user |
|   Residential and outpatient drug-free | • Heroin |
| | • Heroin and opioids |
| | • Other opioids |
| | • Multiple nonopioids |
| | • Single nonopioid |
| | • Alcohol and marijuana |
| | • Minimal use |
| Treatment duration | |
|   Methadone | • 1 week or less |
| | • 2–13 weeks |
| | • 14–52 weeks |
| | • Discharge after 52 weeks |
| | • Long-term maintenance |
|   Residential | • 1 week or less |
| | • 2–13 weeks |
| | • 14–26 weeks |
| | • 27–52 weeks |
| | • 53 or more weeks |
|   Outpatient drug-free | • 1 week or less |
| | • 2–13 weeks |
| | • 14–26 weeks |
| | • 27 or more weeks |
| Weeks of treatment in the year after treatment (residential and outpatient drug-free only) | • None |
| | • 1–39 |
| | • 40–52 |

each independent variable. These coefficients are the log of the odds that an independent variable predicts the dependent variable, holding constant the effects of other independent variables. A more readily interpretable estimate of the effect of each of the independent variables is the odds ratio, the exponential function of the log-odds coefficients. Odds ratios greater than 1.0 indicate that the variable increases the odds of the posttreatment behavior, while odds ratios less than 1.0 indicate that the variable decreases the odds of the posttreatment behavior. In the particular logistic regression approach used in these analyses (Harrell 1980), the odds ratio is calculated for each characteristic in comparison to a selected reference group (i.e., multiple nonopioid users are compared to heroin users). For example, a client with a pattern of multiple nonopioid use might have a higher risk of posttreatment cocaine abuse (odds ratio greater than 1.00) than a similar client who used mainly heroin in the year before treatment. An older black male heroin addict may have a comparatively lower risk of posttreatment cocaine abuse (odds ratio less 1.00) than a young white female nonopioid user. Significance is assessed by calculation of the chi-square for each comparison. In this book, results are described as significant if the probability of obtaining the result by chance is less than 5 percent (see Appendix, Tables A-4, A-5, and A-6).

## Summary

The Treatment Outcome Prospective Study is a national longitudinal assessment of drug abuse treatment outcomes. The data presented here are based on interviews at the time of program admission with 4,184 clients from 12 outpatient methadone treatment programs, 2,891 clients from 14 residential programs, and 2,914 clients from 11 outpatient drug-free programs. The programs and cities were purposely selected to reflect drug abuse treatment in large and medium-sized urban areas with a broad range of drug abuse problems. Although the programs were not a nationally representative sample, they appeared to reflect adequately the range of treatments available and types of clients entering treatment between 1979 and 1981.

Full-time interviewers were hired and trained specifically for the TOPS research to interview clients in each participating program. All applicants for drug abuse treatment were referred to the TOPS interviewer as soon as possible after they first contacted the program. Eighty percent of all applicants were interviewed at intake. Comparison of the data from the program's records of nonrespondents with that of other clients who stayed in treatment only a brief time indicated no significant differences in sex, age, race, or primary drug problem between the two groups.

Posttreatment data were collected on subsamples of each admission cohort: the 1979 admission cohort (12 and 24 months after termination), the 1980 admission cohort (3 and 12 months after termination), and the 1981 admission cohort (between 36 and 60 months after termination). Follow-up samples stratified by modality and treatment duration were constructed to provide estimates with equivalent precision across modality. Eighty percent of the clients were interviewed for the three-month, one-, and two-year follow-ups. About 65 percent of the sample was interviewed for the three-to-five-year follow-up. The estimates in the follow-up analyses are adjusted for nonresponse and weighted to represent the population of clients interviewed at intake.

In addition to providing basic information on treatment effectiveness and other policy questions that are the subject of this book, the Treatment Outcome Prospective Study has made a number of important methodological contributions to the study of drug abuse treatment effectiveness. A major objective of the TOPS research was a full and accurate description of the clients and their behavior. To achieve this goal, a variety of prototypic measures of patterns of drug abuse, depression, criminal behavior, and employment were specially developed for the TOPS study. TOPS also provides a comprehensive study of the nature of drug abuse treatment services in the major modalities across the nation. Such information is not available elsewhere and provides a meaningful context for the interpretation of information about treatment effectiveness across the broad range of types of treatment programs.

Other innovations include refinements in the methodology of conducting studies of the effectiveness of drug abuse treatment. TOPS was the first research study to establish a system of program-based data collection, with interviewers working in treatment programs in close cooperation with staff and clients. Approaches designed to achieve high participation rates in all modalities, including compensation, were systematically tested. Efficient methods of locating clients for follow-up studies for the difficult-to-reach population of drug abusers were refined to achieve completion rates of 80 percent.

The wealth of data available in TOPS supported the generation of a variety of new analytic approaches. The cost-benefit study described in Chapter 7 is the most definitive analysis of the cost-effectiveness of drug abuse treatment yet conducted. The study examines the economic impact of the crime reduction effects of drug abuse treatment with data on criminal activity collected during the TOPS study. More extensive analyses are described in Harwood et al. (1988). Other analytic advances include the conceptualization of the treatment history in terms of a treatment career (Marsden, Hubbard, and Bailey 1988), logistic regression analyses of the impact of treatment duration on treatment effectiveness (Hubbard et al. 1987), and demonstration of the distinctiveness of client populations by modality (Hubbard, Bray, Cavanaugh, et al. 1986). Further analyses of the Treatment Outcome Prospective Study data are in progress and will result in additional advances in approaches to understanding drug abuse treatment effectiveness.

# 3. Treatment in the Major Modalities

Although many studies of the effectiveness of drug abuse treatment have been conducted, there is limited information available about the nature of therapy and services delivered in drug abuse treatment programs (Allison and Hubbard 1985). Program administrators, researchers, and policy-makers are in general agreement that community-based drug abuse treatment helped rehabilitate many drug-dependent individuals (Tims 1981). There is no question that treatment works, but much more needs to be known about how and why treatment works. In general, outcomes have not been linked to the nature of treatment that clients have received (Sells 1979). Variables in the "black box" that is drug abuse treatment need to be better specified, and their role in producing positive outcomes better understood (DeLeon and Rosenthal 1979; Meyer 1983). Much of the available information concerns treatments common during the early 1970s. There may have been major changes in the nature of clients and treatment over the past decade that limit the utility of this information (Butynski and Canova 1988; Jaffe 1984; Greenberg and Brown 1984). The findings presented in this chapter provide more current information about the nature, quality, and quantity of treatment rendered in the major modalities.

During the late 1970s and early 1980s, when the clients participating in this research entered treatment, the treatment system was characterized by three major approaches or modalities: outpatient methadone, residential, and outpatient drug-free programs. These are still the most prevalent forms of publicly funded drug abuse treatment in the 1980s (Butynski and Canova 1988), despite such major changes as increased cocaine abuse, the transition in funding of programs from federal to state governments through block grants, and the emergence of the AIDS epidemic.

This chapter describes the nature of treatment delivered in the three major treatment modalities. Because of the pronounced differences in approaches and client populations across these modalities, analyses of the nature of treatment reported in this chapter and changes in client behaviors reported in later chapters of this book consider each modality separately. Analyses presented in this chapter describe the nature of the treatment system, while subsequent chapters consider how aspects of treatment, such as services received and time spent in treatment, affect outcomes. These issues are discussed in more detail in Allison, Hubbard, and Rachal (1985).

## Treatment in Outpatient Methadone Programs

In the 1960s the success of a methadone maintenance program at Beth Israel Hospital in New York (Dole and Nyswander 1965; Dole, Nyswander, and Warner 1968) demonstrated that heroin addicts could be successfully treated with a daily oral dose of methadone. By the early 1970s, methadone maintenance was an accepted mode of treatment for heroin abuse. The number of methadone maintenance clinics increased rapidly between 1970 and 1973, and by the late 1970s over 75,000 heroin addicts were being treated in methadone maintenance programs across the United States (Lowinson and Millman 1979). In 1982 the 71,000 clients in outpatient methadone programs represented 41 percent of all clients in drug abuse treatment units (NIDA 1983).

In 1972 regulations were established jointly by the Food and Drug Administration and the National Institute on Drug Abuse (NIDA). Federal regulations in the late 1970s defined maintenance treatment using methadone as the "continued administering or dispensing of methadone, in conjunction with provision of appropriate social and medical services, at relatively stable dosage levels for a period in excess of 21 days as an oral substitute for heroin or other morphine-like drugs, for an individual dependent on heroin" (U.S. Department of Health and Human Services 1980). Programs were required to obtain a personal and medical history for each client, as well as a comprehensive examination, including any lab or special examinations the attending physician felt were indicated. Social rehabilitation is clearly one of the goals of methadone maintenance treatment, but the regulations only suggested that programs make available various services such as vocational rehabilitation.

In general, methadone maintenance is delivered on an outpatient basis. The basic approach to treatment has not greatly changed since its inception, but there is variation across programs in philosophy, duration, and dosage. D'Amanda (1983) maintains that these differences in program policy regarding methadone administration affect the quality and effectiveness of treatment. Dole and Nyswander (1965) have maintained that supportive social services such as psychotherapy, vocational training, and educational programs are essential parts of treatment. Newman (1977) agreed that methadone by itself cannot be a complete treatment for heroin addiction but also pointed out that the kinds of services needed and the special role of psychological counseling are still subjects of considerable debate. Lowinson and Millman (1979) similarly assert that appropriate services are necessary to overcome social and psychological disabilities resulting from an addict lifestyle.

A major controversy in the provision of methadone maintenance treatment concerns the adherence to the philosophy of long-term methadone maintenance versus methadone-to-abstinence. The federal regulations governing methadone maintenance treatment have accommodated both positions. The regulations state that "an eventual drug-free state is the treatment goal for many patients; it is recognized, however, that for some patients the drug may be needed for a long period of time" (U.S. Department of Health and Human Services 1980). The two positions clearly have important implications for program planning, services offered, definitions of success, funding, staffing, and a myriad of other issues.

There are two models of methadone treatment that differ in their conceptions of the nature of drug addiction, the proper use of methadone, and the requisite services necessary to foster rehabilitation. Graff and Ball (1976) contrast the "metabolic" and "psychotherapeutic" models of methadone treatment. According to the metabolic model, drug abuse is primarily a "metabolic disease, reflecting a specific physical or biochemical deficit." The symptom is a craving for an opioid drug and is corrected by the administration of a daily dose of methadone. Services and therapy are viewed as adjuncts, and abstinence is not a major goal of treatment. In the psychotherapeutic model, drug abuse is seen as a symptom of a primary emotional disorder. In this model, methadone is adjunctive to the principal psychotherapy. Eventual abstinence from methadone is an important goal of treatment. This distinction is similar to that utilized in the Drug Abuse Reporting Program (DARP) research between adaptive and change-oriented programs, respectively (Cole and James 1975). In adaptive programs, clients are expected to continue indefinitely on methadone and to develop vocational skills that enable them to hold a job; counseling and support services are provided for all clients, and there are no provisions for withdrawal or aftercare. In contrast, the goal of change-oriented programs is the achievement of drug-free living and resocialization to a productive lifestyle; a structured framework of therapeutic activities is provided along with special services for withdrawal and aftercare. While in adaptive programs high doses of methadone are prescribed to block the effects should a client attempt to use heroin, in change-oriented programs methadone is typically prescribed at as low a level as the patient can tolerate.

The controversy over long-term maintenance versus methadone-to-abstinence continues. Comparisons of the nature of methadone treatment over the decade of the 1970s with that of previous years suggests an increasing popularity of abstinence-based methadone programs (Allison, Hubbard, and Rachal 1985; Glasscote et al. 1972).

## Organization and Staffing

Methadone clinics vary in size and structure as well as in how they are organized within the health care delivery system. The 17 clinics in the TOPS study had on average just over 260 clients; 14 of the clinics had between 200 and 400 clients. Of the 17, 10 were affiliated with large hospitals. The clinics, however, tended to be located in the community; only two were on hospital grounds. Six of the remaining clinics were operated by independent community organizations. One clinic was part of a multimodality drug abuse treatment agency administered by a county government.

The clinic staff may well be one of the most important determinants of the success of a program. Lowinson and Millman (1979) recommended that staffing patterns be developed to meet the psychosocial as well as obvious medical needs of the methadone client. Thus, in addition to physicians and nurses, they recommend employing a psychiatric social worker and counselors with specialized areas of expertise. The organization of the methadone clinics within the health care delivery system may, in part, lead to different staffing configurations. The staffing may also contribute in many ways to the philosophy and procedures of the program.

Methadone programs do indeed have medical staff members who compose a significant proportion of the staff as a whole. However, the distribution of hours across other types of personnel suggests two types of staffing patterns in the methadone programs. In four clinics, the medical staff (including physicians, nurses, and other medical professionals) worked less than 20 percent of the hours; in nine clinics, they worked more than 30 percent of the hours; and in the other four clinics they worked between 20 and 30 percent. The hours worked by direct service staff members (including psychologists, social workers, and counselors) varied from more than half the full-time hours (six clinics) to less than one-third the full-time hours (eight clinics). The latter clinics were all affiliated with hospitals. This divergence in staff composition suggests two major types of service orientation—programs that emphasize either medical or social rehabilitation. These orientations could affect treatment outcomes because of the differences in the types of services available to clients.

There is little available information about the educational qualifications and experience of drug abuse treatment clinic directors, although a number of studies have evaluated the effectiveness of a counseling staff with varying educational backgrounds and experience. Most research has provided no definitive evidence regarding the superiority of professionally trained counselors versus counselors who are ex-addicts themselves (see reviews by Allison and Hubbard 1985; Hall 1983; Woody 1983; as well as empirical studies by Brown and Thompson 1973; Longwell, Miller, and Nichols 1978; LoSciuto, Aiken, and Ausetts 1979). However, as Greenberg and Brown (1984) note, there is a trend toward improving the formal education and credentials of counselors. In 1979 about half of the paid counselors in methadone programs had at least a bachelor's degree. Seven percent of the full-time staff hours were provided by social workers with professional training.

Directors of clinics participating in this study had a high degree of formal education as well as extensive experience in drug abuse treatment. All but 4 of the 17 directors who responded had at least a bachelor's degree, and 7 had master's degrees. They had an average of nearly seven years' experience in drug abuse treatment. Ten had been at the same program for at least two years, five of these for at least five years. The average age of clinic directors was 34; about half were women, and about half were black or Hispanic.

Counselors were also fairly well educated, mature in age, and had extensive experience in drug abuse treatment, as indicated by responses of 38 counselors with at least one year experience in the programs. Of the 38 counselors, 23 had bachelor's degrees and 14 had master's degrees. Only two did not report having some college courses. The age range was from 27 to 56, with a median age of 37. Experience in drug abuse treatment programs averaged seven years, with 26 of the counselors having spent almost all of their drug treatment careers in their current programs. Ex-addicts participated to some degree in most of the programs, but the extent of their involvement varied. They were very active in four programs but did no counseling in three others.

These findings suggest that the directors and counseling staff of methadone programs are well educated and have extensive experience in drug abuse treatment. Their long tenures in their current programs suggest a staff stability and maturity that should aid the treatment process. However, the selection criterion that the study examine stable, well established programs may have contributed to the observed stability of staff.

*Approach*

Although the dispensing of methadone is the primary defining characteristic of methadone treatment, the orientation toward methadone and its role in the treatment plan contributes to substantial variability among programs. The programs also vary in policies and practices such as dosage level, urine testing, and take-home policies. These issues are important in determining the overall approach to methadone treatment used by each of the programs.

MAINTENANCE VERSUS ABSTINENCE

The controversy over long-term methadone maintenance versus methadone-to-abstinence has important implications for the nature of treatment provided in methadone programs. Federal regulations governing methadone programs accommodate both positions. The regulations state that although an eventual drug-free state is the treatment goal for many patients, it is recognized that some patients may need methadone for long periods (U.S. Department of Health and Human Services 1980).

The survey of directors of clinics participating in this study indicates a movement toward abstinence not apparent a decade ago, when methadone programs appeared to discourage their clients from attempting to detoxify from methadone (Glasscote et al. 1972). Among 17 clinic directors, 3 described their programs as methadone-to-abstinence programs. Twelve of the directors said they encouraged abstinence to a great extent, and 10 stated that detoxification was generally begun at the request of the client. Despite this apparent support for abstinence, however, all but one of the directors said they also supported long-term maintenance to some extent; five encouraged maintenance to a great extent. Nine of the clinics had at least 75 percent of their clients on long-term (over one year) methadone maintenance. In all but one clinic, over half of the clients were in long-term maintenance. Thus, although programs do not agree on which approach to methadone treatment is better, the programs seem to support maintenance treatment.

This division among methadone programs between methadone-to-abstinence and maintenance programs noted by Brown, Jansen, and Benn (1975) is still reflected in great variation among staff and clients in their treatment philosophy. Some ambivalence was also reflected in the responses of methadone counselors. Of the 38 who answered the question regarding whether they encouraged abstinence, 14 reported encouraging it to some extent, 16 to a great extent, and 7 to a very great extent. Of the total, 6 reported encouraging maintenance to a great extent, 24 to some extent, and 7 did not encourage maintenance at all. Despite the variety of responses, most of the counselors indicated that over half of their clients were on long-term maintenance. Their orientations to abstinence or maintenance did not appear to affect dosage levels or the proportion of the counselor's caseload on long-term maintenance. Inconsistent or unclear staff philosophy on methadone may affect treatment in more subtle ways. For instance, clients were well aware of program rules regarding the use of methadone but did not understand the overall treatment plan or program goals.

This inconsistent view of methadone in the field may indicate the need to specify program philosophy clearly, especially the criteria and alternatives for abstinence and maintenance. A precise position and policy on this critical issue could improve staff functioning and help clarify issues critical to clients in their decisions about the course of their treatment.

TREATMENT PLAN

The treatment plan is considered an essential part of treatment. Federal funding criteria require that plans be developed with the knowledge of the individual client and updated periodically. Lowinson and Millman (1979) suggested that plans for methadone clients be developed by a social worker and reviewed and modified as necessary every three months. A General Accounting Office (GAO) report on all treatment modalities concluded that treatment plans are "often incomplete, vague, or missing . . . and that even when present they are not periodically reassessed" (U.S. GAO 1980, pp. 31–32). Rehabilitation should be fostered by the client's understanding and participation in the development of an individualized treatment plan, including setting goals and behavioral guidelines.

Eleven of the clinic directors in this study said that treatment plans were developed within a week after admission. Most said their plans were updated at least every three months. In checks of clinic records, the majority of the plans were found to have been updated at least once and about one-fourth had been revised four or more times. Most of the recorded treatment plans had been developed by a master's level social worker or other member of the counseling staff. Six program directors reported that the social worker usually developed the plans. The other clinics used counselors and other staff members to do so.

The clinic directors also commented more generally on the treatment process within their programs. Most clinics admitted clients into the program within one or two days of initial contact. However, six clinics had an initial trial or review period of from three days to two weeks before the client was officially admitted to the program. Eleven said that the usual planned duration of treatment in their programs was 18 months or more. Only four of the clinic directors indicated they emphasized formal designation of phases or stages of treatment for clients.

In contrast to the clinic directors' emphasis on treatment plans, three-fourths of the clients indicated they had not received a formal, written treatment plan. However, treatment plans that the clients had signed were found in over 90 percent of their files. In 14 of the 17 clinics, treatment plans were found for over 98 percent of clients. This divergence indicates that clients are not fully involved in developing their treatment plans and perhaps are not aware of what treatment plans are. Indeed, in 7 of the 17 clinics, staff members said that clients were only involved to a limited extent in the development of their plans.

The delivery of treatment in these programs appears to follow what has traditionally occurred in methadone programs. However, records of treatment plans appear to be much better than were found in the GAO study. Still, the finding that clients have minimal knowledge of and involvement in the preparation and review of their treatment plans is troubling. Treatment plans are advocated as an important, if not the most important, element in successful treatment. Yet, most clinics do not appear to be using treatment plans appropriately. Clearly, greater client involvement is necessary. Much of the concern about variability and inconsistency of treatment goals (Brown and Thompson 1975–76), especially in methadone programs, might be reduced if plans were clearly written and discussed in detail with clients.

DOSAGE LEVELS

Hargreaves (1983) reviewed current knowledge about daily methadone dosage levels and the effectiveness of varied dosage levels. Because dosage levels of 100 mg have proven to be therapeutically effective with many clients, he advocates freer use of high dosage levels. Despite the evidence cited by Hargreaves, there has been a trend toward lower dosage levels over the decade of the 1970s (D'Amanda 1983). Usual dosage levels were 20 to 39 mg in many programs by 1980 (Brown et al. 1982–83). The research literature (Goldstein and Judson 1983; Hargreaves 1983; Woody 1983) indicates that dosages around 80 mg are effective for a large proportion of clients. Lowinson and Millman (1979) advocate between 20 and 40 mg at the beginning of the induction phase but also report that higher dosages, such as 70 to 100 mg contribute to a "wider margin of safety." Goldstein and Judson (1983), among others, argue that dosage may be unimportant above a certain level and that other factors may be more critical to positive outcomes.

The programs participating in this study appear to be administering dosage levels at admission that are consistent with those advocated by Lowinson and Millman for the induction phase, but dosage levels are clearly lowered as treatment proceeds. At admission the vast majority of clients were receiving methadone dosages of 10 to 40 mg per day; only 3 percent were receiving dosages over 70 mg. At three months in treatment 40 percent of clients were receiving doses below 30 mg per day, although virtually all researchers advocate dosages of 40 mg or more. Dosage levels for long-term methadone maintenance tended to be low and highly variable across programs.

URINALYSIS

Urinalysis is currently as controversial a subject in drug abuse treatment as it is in the workplace. When the TOPS study began, federal regulations required weekly urinalyses for the first three months in a program and then monthly random urinalyses (Lowinson and Millman 1979). D'Amanda (1983) as well as Lowinson and Millman questioned the benefits of urinalysis, given the costs in staff time, expense of the analysis, and possible negative reaction of the clients. Havassy and Hall (1981) could find no significant differences in the proportion of drug-free specimens between monitored clients and a group that was not required to provide urine specimens. Despite the controversy over its use and questions about its efficiency, all clinic directors reported urine samples were collected weekly during the first month in treatment. Urinalysis results were included in the clinical/medical records for 84 percent of methadone clients.

TAKE-HOME POLICY

A third element of controversy in methadone treatment involves take-home medication policy. After demonstrating a commitment to rehabilitation for 3 to 12 months, clients can be granted take-home privileges (D'Amanda 1983; Lowinson and Millman 1979). Some studies (Dole et al. 1971; Patch, Raynes, and Fisch 1973) indicate that denial of take-home privileges has negative consequences. D'Amanda concluded, however, that after other factors are taken into consideration, take-home medication does not affect retention. He cites the study by Havassy and Hargreaves (1979) as evidence that take-home privileges have minimal effect on behavior. Potential diversion of methadone for illicit resale (Inciardi 1977) is clearly one of the major concerns about take-home privileges.

Despite the controversy about take-home policies, the practice is common in programs in this study. In about half of the clinics, 75 to 100 percent of clients have some take-home privileges after three months in treatment. In three other clinics, 50 to 75 percent have take-home privileges, and in the remaining five responding clinics, fewer than 50 percent have such privileges. Checks of the clinic records confirmed these responses in general.

*Services*

The original design of methadone programs emphasized the need for a full range of services to help rehabilitate clients. The role of methadone itself was seen as a way to stabilize behavior so that clients could benefit from these services. Psychological counseling as well as other supportive services are delivered to clients of methadone programs, but the range and intensity of these services vary across programs. Federal regulations required a minimum of one counseling session per month for each client but did not specify the nature of these sessions nor the nature of any supportive services to be provided. Counseling includes communication on the issue of drug use as well as psychotherapeutic counseling on life problems. Both types of counseling may be necessary for the rehabilitative process and are made available in many programs. Clearly, methadone clients also require medical services; other services may aid in the rehabilitative process, but these ancillary services are less often made available.

COUNSELING

Researchers have described a variety of counseling approaches that are in use in drug treatment programs, but there is little description of what constitutes basic "drug counseling." Lowinson and Millman (1979) attempted to delineate some of the major aspects of drug counseling, for example, developing the client's identification with the program, communicating rules and regulations, identifying rewarding alternatives to drug use, and discussing practical, everyday problems. However, it is obvious that many components of drug counseling are difficult to describe, document, or quantify. In the absence of detailed clinic records, it is also difficult to determine the nature, quality, and quantity of counseling received. In reporting on counseling services, it may also have been difficult for clients to distinguish full counseling sessions from more informal contacts. The latter type of contact, which frequently occurs in programs, particularly in crisis situations, may be a major factor in treatment outcomes and may not be easily quantified or documented. Despite these concerns, Woody (1983) and Kleber (1984) report positive outcomes with a variety of psychotherapeutic approaches combined with drug counseling.

Information about the nature of counseling in programs included in this study is available from reports of clinic directors and clients as well as clinical/medical records. All of the clinic directors reported extensive use of individual therapy or counseling and scheduled individual sessions once a week or more often, generally in half-hour sessions. Three clinic directors, however, reported sessions that lasted from 45 to 60 minutes. Counselors, on the other hand, reported that sessions generally lasted longer. Most of the counseling was received in individual sessions. About 78 percent of clients reported receiving most or all of their counseling in individual sessions. Only 7 percent reported receiving any group therapy or counseling, although in one clinic half of the clients reported receiving an equal mix of group or individual counseling. Many of those clinics that do use group sessions use them intensively. In six clinics therapy groups met less frequently than once a week in sessions lasting from 30 to 60 minutes; six clinics did not use them at all; in the four clinics in which groups met weekly, sessions lasted from 90 to 120 minutes. In five clinics, however, about one-fourth of the clients reported receiving no counseling of any kind during their first three months of treatment.

Practical problem solving rather than intensive psychotherapy was the focus of most of the counseling sessions. Ten of the 16 clinic directors who responded to this question reported that this was the case, while two indicated that changing the client's lifestyle was most important, and three others cited a variety of counseling goals. Only one focused on the physiological/medical aspects of methadone. Despite the focus on problem solving, the clinic directors and counselors also reported at least a moderate emphasis on individual psychotherapy.

Average client caseloads in most of the programs indicate that adequate time is available for counseling sessions. Lowinson and Millman (1979) recommend a caseload of 50 clients, while Woody (1983) suggests that a caseload of 35 is a more "workable" number. With only about 60 percent of a counselor's time available for direct client contact, a caseload of 50 suggests that only about one-half hour a week is available for individual sessions with each client. In about half of the clinics included in this study, caseloads range from 20 to 30, well within acceptable ranges. In only one program was the average caseload 70 or more, and a second program had caseloads averaging 45.

Despite limited caseloads in many programs, several findings suggest that adequate delivery of counseling services may be problematic. Although the client/counselor relationship demands the establishment of trust and support, a check of clinic records revealed that three of every five clients had two or more primary counselors. Unless counselor rotation is a planned approach to treatment, there is considerable discontinuity of the client/counselor relationship. Further, there appears to be little matching of clients and counselors. Only 6 of the 17 clinics reported attempts to assign clients with particular types of problems to specific counselors.

SUPPORTIVE SERVICES

In addition to counseling, clients may also receive services directed at specific problem areas. The need for a variety of ancillary and supportive services for methadone clients was first voiced by Dole, Nyswander, and Warner (1968). Lowinson and Millman (1979) cited education, vocational rehabilitation, job placement, family therapy, and legal services as useful areas of specialization for counseling staff.

Information from clients was obtained on seven types of services distinct from drug abuse counseling: medical, psychological, family, vocational, educational, legal, and financial services. Client self-reports, clinic records, and estimates of treatment directors all document that clients received a variety of services. Judging by the reports of clinic directors, medical services were most frequently received (42 percent of the clients), although this value is inflated by the required physical examination at intake. Other services were reportedly received by 20 percent or fewer of the clients. Clinic directors indicated that 20 percent of clients had received psychological services for mental health or emotional problems and about 20 percent had received financial services; about 15 percent had received some type of educational service; and 10 to 12 percent had received either family, legal, or job-related services in the three months before the interview.

Clinic records indicate that the majority of methadone clients receive one or more types of supportive services during the course of their treatment. Comparisons of the number of services received by clients entering treatment in 1979, 1980, or 1981 indicate that programs may be increasing the intensity of service delivery. About 35 percent of clients in clinics in 1979 received two or more services, compared with 43 percent in 1980 and 51 percent in 1981. However, the programs varied considerably in the number of services actually received by most clients and in the range of types of services available to clients. Aftercare services provided as follow-up by programs after clients leave treatment are in general not available to methadone clients.

*Financing*

The 17 methadone clinics in this study had an average annual budget of $1,945 per client. The per client cost is partially a function of the size of the clinic, because buildings and administrative staff are fixed costs. The costs and budgets of the programs in this study may not reflect the per client costs required by clinics with fewer than 200 clients. All clinics received funding from state governments, and nine had NIDA statewide services grants or other grants or contracts for specific services. Client fees made up more than 10 percent of the budgets of only five programs. Public insurance provided almost half of the funding for the seven clinics of one large program. Clinics also obtained funding from the Bureau of Prisons (three clinics), Comprehensive Employment and Training Act (CETA) programs (three), local government (one), and private donations (one). Thus, although most of the TOPS programs received funding from a variety of sources, all were based largely on public funding.

## Treatment in Residential Programs

Therapeutic communities and other similar residential programs are a second major type of drug abuse treatment program. Within this book, all these types of programs are referred to as residential programs. These programs originated with the therapeutic community Synanon, begun in 1958 by Charles Dederich. Synanon grew out of and was loosely based on the philosophical principles of Alcoholics Anonymous (Bourne and Ramsey 1975; Glaser 1974; Yablonsky 1965). Other therapeutic communities that developed during the 1960s, such as Daytop Village in 1963, Phoenix House in 1967, Odyssey House in 1966, and Gateway Foundation in 1968, were based on the Synanon concept. While Synanon emphasized permanent participation in its program and the rejection of life outside the therapeutic community, reentry or return to society was a major goal in most other therapeutic communities (Brook and Whitehead 1980). By 1979 over 300 therapeutic communities had been established across the country (DeLeon and Rosenthal 1979). In 1982 about 1 in 10 clients were residents in therapeutic communities or similar 24-hour live-in facilities (NIDA 1983).

The basic goal of therapeutic communities is for drug abusers to undergo a "complete change in lifestyle: abstinence from drugs, elimination of antisocial (criminal) behavior, development of employable skills, self-reliance, and personal honesty." To effect this change requires a "total 24 hour community impact" (DeLeon and Rosenthal 1979, p. 40). A number of authors (e.g., Densen-Gerber 1972; Nash 1974; Yablonsky 1965) have written detailed and readable accounts of life in a therapeutic community. Kajdan and Senay (1976) also wrote brief overviews of the nature of the treatment programs in Synanon, Odyssey House, Phoenix House, Gateway House, Safari House, Tinley Park, and a number of other therapeutic communities, especially as they relate to youthful addicts.

More recently, Holland (1986) conducted a survey of characteristics of 32 long-term (12 months or more) residential programs that included information on program goals and treatment process in these clinics.

Briefly, therapeutic communities emphasize a self-help approach and rely heavily on the use of program graduates as peer counselors, administrators, and role models. The programs are highly structured, with nearly every moment accounted for. Members progress through the program in stages that are usually clearly demarcated. Each succeeding stage carries more responsibility (and in some cases, more personal freedom) than the previous one. Group counseling or therapy sessions, which are usually confrontive in nature and stress openness and honesty, are a cornerstone to this approach to drug abuse treatment. Indeed, the name Synanon is reputed to have originated from a client's mispronunciation of the word "seminar," which is what Dederich called his early group meetings (Yablonsky 1965). All members are assigned to some kind of work duties, with the level of responsibility determined by the member's position in the community. Members who are more advanced in the program may be employed or enrolled in school or job-training classes outside the community. Some therapeutic communities provide educational programs within the community (Bookbinder 1975).

Two beliefs about the nature of drug abuse form the basis for the general goals of the therapeutic community. The first is that addiction cannot be cured but can only be put in remission by reliance on self-help and support from other addicts (Yablonsky 1965). Proponents of therapeutic communities such as DeLeon and Rosenthal (1979) feel that if remission is to be achieved, all aspects of lifestyle, attitudes, and behavior contributing to drug abuse can and should be changed.

Therapeutic communities and most residential programs have generally consistent philosophies and approaches. The fundamental goal is to change dysfunctional behavior to an effective and productive lifestyle. The fundamental problem for therapeutic communities concerns how to maintain these goals and approaches as they interact with the general health care system and federal, state, and local bureaucracies (DeLeon and Beschner 1976).

The following sections describe a number of basic elements of residential programs and therapeutic communities, as a first step in a more complete understanding of the treatment process in these programs. The nature of residential treatment described here is based on information from 14 residential facilities. Most of the programs did employ the basic principles of therapeutic communities, although some did not identify themselves as traditional therapeutic communities. Data are only available for 14 facilities because one program with three residences that participated in the study in 1979 did not in 1980 or 1981; because the director and staff of the three residences changed, no information from directors or counselors was collected for the latter years. Further, three facilities did not provide complete staffing and budget data. Thus, interview and clinical/medical data are available from 14 residential facilities, information on directors and counselors is available from 11 of these programs, and budget and staffing information is available for a different set of 11 programs.

*Organization and Staffing*

Like most therapeutic communities, the 14 residential facilities participating in this study were all free-standing programs of limited capacity. Most were independent residences operating through contracts with state or local agencies. Three of the 14 facilities were part of one large therapeutic community with residences throughout a state, and 2 were part of another. The average capacity of the facilities was 64. The facilities ranged in size from 26 beds to 126 beds. With two exceptions, the residences were located in urban areas close to addict populations.

The use of peers as staff members is fundamental to the concept of therapeutic communities. The primary staff members are nondegreed professionals who are former offenders, recovering drug abusers who themselves had been rehabilitated in therapeutic communities. They may be supplemented in larger therapeutic communities, however, by degreed professionals with specific areas of expertise (DeLeon and Rosenthal 1979). Holland (1982a) reported that about 40 percent of staff members in 32 long-term residential programs were recovering substance abusers. Despite their use in therapeutic communities, there have been few studies of the impact of ex-addict versus nonaddict professional counselors.

Staffing data indicate the high proportion of nondegreed personnel hours in residential programs in 1979. Physicians and nurses accounted for less than 5 percent of full-time hours, and about two-thirds of the full-time direct hours were for nonmedical direct service. Fully one-third of total full-time hours were accounted for by nondegreed counselors and less than 20 percent by degreed counselors.

All facilities in this study had over half of their staff hours devoted to direct service, and most of the staff members were nondegreed counselors. Nine of the 11 clinics providing staffing data, however, had at least one counselor with a bachelor's degree. Interviews with directors and counselors who had been with the program at least one year revealed a high level of training among some of the staff members of residential programs. Over half of the 18 counselors in these programs were college graduates, and five had master's degrees. Eleven had at least five years of experience working in drug abuse treatment programs; nine had worked all of their years with their current program.

The ex-addict status of counselors was not determined, but all counselors and most program directors reported that ex-addicts were used in counseling to a great extent. Although there is a strong emphasis on ex-addict staff members in these programs, the level of formal staff training appears to be rising, judging by the numbers of staff members with master's degrees and long years of experience in drug abuse treatment programs. Although integration and coordination of professional and paraprofessional roles were seen in the mid-1970s as potentially major internal problems in the therapeutic community (Brook and Whitehead 1980; DeLeon and Beschner 1976), the coordination of professionals and paraprofessionals appears to be proceeding successfully.

*Approach*

There is general consensus on the goals and approaches used in therapeutic communities and other residential programs. The fundamental goal of the programs is to change dysfunctional behavior to an effective and productive lifestyle. The main elements are in general:

• a long-term intensive communal experience, including group therapy supported with other appropriate services and activities
• a major therapeutic role for paraprofessionals who have had experiences similar to those of residents
• a commitment to reenter the larger society through the therapeutic community subculture.

Although there is a large degree of agreement on the general approach to treatment among advocates of the therapeutic community, there is some disagreement about several specific issues, notably the orientation toward resocialization, duration of treatment, and phases of treatment, particularly reentry (Johnson 1976).

RESOCIALIZATION

Cole and James (1975) identified three approaches to residential treatment, each with a somewhat different approach to resocialization. The programs differ in the extent to which the return to society as a productive, independent member is considered to be feasible and is encouraged. The goals of the traditional therapeutic community were to achieve changes in the addict's value system and lifestyle, help the client develop self-control, and return the addict to unsupervised community living as a self-sufficient, effectively functioning member of society. The modified therapeutic community had more limited goals: to aid the addict in attaining a drug-free state and to develop practical skills and tools to enable the addict to function in society. Expectations of total resocialization are usually regarded as overly ambitious. Short-term residential treatment programs appear not to emphasize resocialization. Their goals were to assist the addict in eliminating drug use, reestablishing family relationships, and providing the addict with skills to enable him/her to survive in the environment without resorting to criminal activity. Short-term treatment is generally expected to last from 3 to 6 months, in contrast to the expected duration of perhaps one year in other types of therapeutic communities.

These orientations have very different implications for the nature of treatment delivered, the intensity of program services, and even the nature of client populations that enter the different types of programs. Longer-term programs, such as the traditional and modified therapeutic communities, are likely to have distinct residential and reentry phases as well as higher expectations that clients would avoid criminal activities, have positive relations with others, and function without the aid of support groups.

In the DARP study during the early 1970s the therapeutic communities were evenly divided among the three types of programs (Cole and James 1975). However, only three programs in the current study were described as modified, and the remainder were classified as traditional. Thus, it appears that most of the therapeutic communities during the late 1970s and early 1980s had a philosophy of resocialization similar to that of the traditional therapeutic communities.

Therapeutic communities also vary in the planned duration of treatment. Traditional therapeutic communities require at least 15 months in residence for graduation (Cole and James 1975; DeLeon and Rosenthal 1979), while the modified therapeutic community had only a 6- to 9-month requirement, and the short-term program a 3- to 6-month requirement. Information on planned duration of treatment (Holland 1982b) indicated that 35 percent were short-term (less than 6 months), 28 percent middle-term (6 to 11 months), 25 percent long-term (a year or more), and the remaining 12 percent had multiple options. These data and observations by DeLeon and Rosenthal suggest that more residential programs are experimenting with shorter treatment. Data from the residential programs participating in this study also support this view. Although 9 of the 14 residential programs reported a planned duration of 12 months for most clients, four had planned durations of 10 to 12 months, and one required less than 4 months in residence. Only one residence indicated a planned duration for most clients of 18 months or more.

## DURATION AND PHASES OF TREATMENT

Where most therapeutic communities previously adopted longer standard treatment plans, many programs now seem to be moving to shorter or more flexible plans. Concerns with cost, availability of beds, requirements to serve more clients, and accreditation for health insurance reimbursement make duration of treatment a key issue. Further, as Holland (1982b) notes, differences in the planned duration of treatment are associated with substantial differences in the nature of the treatment process in programs of varying length. Longer-term programs were much more likely to have both residential and reentry phases, and these phases were likely to be compressed or the reentry phase absent in programs of shorter duration. These types of variations in treatment length and service intensity should be fully investigated before shorter-term residential treatment can be confidently recommended.

Data from the programs participating in this study appear to support the findings of Holland and the concepts of Cole and James regarding the nature of reentry phases in residential programs. There is less emphasis on phases of treatment (probably including reentry) and resocialization in programs in which there is a planned shorter duration of treatment. The differences in program philosophies, together with differences in planned durations and treatment services, could significantly affect treatment outcomes. Assessing the optimal time in treatment and the emphasis on resocialization and reentry is a complex task that should be undertaken with a detailed knowledge of client characteristics and behaviors and the treatment process in varied types of residential programs.

Drug abuse treatment in most therapeutic communities is divided into three phases—residence, reentry, and aftercare (Holland 1982b). Entry into the program requires a rigorous review to determine readiness to become a member of the community (Brook and Whitehead 1980). Once accepted, the new member has little responsibility and performs basic housekeeping chores. As residents progress through treatment, they gain more responsibility and privileges (Yablonsky 1965).

These procedures appear to be followed in the residential programs participating in this study. Most of the programs exerted control over all phases of treatment. Three of the residences admitted clients within the first few days after application. The other residences typically required at least a one- to two-week trial period. The high dropout rate for therapeutic communities suggests that even this process cannot easily identify applicants who will remain in treatment. This trial phase is one area that might warrant further investigation to develop more accurate methods of assessing an applicant's motivation and ability to complete the program.

As in other types of drug abuse treatment programs, treatment plans are required in residential programs and are to be updated every 30 days. Without exception, the residential treatment directors stated that individualized, formal treatment plans were prepared for all clients in their clinics. Most clinics prepared the plans within a week after the client entered the program. Indeed, 98 percent of the client files contained such plans signed by the clients. In stark contrast, however, nearly two-thirds of the clients said they had not received such a treatment plan, even though most counselors and directors reported that clients were involved to a great extent in the preparation of their plans. It may be that the plans were signed along with other documents and, therefore, the clients failed to notice or remember them. Giving residents a clearer picture of the goals and requirements of treatment and, perhaps, more involvement in the development of their plans, might increase retention in treatment and treatment effectiveness.

The use of privileges and sanctions is a fundamental method of motivating behavior through the stages of the therapeutic community experience (Brook and Whitehead 1980; Glasscote et al. 1972). In comparing therapeutic communities of varying duration, Holland (1982b) found that longer-term programs are more likely to use sanctions and privileges and to emphasize peer responsibility for explaining, clarifying, and giving feedback on behavior.

All of the programs used some kind of loss of privilege as a sanction. Verbal reprimands were in general not used. Peer pressure was the most commonly used type of influence. All of the program directors reported that violation of program rules and regulations was an important reason for dismissing clients. Clearly the programs tended to be nonpermissive. They did, however, vary in the nature and extent of use of sanctions and privileges. These variations may have important implications for treatment process and the impact of treatment on client behaviors.

*Services*

The 24-hour community experience is the fundamental aspect of residential programs (DeLeon and Beschner 1976). Within this experience, elements of the therapeutic process include encounter groups, individual therapy, educational sessions, and residential job functions. Glasscote et al. (1972) described treatment in residential programs as a combination of

psychodynamics (group transactions) and behavior modification implemented by the system of privileges and sanctions. Critics contend that
therapeutic communities need to broaden their approaches and become
more flexible (Deitch and Zweben 1976). Coulson (1975–76), for instance,
recommended the replacement of confrontive therapy techniques with
more constructive methods including positive reinforcement. Glasscote
et al. (1972) were concerned with the "demeaning and punitive" approach to residents. DeLeon and Beschner (1976) reported concern at a
planning conference about the impact of the confrontational approach for
younger residents. Thus, despite general agreement about the overall
approach to the therapeutic community, there is some controversy about
specific therapies.

Individual and group counseling are the focus of most of the therapeutic offerings in residential programs. Brook and Whitehead (1980)
found that clients in the major therapeutic programs spent about three
hours per day in therapy of some kind. Holland (1982a) reported about 12
hours per week were spent in treatment activities (group or individual
counseling), 13 hours a week in reentry activities (vocational counseling
and use of community resources), and 8.5 hours in interpersonal
activities.

In the programs in the current study, counseling is delivered mostly
in group sessions, but individual counseling is available as well in all
programs. All but one director reported group counseling at least twice a
week, and 4 of the 11 reporting directors scheduled sessions four or more
times a week. Session length varied from 90 minutes in three residences
to three hours in two others. The remaining six had two-hour sessions.
Similarly, all but one of the directors reported offering individual counseling at least once a week. Four residences had sessions more than once a
week. Most of the sessions were 45 to 60 minutes in length. Counselor
caseloads were all less than 15.

Counseling is "mostly group," according to almost 60 percent of the
clients surveyed. Both directors and counselors report at least moderate
emphasis on all types of group therapies, including sensitivity, encounter,
and task-oriented or problem-solving therapies. However, there is some
variation across the programs as to the proportion of counseling hours
that are spent in individual and group sessions. About one-fourth of the
clients report receiving at least half their counseling in individual sessions, and about 1 in 10 report receiving mostly individual sessions. The
individual sessions had a strong focus on social support and behavior
modification, but five directors reported at least a moderate emphasis on
individual psychotherapy using traditional techniques.

The directors and counselors emphasized all areas of well-being, including physical health, coping skills, social functioning, self-esteem, self-understanding, and abstinence from drugs. Abstinence was ranked most highly, followed by self-understanding, self-esteem, and coping skills. Less highly ranked were physical health and social functioning.

These findings indicate that counseling in therapeutic communities has moved beyond the traditional reliance on group counseling. The inclusion of group counseling may allow therapeutic communities to address in more detail the specific problems of new types of clients entering the programs (DeLeon and Beschner 1976). In fact, 6 of the 11 reporting directors indicated that extensive attempts were made to match clients with their counselors.

DeLeon and Rosenthal (1979) have noted that the therapeutic regimen includes a wide array of services in addition to counseling, including tutorial-learning sessions, and remedial and formal educational classes. Holland (1982a) found reentry activities focusing on vocational and educational programs, interpersonal skills training, and family and other types of counseling. The therapeutic community planning conference recommended increased attention to family, educational, and vocational services.

Clients in the residential programs participating in this study reported receiving a variety of types of services. According to clients' self-reports, clinical/medical records, and estimates by treatment directors, about three-fourths of the clients received medical services during the first three months of treatment, about three-fifths psychological services, about one-third educational services, and one-fourth or fewer clients received family, legal, job, or financial services. Most of the individual residences delivered a variety of services, and none could be rated either high or low in their provision of services. Ninety percent of the clients reported they received at least one type of service in the first three months of treatment. About 35 percent received four or more types of services, and about 40 percent reported receiving at least two types of service over the course of treatment. The directors of all but one residence said they frequently or always provided aftercare services for their clients, generally for six months. The nature of aftercare services was not immediately apparent, however, and client reports of the availability of aftercare experiences did not always agree with directors' reports.

*Financing*

The average cost per bed for the 12 residences providing budget data for this study in 1980 was $6,135, somewhat under the national average cost of $7,329 per bed for residences in 1982 (NIDA 1983). It is also considerably under the $25 per day median client cost for long-term residential programs analyzed by Holland (1982b). The lower per bed costs of residential facilities in this study may be due to the larger sizes of the facilities, because fixed costs such as rent, administrative staff, and utilities are distributed over a larger number of clients. Indeed, the two highest per bed costs, $9,038 and $8,372, were found in the smallest residences.

All 12 of the clinics with available funding data had NIDA statewide services contracts. Ten had state funding, and two, local government funding. Four received some private donations. Nine received support from public welfare, and five had revenue from client fees. Other sources included Bureau of Prisons (four clinics), Law Enforcement Assistance Administration (LEAA) (one), and Comprehensive Employment and Training Act (CETA) (three). Most of the programs clearly received a large proportion of their funding from public sources.

## Treatment in Outpatient Drug-Free Programs

Outpatient drug-free programs emphasize counseling, do not include medication as a major component of treatment, and serve clients who continue to reside in the community. Within these broad boundaries, there are various approaches to drug abuse treatment. Cole and James (1975) describe two types of outpatient drug-free programs—"change-oriented" and "adaptive." Change-oriented programs have as their goal the complete resocialization of the addict to enable him/her to live a drug-free life in the community, while adaptive programs consider resocialization not to be a realistic goal. These programs are less structured and may be thought of as extended crisis care. No information is available about the percentage distribution of outpatient drug-free programs across these two major types, but the types encompass a diverse set of programs. Perhaps because of this diversity, research literature on outpatient drug-free programs is extremely sparse. Kleber and Slobetz (1979) describe the range of outpatient drug-free programs, which range from drop-in "rap" centers to highly structured programs. Most provide a variety of services, with some form of counseling or psychotherapy as the backbone of treatment. Services for physical and mental health, educational, vocational, legal, and other problems may be provided within the program or through referral to other social service agencies.

Outpatient drug-free programs originally began in response to a need for community-based treatment clinics to which addicts could turn in crisis situations. These "crisis clinics" then evolved into longer-term counseling and treatment programs. The clinics were often staffed by ex-addicts from the community (Quinones et al. 1979). By 1979, outpatient drug-free programs were the most popular modality, accounting for about 58 percent of all clients being treated (Kleber and Slobetz 1979). Despite their prominence, and perhaps because of their diversity, there is little research literature about the nature of drug abuse treatment delivered in outpatient drug-free programs.

Ten outpatient drug-free clinics participated in this study. One of these had closed before the special data collection for the treatment program substudy. Thus, client interview data are available from all ten programs, but staff interviews and clinical/medical record data are available from only nine programs.

*Organization and Staffing*

The ten outpatient drug-free programs had an average of 160 clients enrolled, with 80 in the smallest program and 240 in the largest. Three clinics were affiliated with community mental health centers. Four programs were free-standing, community-based programs that had specialized treatment emphases (such as vocational rehabilitation or emergency treatment) or served specific populations (such as criminal offenders). Two programs were parts of more comprehensive drug abuse treatment programs, and the remaining program was hospital-based.

Given that outpatient drug-free programs emphasize counseling in place of medication, the percentages of psychologists and social workers on the staffs of these programs were higher than in other treatment modalities. The percentage of medical personnel in programs participating in this study was relatively low. In five programs the percentage of staff time consumed by medical personnel was 2 percent or less and in three other programs for which data were available, ranged from 8 to 12 percent. In contrast, psychologists, social workers, and other counselors (including vocational rehabilitation counselors) accounted for one-half to two-thirds of the total staff time in five clinics and almost all staff time in the three other clinics for which data were available. The remaining staff hours were devoted to program administration. These staffing patterns indicate the principal focus of treatment in these programs is the social and psychological rehabilitation of the client.

The treatment staff in the outpatient drug-free programs appears to be composed of well educated, highly experienced, and relatively stable employees. The directors averaged 6.5 years of experience in their current program and just over 7 years in drug abuse treatment. Two directors had bachelor's degrees, six had master's degrees, and one had a Ph.D. They averaged 38 years of age; 6 of 10 were women and all but one were white. Of the 19 counselors who provided information, all had been employed in their current programs at least one year. They averaged nearly five years in their current programs and just over six years in drug abuse treatment. Two had Ph.D.s, nine had master's degrees, one had some graduate coursework, two had bachelor's degrees, and the other five had high school diplomas or some college coursework. They averaged 37 years of age; 11 were men and 15 were white. Three of the five minority counselors were employed in one program.

Ex-addict counselors were not used to a great extent in outpatient drug-free programs. Five of the nine directors and 11 of the counselors said they were not used at all, and most others said they were used to "some extent." These findings are in contrast to the description of outpatient drug-free programs provided by Quinones et al. (1979). Clearly the emphasis is on employing professionally trained treatment staff.

*Approach*

Outpatient drug-free programs vary in the extent to which they focus on the goal of complete resocialization. "Change-oriented" programs attempt to foster complete resocialization, while "adaptive" programs focus on reducing the addict's need for drugs to cope with society but do not attempt complete resocialization (Cole and James 1975). In DARP, about 30 percent of the clinics could be classified as change-oriented. Similarly, three of eight of the clinic directors in this study who responded to this question classed their programs as change-oriented. Given the small number of outpatient drug-free clinics in this study and the fact that neither the DARP nor the TOPS samples were statistically representative, one cannot draw any firm conclusions from this finding. Most outpatient drug-free programs, however, do appear to be of the adaptive type.

As with other types of treatment programs included in this study, a majority of the outpatient drug-free clients responded that they had not received a written treatment plan. In contrast, 90 percent of the clinical records contained formal, written treatment plans that had been signed by the clients. The treatment directors reported that the intended duration of the treatment plans was on average about nine months and that they were updated periodically. Six of the nine responding directors stated that treatment plans were revised every three months. These revisions were not always noted in clinic records.

*Services*

Counseling is the cornerstone of outpatient drug-free treatment (Kleber and Slobetz 1979), although the programs may also offer services such as crisis intervention, day care, and assistance with such specific needs as housing, employment, welfare, and legal problems (Brill 1981; Safer and Sands 1979; Sandorf et al. 1978).

Nearly 80 percent of the clients said the counseling received in outpatient drug-free programs was primarily individual counseling, although the percentage varied from 40 to 100 percent. Fifteen of the counselors scheduled individual sessions once a week, four held them twice a week, and one scheduled them less than once a week. In addition, most of the counselors stated that group counseling sessions were held once a week. Most of the individual counseling sessions lasted one hour, while most of the group sessions lasted 90 minutes.

The directors noted that the traditional, analytic approach of individual psychotherapy was heavily emphasized in individual counseling sessions. However, other methods were also used, ranging from sensitivity groups to encounter groups to group counseling sessions using a problem-solving approach. The majority of the directors said their major goal was resocializing the client, and their secondary goal was practical problem solving. The counselors generally agreed that there were systematic attempts to match clients with specific counselors. The fact that two-thirds of the clients indicated that they had one primary counselor indicates that there was sufficient opportunity for most clients and their counselors to develop a good rapport.

Although counseling is the cornerstone of outpatient drug-free treatment, it is clear that the clients have problems aside from drug abuse that might benefit from attention. Indeed, a majority of clients received psychological services (79 percent according to client self-reports) and sizable proportions received medical (28 percent), family (46 percent), legal (6 percent), educational (19 percent), job (13 percent), or financial (9 percent) services. Many of the services were available within the clinics, but some were available only though referral to other programs or agencies.

Certain of the programs concentrated on specific problems of the clients. For instance, one of the programs specialized in vocational rehabilitation. With over 44 percent of outpatient drug-free clients unemployed, these services are critical for client rehabilitation. Over half of the outpatient drug-free clients report receiving services for two or three kinds of problems during the first three months of treatment. Comparison of client responses across the three cohort years suggests a trend toward expansion of services.

Clinics varied considerably with respect to the provision of follow-up or aftercare services. Of eight clinic directors who responded to this question, one said they always provided these services, two said they frequently did, four said they occasionally did, and one said they did so only rarely. The posttreatment period over which these services were delivered averaged eight months.

*Financing*

The average annual cost per client of treatment in the outpatient drug-free programs participating in the study was $2,000, 25 percent higher than the national average cost of $1,600. This is in direct contrast to the comparatively lower costs per client found in this study compared to data from the national census of methadone and residential programs. These cost data, combined with information on staff members, confirm that the outpatient drug-free programs chosen for this study were more oriented toward intense professional therapeutic approaches than the typical outpatient drug-free program.

## Conclusions

The current treatment system has evolved over the past decades in response to variations in drugs being abused and public reactions to drug abuse and addiction. The current system consists of three major treatment modalities or approaches—outpatient methadone, residential, and outpatient drug-free programs. Despite a large degree of variation within each modality, all are distinct in the nature of treatment being provided and the nature of client populations (described in the next chapter).

Outpatient methadone programs provide services after stabilization with the prescription of methadone to heroin-dependent individuals. Residential programs rely heavily on the use of program graduates to provide in 24-hour live-in facilities highly structured treatment that is oriented toward a total change in lifestyle. Outpatient drug-free programs emphasize counseling delivered to clients who continue to reside in their homes and do not depend on medication. Within these broad definitions, there is great variation in treatment size and structure, therapeutic approach, services and financing.

Outpatient programs on average were larger than residential programs. The average outpatient methadone program participating in this study had 260 clients, compared to 160 for outpatient drug-free and 64 for residential. Outpatient methadone programs provide a high degree of medical care; residential and outpatient drug-free programs focus more on counseling services, provided by ex-addicts in the case of residential programs and by a professionally trained staff in the case of outpatient drug-free programs.

The majority of clinic directors described abstinence from drugs and complete reintegration to society as achievable goals of treatment, but the modalities differ in their emphasis on these goals. Methadone programs varied in their support of maintenance versus abstinence as goals, while outpatient drug-free programs focused on either resocialization or adapting to society (developing more adequate coping skills). Outpatient methadone and outpatient drug-free programs relied on individual counseling, while residential programs used group counseling for most of their clients. The average annual cost per client for treatment in the outpatient drug-free programs was $2,000, $1,945 for outpatient methadone, and $6,135 for residential.

Several problem areas were revealed in the examination of the nature of treatment received in these programs. First, all program directors stated that treatment plans were required, and indeed almost all client files contained signed treatment plans. Many clients, however, were unaware such plans existed or did not know the nature of their contents. This finding suggests that many clients were unaware of the nature of treatment being provided to them and were not full participants in the treatment process.

Few clients participating in these programs received aftercare services to assist in the reintegration into society, although the effectiveness of aftercare in reducing relapse has been demonstrated (Brown 1979; Brown and Ashery 1979). Thus, many programs appear not to focus successfully on the transition between program completion and reentry to the community.

Comparison with current data (Butynski and Canova 1988) reveals that expenditures for drug abuse treatment have decreased since the time this study began. This suggests that the quality of treatment may have deteriorated since the early 1980s. Thus, programs participating in this study may provide a better framework for the evaluation of the potential effectiveness of drug abuse treatment than the current system, which is less well funded. The impact of per client expenditures on the quality of treatment needs further investigation, however, as does the impact of other structural elements such as program size, service intensity, and type of services.

Counseling is the cornerstone of most drug abuse treatment programs. However, the high rate of counselor turnover suggests that the necessary continuity in staff may not be being provided. On the whole, however, program staff members appear to be well qualified and highly educated, and degreed and nondegreed staff members seem to have been successfully integrated.

These findings have several implications for the more effective delivery of drug abuse treatment services. First, programs should develop clear treatment plans and counsel clients on these treatment plans. Improving clients' knowledge about the treatment process may strengthen their involvement in treatment and compliance with behavioral objectives for the program. Second, aftercare services appear to be important in decreasing relapse and fostering reintegration into society. Programs should place greater emphasis on reintegration and advocate effective aftercare services. Finally, further detailed research on drug abuse treatment approaches, services, and settings associated with positive treatment outcomes should be encouraged, to provide improved information about the components of effective treatment.

# 4. Clients in the Major Modalities

Research on drug abuse treatment populations has shown that the major modalities treat very different types of clients. Upon entry to treatment, the clients in the modalities vary on such sociodemographic characteristics as age and race, on drugs of abuse, length and severity of addiction, criminal activity, and other behaviors (Hubbard, Bray, Cavanaugh, et al. 1986; Simpson 1981b). Knowledge about the nature of the client populations in the three modalities is fundamental to the design of appropriate treatment and is indicative of expected treatment outcomes (DeLeon and Rosenthal 1979; Lowinson and Millman 1979). The nature and extent of client problems determine the nature of services needed for clients in each modality, and, other things being equal, higher effectiveness rates would be expected from those client populations with lower problem severity. Treatment needs and prospects for successful outcomes, for instance, vary by such characteristics as sex (Beschner and Thompson 1981; Finnegan 1979), age (Friedman and Beschner 1985), race and ethnicity (Austin et al. 1977; Espada 1979), and prior treatment experience (Simpson, Savage, and Joe 1980). Unless variation in sociodemographic characteristics and problem severity is explicitly examined across modalities, effectiveness rates for programs and modalities cannot be meaningfully compared. Information about client characteristics and behaviors at entry to treatment also, of course, serves as a baseline from which to assess the magnitude of effects during and after treatment.

For these reasons, analyses reported in this book separately consider the three modalities, and in this chapter we examine in detail the characteristics of clients entering each modality. This information documents changes occurring in the drug-abusing population during the 1970s toward more multiple drug use and greater problem severity. The federal legislation establishing block grants in 1981 marked the end of a decade of major changes in the community-based treatment that had developed and flourished in the 1970s. There was general consensus in a survey of experienced state agency directors and treatment program administrators that significant changes had occurred during the 1970s in the client populations entering publicly funded drug abuse treatment programs. The directors and administrators felt that more young, female, and multiple-substance-abusing clients were entering treatment. They also felt that the clients were more disturbed in psychological functioning and had a greater variety of drug-related problems (Greenberg and Brown 1984).

These tendencies are substantiated to a large degree in analyses of the client population entering drug abuse treatment in the late 1970s and early 1980s described in this chapter. Data from the intake survey of clients in the three major modalities and for the three admission cohorts (1979, 1980, 1981) are examined. For most comparisons, data on the three admission cohorts are combined and the modalities considered separately. Some analyses consider the differences among the three admission cohorts to indicate recently occurring changes in the nature of the overall drug abuse treatment populations. Other analyses compare data from the Treatment Outcome Prospective Study (TOPS) and Drug Abuse Reporting Program (DARP) admission cohorts to ascertain the nature of longer-term changes in client populations over the past two decades. These analyses are thus based on 4,184 clients entering outpatient methadone, 2,891 clients entering residential, and 2,914 clients entering outpatient drug-free programs in 1979, 1980, and 1981. Most of the behavioral measures are self-reports of characteristics and behaviors in the year before entering treatment. For the sake of comparability with the DARP data, which are based on the two months before the interview, data on behavior three months before the intake interview are used in the TOPS-DARP comparisons. Analyses are presented in more detail in Hubbard, Bray, Cavanaugh, et al. (1986).

## Sociodemographic Characteristics

Publicly funded drug abuse treatment serves a predominantly young adult male clientele. There are only minor variations in age and sex composition across the three modalities. Modality differences are greater, however, on other sociodemographic characteristics, drug use, and other behaviors, as described later in this chapter.

The majority of clients entering the programs in this study were under 30 years of age. The average age, however, ranged from 37 for outpatient methadone to 27 for residential, and 25 for outpatient drug-free clients. As shown in Table 4-1, outpatient methadone programs were somewhat more likely to have clients over age 30 (40.5 percent were age 30 or over), while residential and outpatient drug-free programs were more likely to have very young clients (19.1 percent and 27.3 percent, respectively, were under 21). Seventy-one percent of all clients were male, varying from 67.0 percent in outpatient drug-free programs to 68.4 percent in outpatient methadone programs to 77.7 percent in residential programs.

The programs had large proportions of black and Hispanic clients, but many non-Hispanic whites were also being served, even in the large inner city urban programs. Non-Hispanic whites constituted 40.8 percent of clients in methadone programs and 52.9 percent in residential programs but almost 80 percent in outpatient drug-free programs. Blacks were heavily represented in the outpatient methadone (36.8 percent) and residential (39.5 percent) programs. Methadone programs had the largest proportion of Hispanics, who made up about one-fifth of their clientele (Table 4-1).

Only about one-half of clients entering drug abuse treatment had high school diplomas. Slightly higher proportions of outpatient drug-free clients (56.7 percent) were high school graduates than were clients entering methadone (48.3 percent) and residential (48.6 percent) programs (Table 4-1). This was true even after excluding clients under 18 years of

Table 4-1  Sociodemographic Characteristics of Clients Entering Treatment, by Modality

| Characteristic | Outpatient Methadone ($N=4,184$) | Residential ($N=2,891$) | Outpatient Drug-Free ($N=2,914$) |
|---|---|---|---|
| | % | % | % |
| Age | | | |
|   Under 21 | 2.1 | 19.1 | 27.3 |
|   Over 30 | 40.5 | 25.2 | 21.2 |
| Sex | | | |
|   Male | 68.4 | 77.7 | 67.0 |
| Race/ethnicity | | | |
|   White (non-Hispanic) | 40.8 | 52.9 | 79.7 |
|   Black | 36.8 | 39.5 | 10.3 |
|   Hispanic | 21.4 | 6.8 | 8.4 |
| High school graduate or GED | 48.3 | 48.6 | 56.7 |
| Marital status | | | |
|   Married or living as married | 40.0 | 15.5 | 21.9 |
|   Never married | 33.7 | 54.8 | 54.9 |

*Note:* Only selected categories of each characteristic are shown. Because the number of respondents differs slightly for each of these characteristics, only total population sizes for the three modalities are presented here.

age. The educational level of clients was considerably lower than that of the general U.S. population. In 1977, 84 percent of the population aged 22 to 34 and 75 percent of those aged 35 to 44 were high school graduates (U.S. Bureau of the Census 1979). Although the educational attainment of drug abuse treatment clients was low, it was not much different from that of similar socioeconomic groups. Among black males with incomes below the poverty level, for instance, 58 percent of those aged 22 to 34 and 39 percent of those aged 35 to 44 had graduated high school.

About one-half of residential and outpatient drug-free clients and one-third of outpatient methadone clients had never been married. Only about 40 percent of outpatient methadone clients, 15.5 percent of residential clients, and 21.9 percent of outpatient drug-free clients were currently married or living as married (Table 4-1). About one in four clients in all modalities was separated, widowed, or divorced. About one-half of clients in methadone programs and 7 of 10 in residential and outpatient drug-free programs had no dependents (defined as "spouse, children, other family members, or others living with you"), but many had lived with their families in the year before entering treatment. Two-thirds of methadone, one-third of residential, and over half of outpatient drug-free clients reported living with their families in the year before treatment. Closer examination of the living arrangements of these clients revealed two distinct groups. One group, more common in residential treatment, was not married, had few dependents, and did not live with their families. A second group of clients, commonly entering methadone treatment, was married, had two or more dependents, and lived with their families.

Thus, although the majority of the clients in each of the modalities were young adult males, the race/ethnic status and marital status of the modalities differed. Outpatient drug-free clients were primarily non-Hispanic whites, while larger proportions of minorities were represented in outpatient methadone and residential programs. Residential clients were least likely to be married, perhaps indicating the difficulty of married clients in leaving home and family to live in a 24-hour facility. Each modality has substantial proportions of clients who may have special needs. The young average age of clients, the representation of females, and the large proportions of race and ethnic minorities indicate the need for specialized services, such as family services, day care, and financial counseling. The low educational status of these clients indicates that many need additional education and training in order to assume productive lives. Living arrangements suggest two sets of service needs. The married clients who had dependents and lived with their families would be more likely to need family services during treatment, while the unmarried clients with no dependents and living away from family may lack family or social support that facilitates the rehabilitation process.

## Admission Characteristics

Many characteristics of the clients at admission, including prior treatment experience (Hubbard, Bray, Cavanaugh, et al. 1986; Savage and Simpson 1978; Simpson, Savage, and Joe 1980), the source of referral (Collins, Hubbard, et al. 1982; Collins et al. 1988), and the client's method of paying for treatment could influence the course and outcome of a particular treatment episode. The number of prior treatment episodes is an indicator of the stage and severity of the addiction and its amenability to change (Hubbard, Bray, Cavanaugh, et al. 1986; Marsden, Hubbard, and Bailey 1988). Further, an extensive literature has examined the treatment outcomes of the client referred from the criminal justice system compared to others (see review in Collins, Hubbard, et al. 1982; Collins et al. 1988), focusing on the role of coercion in treatment effectiveness (Collins and Allison 1983).

Many clients have been in treatment before, as shown in Table 4-2. Three-fourths of methadone clients, slightly over one-half of residential

Table 4-2  Admission Characteristics, by Modality

| Characteristic | Outpatient Methadone (N=4,184) | Residential (N=2,891) | Outpatient Drug-Free (N=2,914) |
|---|---|---|---|
| | % | % | % |
| Previous treatment for drug abuse | 75.2 | 52.7 | 34.0 |
| Referral through the criminal justice system | 2.6 | 31.2 | 30.9 |
| Public assistance as the primary source of income[a] | 23.9 | 11.2 | 13.6 |
| Private health insurance coverage | 16.9 | 14.2 | 28.4 |

*Note:* Clients may report more than one type of characteristic. Because the number of respondents differs slightly for each of these characteristics, only total population sizes for the three modalities are presented here.
a. Public assistance includes Supplemental Security Income, Social Security, or unemployment insurance.

clients and one-third of outpatient drug-free clients had at least one treatment experience before entering the programs included in this study.
Many had been in drug abuse treatment three or more times (43.6 percent
of methadone, 25.4 percent of residential, and 14.5 percent of outpatient
drug-free clients). Thus, although most outpatient drug-free clients were
entering treatment for the first time, for many clients, particularly for
outpatient methadone and residential clients, treatment had been a recurrent phenomenon.

Many clients had also received treatment for alcohol-related problems or mental health problems before entering treatment (data not
shown). Across the three modalities, one-fifth of clients had received
treatment for alcohol-related problems and one-fourth for mental health
or emotional problems other than drug abuse or alcohol abuse before
entering the program included in this study (Marsden, Hubbard, and
Bailey 1988).

Many of the clients in the three major modalities were self-referrals or
referred to treatment by family and friends, but substantial proportions,
particularly in residential and outpatient drug-free programs, had been
referred to the program by the criminal justice system. The criminal justice system may refer drug abusers to treatment as an alternative to incarceration. About half of methadone clients were self-referrals, one-third
were referrals from family or friends, and about 3 percent were referrals
from the criminal justice system. Among residential clients, one-fourth
were self-referrals, one-fifth were referrals by family and friends, and
almost one-third were referred by the criminal justice system. Among
outpatient drug-free clients, about one-fifth were self-referrals, one-fifth
referrals by family or friends, and almost one-third were referrals from
the criminal justice system (Table 4-2). Thus, for residential and outpatient
drug-free programs, the criminal justice system was the most common
source of referral.

These data on principal source of referral may understate the influence of the criminal justice system on clients. Although admission may
have not been the result of a formal referral from the criminal justice
system, many clients had a criminal justice status at admission—probation, parole, or incarceration. At intake, one in five methadone, half of
residential, and two of five of outpatient drug-free clients reported being
involved with the criminal justice system. Three of every 10 residential
clients and 2 of every 10 outpatient drug-free clients reported they were
on probation at the time of contacting the program. Thirteen percent of
residential clients compared to less than 1 percent of clients in other
modalities were in jail or prison at the time of initial contact with the

program. Further, analyses suggest that residential programs may serve as a transition from jail for those with drug problems. About half of residential clients were incarcerated in the three months before entering treatment and, as noted in Table 4-2, almost one-third were formal referrals from the criminal justice system. Even if a formal referral mechanism is not used, the recommendation of criminal justice system personnel may be the immediate reason for entering a drug abuse treatment program.

Most individuals with severe drug abuse problems cannot pay for treatment or afford private health insurance and are unlikely to have jobs that provide group health insurance as a fringe benefit. Many of those who have medical insurance may not be covered for drug abuse treatment or may have exhausted their maximum reimbursement in previous treatment episodes. As noted in Table 4-2, 16.9 percent of methadone and 14.2 percent of residential clients had private insurance coverage for their treatment. A much higher proportion of outpatient drug-free clients had coverage, 28.4 percent. Less than one-half of clients had any health insurance; about one in five had state, Medicaid, or other public coverage. Public insurance for methadone treatment was most common in the New York and California programs. In addition, also shown in Table 4-2, almost one-fourth of outpatient methadone clients, 11.2 percent of residential clients, and 13.6 percent of outpatient drug-free clients reported that their primary source of income was some sort of public assistance, including Supplementary Security Income, Social Security, or unemployment insurance. The lack of client resources to pay for treatment will continue to require the substantial investment of public monies in community-based drug abuse treatment.

These comparisons of the admission characteristics of clients entering drug abuse treatment suggest further points of differentiation among the three major modalities. Few outpatient methadone clients were referred from the criminal justice system, compared with almost one-third of residential or outpatient drug-free clients. The majority of outpatient methadone clients were reentering treatment, while the majority of outpatient drug-free clients were entering treatment for the first time; residential clients were about equally likely to be first-timers or reentrants. Many clients in each of the modalities, however, were receiving public assistance or were uninsured. These differences in referral source and prior drug treatment experience suggest that clients in the major modalities differ as to the motivations for seeking treatment, criminal justice history, and the severity of drug abuse and related problems. These differences further underscore the need to control for client differences in cross-modality comparisons. The numbers of uninsured and low income clients suggest a continued need for public investment in drug abuse treatment. Most clients entering the publicly funded treatment system appear unlikely to have either private insurance coverage or sufficient funds to pay fees for services. Public support, either through direct funding of treatment programs or reimbursement through publicly funded health insurance, is needed to insure access to treatment for clients with limited resources.

## Drug Abuse

The nature and extent of drug abuse among clients entering a treatment program are critical to the design, implementation, and outcome of the regimen. Outpatient methadone programs were designed to treat a particular type of drug abuser—the client with a history of opioid addiction—but residential and outpatient drug-free programs treat a greater variety of drug abusers in addition to the opioid abuser. Indeed, the broad-based orientation of residential programs (DeLeon and Rosenthal 1979) attracts clients with a wide range of drug abuse patterns, often coupled with psychological disturbance and social dysfunction.

Drug abuse patterns may be described in a variety of ways. In this book the basic measures are regular (weekly or daily) use of specific drugs and patterns of multiple drug use before, during, and after treatment. We also describe drug abuse patterns in terms of clients' self-reports of the number of drugs abused and the primary drug of abuse. Weekly or daily drug use is not in itself an indicator of dependence or addiction, but it is indicative of abusive levels of use. Although the concept of a primary drug of abuse does not capture the complexity of drug abuse, the concept is simple and has a long history in drug abuse treatment research. A detailed description of the nature and extent of drug abuse among clients entering treatment is available in Bray et al. (1982), Craddock, Bray, and Hubbard (1985), Hubbard, Bray, Craddock, et al. (1986), and Hubbard et al. (1984).

Weekly or daily use of heroin is the dominant pattern of drug abuse among outpatient methadone clients. But the drug abuse patterns of residential and outpatient drug-free clients before entering treatment are more diverse. About two-thirds of outpatient methadone clients were regular users of heroin in the year before admission (Table 4-3). Virtually all methadone clients who did not report regular heroin use in the year before entering treatment, however, reported daily use of heroin at some point in their lives. Many of these former daily heroin users who did not report frequent heroin use in the year before treatment were transferring to this program from another treatment program or other restricted environment in which their drug use was limited. Thus, they had used heroin regularly in the past but not in the reference period, the year before entering this program.

Compared to the dominance of heroin among outpatient methadone clients, 30.9 percent of residential clients and 10.3 percent of outpatient drug-free clients used heroin regularly in the year before entering treatment. However, there are no dominant drugs of abuse among residential and outpatient drug-free clients. Weekly or daily cocaine use, abuse of opioids other than heroin, and nonmedical use of tranquilizers were reported by over a quarter of the clients in methadone and residential

Table 4-3  Regular (Weekly or Daily) Drug Use in the Year before Admission, by Modality

| Drug | Outpatient Methadone (N=4,184) | Residential (N=2,891) | Outpatient Drug-Free (N=2,914) |
|---|---|---|---|
| | % | % | % |
| Heroin | 66.5 | 30.9 | 10.3 |
| Methadone | 18.7 | 5.1 | 1.9 |
| Other opioids | 28.3 | 29.7 | 15.1 |
| Cocaine | 27.6 | 30.0 | 16.8 |
| Minor tranquilizers | 24.9 | 28.1 | 17.3 |
| Major tranquilizers | 1.3 | 3.8 | 1.9 |
| Barbiturates | 5.9 | 15.1 | 7.9 |
| Sedatives | 6.0 | 17.4 | 13.9 |
| Amphetamines | 9.0 | 30.0 | 22.7 |
| Hallucinogens | 0.9 | 9.7 | 5.8 |
| Inhalants | 0.4 | 1.8 | 1.5 |
| Marijuana | 55.0 | 65.0 | 68.1 |
| Alcohol | 47.4 | 65.0 | 61.7 |
| Multiple drugs[a] | | | |
| Two or more drugs | 78.6 | 80.7 | 69.8 |
| Four or more drugs | 32.2 | 40.1 | 20.1 |

*Note:* Clients may report regular use of more than one drug. Because the number of respondents differs slightly for each of the drugs, only total population sizes for the three modalities are presented here.
a. Alcohol is included in the number of drugs.

programs. Over half of the methadone clients and about two-thirds of the residential and outpatient drug-free clients used alcohol and/or marijuana at least once a week in the year before entering treatment. The weekly or daily use of alcohol is included in the table for the sake of comparability with the other drugs, although weekly use of small amounts of alcohol would by no means be considered to constitute abuse. Alcohol use and abuse is examined in more detail in the next section on consequences and concomitants of drug abuse.

The majority of clients in all three modalities abused two or more drugs regularly in the year before entering treatment. Multiple drug abuse appears to be particularly common among residential clients. Substantial proportions, higher among residential than other clients, abused four or more drugs in the year before treatment. Because alcohol and marijuana were included in these totals, these figures may somewhat overestimate the extent of multiple drug abuse, but it is clear that most clients do not exclusively abuse a single drug.

In accord with the figures presented in Table 4-3 for drugs used weekly or daily, self-reports of clients regarding their primary drug of abuse reveal that two-thirds (68.0 percent) of methadone clients stated that heroin was their primary drug of abuse before admission. Among residential and outpatient drug-free clients, there was no dominant primary drug of abuse. Heroin was also cited most often by residential clients (25.6 percent), followed by other opioids (12.0 percent) and amphetamines (10.7 percent); other drugs were less frequently cited. Among outpatient drug-free clients, marijuana was most commonly cited as the primary drug of abuse (19.3 percent), followed by tranquilizers/barbiturates/sedatives (13.4 percent); other drugs were cited by fewer than 10 percent of outpatient drug-free clients.

Drug abuse was also described in terms of a seven-category index developed to capture the patterns of multiple drug abuse engaged in by a majority of clients (Simpson and Sells 1979). Construction of this index is described in detail in Hubbard, Bray, Craddock, et al. (1986) and Bray et al. (1982). Briefly, information about the regular use of eight drug types was used to create a hierarchical index. Table 4-4 presents the distribution of clients among the seven drug abuse patterns in the year before treatment.

The abuse patterns for the majority of outpatient methadone clients, as expected, included some type of opioid abuse in the year before entering treatment—80 percent used heroin, other opioids, or a combination of the two. About half of residential clients and almost one-fourth of outpatient drug-free clients reported a pattern of abuse that included some type of opioid. As noted earlier, most of the methadone clients who did not report heroin abuse in the year before entering treatment were former daily abusers who were not currently using heroin and who were transfers from jails or another methadone program to the programs selected for this study. Thus, many had been regular heroin abusers at some time, but in the year before entering treatment they had been in environments that curtailed their current heroin use. Of the three types of opioid abuse, most methadone clients used only heroin in the year before entering treatment, residential clients were fairly evenly divided among the types, and outpatient drug-free clients were concentrated in the other opioid abuse pattern.

There was no predominant type of drug abuser among residential clients or outpatient drug-free clients. However, one-third of outpatient drug-free clients used alcohol or marijuana regularly and about one in five abused a single nonopioid in the year before entering treatment. Actual drug use patterns may be more complex than these categories imply. Each of the seven categories can include use of other drugs, and each category encompasses less severe patterns of use.

Most clients thus abused a variety of drugs in the year before entering treatment. Regardless of the drug abuse pattern, the majority of clients used alcohol and marijuana at least weekly. Although heroin was the predominant drug of abuse among methadone clients, drug abuse patterns were more diverse among residential and outpatient drug-free clients. The pronounced differences in abuse of specific drugs, drug abuse

Table 4-4 Drug Abuse Patterns in the Year before Admission, by Modality

| Drug Use Pattern | Outpatient Methadone (N=4,184) | Residential (N=2,891) | Outpatient Drug-Free (N=2,914) |
|---|---|---|---|
| | % | % | % |
| Heroin/other opioids | 19.0 | 12.7 | 3.5 |
| Heroin | 52.4 | 20.0 | 7.7 |
| Other opioids | 8.9 | 16.8 | 11.4 |
| Multiple nonopioids | 1.2 | 12.6 | 10.8 |
| Single nonopioid | 4.2 | 16.2 | 22.0 |
| Alcohol/marijuana | 9.0 | 15.1 | 35.7 |
| Minimal | 5.2 | 6.8 | 8.9 |
| Total | 100.0 | 100.0 | 100.0 |

patterns, and primary drug of abuse further confirm the fact that the modalities treat very different populations of drug abusers. The substantially higher involvement of residential clients in multiple drug abuse indicates the need for a broad-based treatment approach for a wide variety of drugs including alcohol.

## Consequences and Concomitants of Drug Abuse

Individuals entering drug abuse treatment have multiple problems. Information about client behaviors and problems other than drug abuse upon admission illustrates how program planning should consider client needs for services. This information also serves in creating a baseline for determining how the nature and extent of treatment affects the goal of building productive lives. The habilitation and rehabilitation of clients must be assessed not only in terms of changes in drug abuse but in terms of changes in such indicators as criminal activity, employment, alcohol abuse, and depression.

### Criminal Activity

Drug abusers entering publicly funded treatment are substantially more likely than the general population to be engaged in criminal activity (Collins, Rachal, et al. 1982; Collins et al. 1987). Indeed, the key impetus for public funding of drug abuse treatment is that it is expected to result in decreases in drug abuse and therefore in criminal activity. Despite the assumed relationship between drug abuse and criminal activity, Caplovitz (1976) showed that a number of addicts held jobs and supported their habits in large part through legitimate earnings. Poor educational backgrounds and work histories of many drug abusers, however, mean that many clients were employed only temporarily or part-time for low wages. Meeting the cost of maintaining an expensive drug habit, though, requires resources far beyond what most people can earn legitimately. Many drug abusers thus pay for their expensive drug habits through such income-generating crimes as robbery, theft, and burglary (Ball et al. 1981; Collins, Hubbard, and Rachal 1985; Gandossy et al. 1980; Hunt, Lipton, and Spunt 1982; Panel on Drug Use and Criminal Behavior 1976).

Client involvement in criminal activity was assessed in this study in terms of self-reported commission of 11 types of crimes. Most analyses reported here are based on commission of a subset of these crimes— income-generating or "predatory crimes" committed in the year before entering treatment. Predatory crimes are defined as acts such as aggravated assault, robbery, burglary, larceny, auto theft, forgery/embezzlement, and dealing in stolen property. We exclude drug-defined acts such as drug sales and driving while intoxicated and consensual crimes such as gambling and prostitution. Based on this definition, 41 percent of all clients claimed to have committed at least one predatory crime in the year before admission. Residential clients were the most likely to admit to such crimes in the year before admission: almost 60 percent, compared with about 36.5 percent of outpatient drug-free clients and 33.4 percent of outpatient methadone clients (Table 4-5). Not only were residential clients more likely to commit such crimes, they committed more of them. Forty-seven percent of residential clients admitted three or more predatory crimes in the year before treatment, compared with 23.6 percent of methadone clients and 22.0 percent of outpatient drug-free clients.

As with the general population, males and younger clients were more likely to have committed crimes in the year before treatment. Forty-four percent of males and 35 percent of females reported committing a predatory crime in the year before treatment, and males reported a higher frequency of offenses. Similarly, about 56 percent of clients under age 21 reported committing a predatory offense in the year before treatment, compared to 42.3 percent of those aged 21 to 30 and 33.3 percent of those over age 30. This lower level of criminal activity among older clients is also apparent in the general population and may be the result of offenders' "maturing out" of their criminal behavior or may reflect long periods of incarceration of the criminally active. Despite this decrease with age, sizable proportions of clients in each age category committed large numbers of predatory illegal acts in the year before treatment.

Criminal activity was associated with the nature of drug abuse in the year before treatment. In general, criminal activity was much more likely among those with more serious drug abuse patterns than those with alcohol/marijuana or minimal drug use patterns. Twenty-three percent of minimal users and 35.2 percent of alcohol/marijuana users admitted to predatory criminal activity in the year before treatment, compared with much higher percentages among other types of drug abusers. However, criminal activity was not highest among heroin abusers, who are generally described to be most seriously involved in drug abuse. Instead, multiple nonopioid abusers were most likely to be criminally involved; 53.3 percent of that type of drug abuser were criminally active. These findings demonstrate the close correspondence of criminal activity with more serious drug abuse.

A logistic regression analysis was performed to examine the risk factors for criminal activity in the year before treatment. Coding specifications for variables included in this analysis are described in Chapter 2.

Age, race/ethnicity, sex, drug abuse pattern, drinking level, depression, weeks worked, and number of prior drug abuse treatments were included in a separate regression model for each of the modalities. The dependent variable was any predatory crime in the year before treatment. In general, the results reported above for specific characteristics were confirmed. Males were substantially more likely to be involved in criminal activity than females, and those under 20 were two to four times more likely than those over age 30 to be criminally involved. Heroin abusers were significantly more involved in criminal activity than minimal drug users, and those with prior episodes of drug abuse treatment were substantially more likely to have committed crimes than those who were entering treatment for the first time. Other pretreatment behaviors such as drinking level, depression, and weeks of full-time work may have complex and important relationships to criminal activity but were not significant predictors of criminal activity in these analyses. Thus, age, sex, and drug abuse pattern exert important independent effects on the likelihood of criminal activity in the year before treatment. Perhaps most importantly, they offer further confirmation of the drug abuse–crime relationship.

Consistent with the relatively high proportions of clients who report criminal activity in the year before entering treatment, many report that most of their income was from illegal sources. Over one-half of outpatient drug-free clients and over one-third of outpatient methadone and residential clients reported that their primary source of income was from jobs, but one-third of residential clients, almost one-fourth of outpatient methadone, and more than 1 of 10 outpatient drug-free clients reported that their primary source of income was from illegal activity (Table 4-5). These findings contrast with those of earlier research (Burt Associates 1977; Mandell, Goldschmidt, and Grover 1973; Sells 1974), which found that criminal activity was the primary source of income for between 36 and 59 percent of clients and that jobs were the primary source for 14 to 23 percent of clients. Thus, the clients participating in this study were, in general, more dependent on jobs for income, compared with those in other studies. As noted previously in this chapter, many clients were also dependent on public assistance for support; almost one-fourth of methadone clients and more than 1 in 10 residential and outpatient drug-free clients reported that their primary source of income was from public sources. These findings indicate the need for continued emphasis on vocational and job placement services to help decrease client dependence on crime and public assistance as means of support.

*Employment*

A major goal for clients both during and after treatment is to earn a legitimate income in productive work, maintain a household and care for dependents, or attend school or training programs. Exceptions are, of course, made for those who are handicapped or too young or too old or otherwise unable to perform these roles. Indeed, improvements in employment and productive activity are important indicators of treatment effectiveness. The TOPS intake interview included a number of items with which to assess employment behavior in the year before treatment and the week immediately before treatment, as well as some aspects of clients' employment histories. Here we focus on labor force status in the week before admission and weeks of full-time work in the year before admission.

A review of prior studies of labor force participation of clients conducted between 1970 and 1977 revealed that employment rates ranged between 18 and 40 percent in methadone programs and between 16 and 23 percent in residential programs (Hubbard, Harwood, and Cruze 1977). This study shows a similar but somewhat lower level of employment during the years 1979 to 1981. In the week before admission, 35.9 percent of outpatient drug-free, 29.2 percent of outpatient methadone, and 12.2 percent of residential clients were employed at a legal job. In the week before entering treatment, four of five outpatient drug-free clients, two-thirds of residential clients, and three of five outpatient methadone clients were in the labor force or involved in productive activities. In addition to employment or looking for work, these activities include school or training, homemaking, disability or retirement, or institutionalization. About one-third of the residential clients were institutionalized in the week prior to entering treatment, either in jail or in other treatment programs. Thus, at most 20 to 30 percent of clients were not involved in some kind of productive activity immediately before entering treatment.

About 60 percent of clients reported some weeks of full-time work (35 or more hours) in the year before entering treatment. For many of these clients, however, full-time employment was for only part of the year. Table 4-5 shows data on full-time employment throughout the year before treatment (employed full time for 40 weeks or more). Clients entering outpatient drug-free treatment were the most likely to be employed full time (25.4 percent) despite the fact that about 25 percent were students, homemakers, or disabled. The rate was similar for outpatient methadone clients (23.6 percent). Residential clients were least likely to have been fully employed (14.7 percent). Younger clients (those under age 30) and whites were more likely than other clients to be fully employed. Some clients had held a job for a long time, but many were at a serious disadvantage for obtaining employment during and after treatment.

A logistic regression analysis predicted the likelihood of being employed 40 or more weeks full time in the year before entering treatment for clients in each of the modalities. Independent variables included age, race/ethnicity, sex, drug use prior to treatment, and prior treatment admissions. Compared to other factors in the regression model, sociodemographic factors were the most predictive of high levels of employment. In all modalities, whites, males, and clients who were over 30 had the highest relative odds of working full time for 40 or more weeks. Other results were inconsistent across modalities. For outpatient methadone clients, those who were reentering treatment for at least the third time were substantially less likely than those who were entering for the first time to be fully employed; multiple nonopioid abusers were less likely than heroin abusers to be employed. For residential clients, a different pattern was observed; multiple nonopioid abusers were substantially more likely than heroin abusers to be employed. A similar finding was apparent for outpatient drug-free clients although the results were not significant. For outpatient drug-free as for methadone clients, first-time entrants were more likely to be employed than reentrants.

*Alcohol Use*

Alcohol use is widespread among clients before, during, and after treatment. Estimates of the extent of alcohol use vary, depending on the treatment population and the definition employed. However, 20 to 50 percent of clients may be alcohol abusers (Belenko 1979; Hunt et al. 1986; Stimmel et al. 1983). The extent of alcohol abuse among clients is an important consideration, because alcohol abusers are more frequently discharged from treatment programs (Bihari 1973) and have poorer treatment outcomes than those who do not abuse alcohol (Rawson et al. 1981). Clients who are dually addicted or who have a history of alcohol abuse have higher rates of psychopathology, medical complications, and criminal activity than those without drinking problems (Roszell, Calsyn, and Chaney 1986). Further, clients may often substitute alcohol as their drug usage decreases (Judson et al. 1980; Simpson and Lloyd 1977).

The majority of clients drank alcohol in the three months before admission. Outpatient drug-free clients were most likely to have consumed alcohol (83.8 percent), followed by residential clients (68.7 percent), and outpatient methadone clients (66.0 percent). However, the proportion of heavy drinkers offers more information on the likelihood of potential problems. About two of every five (41.7 percent) residential clients, one-third (35.7 percent) of outpatient drug-free clients, and a fourth (25.0 percent) of outpatient methadone clients were classed as heavy drinkers in the three months before admission (Table 4-5). That is, they drank five or more drinks at a sitting, once a week or more often. These rates suggest that clients were more than three times as likely as persons in the general population (Clark and Midanik 1982) to be heavy drinkers. Alcohol use at admission to treatment was higher among males, nonopioid abusers, depressed clients, and those with fewer prior drug treatment admissions and many drug-related problems (Schlenger et al. 1984).

*Depressive and Suicidal Indicators*

The prevalence and course of depressive symptoms among clients is a major topic of concern. Serious depression can affect the course of treatment and jeopardize successful outcomes (Dorus and Senay 1980; Woody and Blaine 1979). Because short indexes of depression had not been validated and the time available in the interviews was limited, only three questions were included in the TOPS survey to assess the preva-

Table 4-5 Concomitant Behaviors in the Year before Admission, by Modality

| Behavior | Outpatient Methadone (N=4,184) | Residential (N=2,891) | Outpatient Drug-Free (N=2,914) |
|---|---|---|---|
| | % | % | % |
| Predatory criminal activity | 33.4 | 59.8 | 36.5 |
| Illegal activity as primary source of income | 23.2 | 33.9 | 12.0 |
| Fully employed (40 weeks or more) | 23.6 | 14.7 | 25.4 |
| Heavy alcohol use | 25.0 | 41.7 | 35.7 |
| Suicidal thoughts or attempts | 28.9 | 43.8 | 47.6 |
| Multiple (3 or more) drug-related problems | 40.9 | 63.3 | 50.1 |

*Note:* Clients may report more than one type of behavior. Because the number of respondents differs slightly for each of the behaviors, only total population sizes for the three modalities are presented here.

lence of such symptoms before, during, and after treatment. The three items have, however, been shown to be valid indicators of depressive symptoms as measured by standard depression inventories (Allison et al. 1986). These three items are self-reports of feeling so depressed that one could not get out of bed in the morning; having thought of suicide; or having attempted suicide. A comprehensive description of depression and suicidal indicators among clients is provided in Allison, Hubbard, and Ginzburg (1985).

Sixty percent of clients reported some symptom of depression in the year before admission; the prevalence was somewhat higher among residential (63.3 percent) and outpatient drug-free clients (61.5 percent) than among outpatient methadone clients (53.7 percent). Considering only the two indicators, suicidal thoughts and attempts at suicide (Table 4-5), rates among residential (43.8 percent) and outpatient drug-free clients (47.6 percent), however, were almost double that for methadone clients (28.9 percent). Across the three modalities, 14 to 25 percent of clients had felt depressed, 23 to 34 percent had thought about suicide, and 6 to 14 percent had attempted suicide in the past year. Symptoms of depression were more common among young and female clients, and among Hispanics and non-Hispanic whites.

A logistic regression model to examine the risk factors for suicidal thoughts or attempts in the year before entering treatment revealed that non-Hispanic whites were 2 to 3 times more likely than blacks to report such thoughts across the three modalities; females about twice as likely as males; and multiple nonopioid abusers about twice as likely as heroin abusers to do so. Independent variables included in this regression were age, race/ethnicity, sex, drug abuse pattern prior to treatment, prior treatment episodes, and source of referral. The magnitude of the effects of other characteristics varied by modality and was, in general, lower than the magnitude for the above characteristics. Knowledge of these risk factors should help clinicians identify client types entering treatment with a higher risk of depressive symptoms. The prevalence of depressive symptoms demonstrates the need for mental health services in drug abuse treatment programs, particularly in residential and outpatient drug-free programs.

*Drug-Related Problems*

Various serious medical, social, economic, and mental health problems in addition to depression are closely associated with drug and alcohol abuse and affect the course of client behaviors before, during, and after treatment. It is generally agreed that assisting clients with these problems should be a major goal of treatment and that to be successful, treatment must be oriented to a variety of client needs and to services that effectively meet those needs.

Interviews obtained the frequency of occurrence of six types of drug-related problems in the year before admission to treatment—medical; mental health or emotional; family or friends; police or legal; job, work, or school; and financial or money. These categories describe a variety of problems experienced by clients, many of which are interrelated but emerge from their drug abuse. Unlike the assessments of clinicians using such instruments as the Addiction Severity Index (McLellan et al. 1985), in the TOPS interviews the clients described the severity of their problems and the degree to which the problem was attributed to drug abuse.

About 80 percent of clients reported a drug-related problem in the year before entering treatment. Residential clients were slightly more likely than others to report having experienced a problem, but the differences among the modalities were not large. Problems with family and friends were the most commonly cited type of problem, reported by 66.9 percent of residential clients, 56.1 percent of outpatient drug-free clients, and 45.7 percent of methadone clients. Financial and money problems were second in importance, reported by 62.0 percent of methadone clients, 57.5 percent of residential clients, and 44.1 percent of outpatient drug-free clients. Mental health problems were cited by over 50 percent of residential and outpatient drug-free clients and about one-third of methadone clients. Other types of problems were less frequently cited but, in general, were experienced by 40 percent or more of clients. Medical problems were least frequently cited (41.6 percent of residential clients and about one-third of other clients). Most clients reported problems in more than one area, and residential clients were most likely to report multiple problems. Two-thirds of residential clients reported problems in three or more areas compared to about 50 percent of outpatient drug-free clients and 40 percent of methadone clients (Table 4-5).

A logistic regression analysis to examine the risk factors associated with experiencing three or more types of drug-related problems in the year before treatment revealed fairly consistent findings across the three modalities. Independent variables included age, race/ethnicity, sex, drug abuse pattern in the year before treatment, and prior treatment episodes. Non-Hispanic whites were two to three times more likely than blacks to report many drug-related problems, as were those with multiple prior admissions compared to those entering treatment for the first time. Heroin/other opioid abusers were two to five times more likely than heroin abusers to report multiple drug-related problems. Other effects were less strong or not significant.

## Changes in Treatment Populations

Observations from treatment directors and administrators have indicated that the treatment population is becoming more likely to abuse multiple drugs, is more disturbed psychologically, and more commonly has a greater number of personal, health, and other problems related to drug abuse. Further, more young and female clients appeared to be entering treatment (Greenberg and Brown 1984). To investigate the assertion that clients during the 1980s had more severe problems, we compared TOPS data with Drug Abuse Reporting Program data from the 1970s and compared the three admission cohorts within TOPS (Hubbard, Bray, Cavanaugh, et al. 1986). From both of these analyses, we expect indications of a movement toward more multiple drug abuse and greater problem severity along a number of dimensions. This section describes these comparisons and examines the implications for the provision of treatment services.

### Changes since the 1970s

Examination of changes in client populations since the 1970s is based on comparisons of data on treatment populations from the TOPS and DARP studies. The DARP study, described in more detail in Chapter 1, provides information about populations entering treatment from 1969 to 1974, while the TOPS study provides information for 1979 to 1981. To ensure the most accurate comparison, the TOPS data set was made roughly comparable to the DARP data set by excluding from the TOPS data those clients who received no treatment, were confined in the two months before treatment, reported being in methadone maintenance in the two months before treatment, and reported no drug use in the two months before treatment. Abusers receiving detoxification services were excluded from both data bases. The comparison populations consisted of 21,313 DARP clients who entered treatment from 1969 to 1974 and 6,364 TOPS clients who entered treatment from 1979 to 1981. The TOPS and DARP samples were compared on a variety of sociodemographic and behavioral measures, including drug abuse, alcohol use, and criminal activity.

In contrast to DARP clients, TOPS clients were more likely to be female (methadone only), white, older, and returning to treatment rather than entering treatment for the first time (particularly for methadone clients). TOPS clients were, for instance, 2 to 3 times more likely than DARP clients to have three or more previous admissions. TOPS clients were somewhat less likely to be involved in the criminal justice system and to have an illegal source of income than DARP clients. The major difference between TOPS and DARP clients was, however, in the nature of drug abuse on entry to treatment. TOPS clients were much more likely to engage in multiple drug abuse and less likely to abuse opioids daily. Among DARP methadone clients, 45 percent were principally daily abusers compared with 21 percent of TOPS methadone clients: 49 percent of DARP clients used nonopioids along with their daily opioid use compared to 60 percent for TOPS. Among residential and outpatient drug-free clients, opioid abuse was much less common among TOPS clients than DARP clients; 23 percent of DARP residential clients and 17 percent of DARP outpatient drug-free clients were daily opioid users, compared with 6 percent of TOPS residential and 2 percent of TOPS outpatient drug-free clients. In contrast, 17 percent of DARP residential clients compared to 41 percent of TOPS residential clients were nonopioid abusers. The rates of nonopioid abuse were 48 and 64 percent for DARP and TOPS outpatient drug-free clients.

These differences support observations that the drug abuse treatment population is now more likely to be composed of multiple drug abusers and to have greater proportions of females. However, against expectation, the population appears to be getting older with longer treatment histories. These differences in client populations, even in the decade between DARP and TOPS, require major reorientations in program services to meet the needs of an increasingly mature, multiple drug, and nonopioid-abusing population.

*Changes during the 1980s*

Although the TOPS study included only three consecutive annual admission cohorts, observed differences among the cohorts may be indicative of emerging trends in client populations that will now need to be considered in the orientations and services of drug abuse treatment. For the most accurate comparisons across the three cohorts, we consider here only clients in those 17 programs in five cities that participated in all three years. The resulting subsample consisted of 2,172 TOPS clients from the 1979 admission cohort, 2,389 from the 1980 cohort, and 1,803 from the 1981 cohort.

Although there are some exceptions by modality, between 1979 and 1981 there tended to be an increase in the proportions of female clients, clients over age 30, and non-Hispanic whites. There were, in general, more referrals from the criminal justice system and more clients with no prior treatment experience, although fewer clients reported criminal activity in 1981 compared with 1979. Changes in drug abuse were not substantial, although fewer clients reported heroin abuse as the primary drug problem in later cohorts. Few differences in employment were observed in comparisons of the three cohorts.

Cohort differences were further examined by means of a logistic regression procedure that used the 1979 cohort as the reference group. Models were estimated to examine for each of the modalities the impact of cohort (1980/1979, 1981/1979) on each of the following characteristics and behaviors: high drug abuse severity, three or more types of drug-related problems, suicidal thoughts or attempts, heavy alcohol use, predatory crime, and 40 or more weeks of full-time work. Independent variables included age, sex, race/ethnicity, pretreatment drug abuse pattern, number of prior treatment episodes, and source of referral.

Only 3 of the 18 regressions that compared 1979 and 1980 measures were statistically significant; outpatient methadone and outpatient drug-free clients in 1980 were not as likely to have high drug abuse severity as in 1979, and outpatient methadone clients were less likely to be fully employed in 1980 than in 1979. More cohort differences were observed in comparisons of 1981 and 1979 data. Of the 18 regressions, nine showed statistically significant cohort effects. Five of these effects were evident for methadone clients, indicating that between 1979 and 1981 there was a lower likelihood of high drug abuse severity, multiple drug-related problems, suicidal thoughts or attempts, and heavy alcohol use, and a greater likelihood of predatory crime. A greater likelihood of drug-related problems and a lower likelihood of predatory crime were indicated for residential clients, and a lower likelihood of drug abuse severity and predatory crime were indicated for outpatient drug-free clients between 1979 and 1981.

These results are counter to impressions of program personnel that the problems of clients would become more severe during the 1980s (Greenberg and Brown 1984). The major increases in the proportions of clients with multiple drug abuse and multiple problems that occurred between 1970 and 1980 may have peaked. These comparisons are based on a limited period of time, however, so the results are only indicative of changes that might occur throughout the 1980s. Regardless of the trends, it is clear that treatment programs must provide services that meet the needs of increased numbers of females, multiple drug abusers, and those with multiple problems.

## Distinctiveness of Client Populations by Modality

One issue complicating the comparison of effectiveness rates across modalities is that the modalities have very different client populations.

That is, although the modalities serve diverse client types and have clienteles that vary in the type of drug abuse and in problem severity, certain client types are disproportionately represented in the modalities. Outpatient methadone programs, for instance, were designed to treat heroin and other opioid addicts, and while residential and outpatient drug-free programs also treat opioid addicts, the drug abuse patterns of their clientele are typically more diverse. Further, drug-related problem severity may be greater among outpatient methadone clients and residential clients than among outpatient drug-free clients. Simpson (1981b) finds that clients in the major modalities in the DARP study vary in type of drug abuse, age, and race. Daily opioid users and blacks are overrepresented in methadone maintenance programs, while younger clients are overrepresented in outpatient drug-free programs.

Because these client characteristics may be related to treatment outcome and because modality differences are so extreme on many client characteristics, the modalities are in general examined separately in analyses reported in this book. In order to examine in more detail the nature and extent of differences in client populations across modality, however, a series of logistic regressions was used to predict the following types of client characteristics and behaviors in the year before treatment: high drug abuse severity (daily use of three or more drugs or weekly use of four or more drugs), three or more types of drug-related problems, suicidal thoughts or attempts, heavy alcohol use, involvement in predatory illegal acts, and 40 or more weeks of full-time employment in the year before treatment. Independent variables included in the models were age, sex, race/ethnicity, pretreatment drug abuse patterns, number of prior treatments, and source of referral. Regression models were estimated that compared the effects on each of the behaviors of residential treatment relative to methadone treatment and outpatient drug-free treatment relative to methadone treatment.

Each of the 12 regressions yielded statistically significant modality effects except for the outpatient drug-free/methadone comparison for employment. Residential clients compared with methadone clients were more likely to have higher drug abuse severity, a high number of drug-related problems, suicidal thoughts or attempts, heavy alcohol use, involvement in predatory illegal acts, and 40 or more weeks of full-time employment. Compared with methadone clients, outpatient drug-free clients were less likely to have high drug abuse severity and were more likely to have a high number of drug-related problems, suicidal thoughts or attempts, heavy alcohol use, and involvement in predatory illegal acts. Thus, outpatient methadone clients were less likely than other clients to demonstrate various behaviors frequently characteristic of drug-abusing populations and tended to be lower in problem severity. Residential clients illustrated greater problem severity along a number of dimensions. These findings indicate that the modalities do serve very different client populations.

## Time Spent in Treatment

A number of studies of drug abuse treatment effectiveness have found more positive outcomes among those who stay in treatment for longer periods of time. Longer stays have been found to result in greater decreases in drug use, criminal activity, and unemployment in prior studies (Cushman 1977; Dole, Nyswander, and Warner 1968; McLellan et al. 1986; Ogborne and Melotte 1977; Riordan et al. 1976; Simpson 1979, 1980, 1981b), as well as in the analyses reported here. Indeed, our analyses demonstrate that time in treatment is among the most important predictors of positive outcomes.

Despite this consistent finding, studies of factors related to time in treatment itself yield highly inconsistent results. For example, client age has been found to be positively related (Joe and Gent 1978; Sansone 1980), negatively related (Babst, Chambers, and Warner 1971), and unrelated (Gearing 1972) to treatment tenure. If client characteristics could be found that are consistently related to treatment tenure, efforts could be directed toward increasing tenure and thereby treatment effectiveness.

Clients in the three modalities differ not only in background characteristics and pretreatment behaviors, but also in time spent in treatment. Given the substantial differences in program goals and clientele, this is not unexpected. As shown in Table 4-6, the average length of stay is longest for clients in outpatient methadone programs (mean of 38.4 and median of 28.3 weeks), followed by residential programs (mean of 21.3 and median of 11.0 weeks) and outpatient drug-free programs (mean of 14.6 and median of 7.9 weeks). These median values are comparable to those reported in the DARP study of clients entering treatment in the early 1970s—27 to 31 weeks for outpatient methadone, 12 to 15 weeks for residential, and 10 to 12 weeks for outpatient drug-free clients (Simpson 1979, 1981b). It appears, therefore, that the average numbers of weeks spent in different types of treatment did not change in the 10 years between the DARP and TOPS studies.

Most of the difference in average time in treatment between methadone clients and others is explained by the fact that 34.1 percent of the methadone clients but only 13.4 percent of residential and 6.6 percent of outpatient drug-free clients stayed in treatment at least one year (Table 4-6). More than 80 percent of residential and outpatient drug-free clients, on the other hand, stayed in treatment less than 6 months. Over 22 percent of clients assigned to outpatient drug-free treatment but only 11 percent of outpatient methadone and 10 percent of residential clients stayed in treatment for 1 week or less and received essentially no treatment. These results suggest the need for more intensive efforts early in outpatient drug-free treatment. While residence and medication are potential motivating factors in the other modalities, outpatient drug-free programs must convince a client that counseling is beneficial. A very positive initial experience is necessary to motivate outpatient drug-free clients to return for subsequent sessions. It is important to note that half the outpatient drug-free and methadone clients and 38 percent of the residential clients who stayed in treatment at least 3 months eventually completed treatment. Because completion of treatment is an important predictor of effectiveness, efforts to retain clients for at least 3 months should increase the overall benefits.

Given the modality differences in average lengths of stay in treatment, regression analyses of the factors related to time in treatment were conducted separately for the three major modalities. Predictor variables

Table 4-6  Time in Treatment, by Modality

| Time in Treatment | Outpatient Methadone (N=2,698) | Residential (N=1,873) | Outpatient Drug-Free (N=2,040) |
|---|---|---|---|
| | % | % | % |
| 1 week or less | 10.7 | 9.6 | 22.4 |
| 2–4 weeks | 8.4 | 22.5 | 18.8 |
| 5–13 weeks | 12.5 | 23.2 | 22.6 |
| 14–26 weeks | 16.0 | 17.9 | 19.0 |
| 27–52 weeks | 18.3 | 13.4 | 10.6 |
| 53 or more weeks | 34.1 | 13.4 | 6.6 |
| Total | 100.0 | 100.0 | 100.0 |
| Mean (weeks) | 38.4 | 21.3 | 14.6 |
| Median (weeks) | 28.3 | 11.0 | 7.9 |

*Note:* Estimates are based on data from the population of clients entering treatment in 1979 and 1980.

included age, race/ethnicity, sex, marital status, educational level, pre-treatment drug abuse, pretreatment alcohol use, source of referral, and pretreatment depression. These regression analyses yielded a number of significant predictors of time in treatment, although the predictors were not always consistent across the three modalities in significance level or direction. In fact, the only consistent finding across the three modalities was that heavy alcohol users were less likely to remain in treatment for lengthy stays than abstainers or less frequent users. In general, younger clients stayed shorter periods of time, but this finding was significant only for residential and outpatient drug-free clients. Females stayed significantly longer in outpatient methadone and outpatient drug-free programs; however, they were likely to have shorter stays in residential programs although the relationship was not significant. The finding that women stay shorter periods in residential programs is consistent with the finding of a body of prior research that cites the demands of family life on women as reasons for their dropping out of residential programs. They may be more likely to complete outpatient programs in which they can maintain family ties more easily.

Criminal justice system referrals stayed significantly longer in residential and outpatient drug-free programs than referrals from other sources, while criminal justice referrals stayed significantly shorter periods in outpatient methadone programs. Although these findings are also inconsistent, there are relatively few criminal justice referrals to outpatient methadone programs. Also inconsistent was the relationship between marital status and length of stay. Married clients were significantly more likely to have long stays in outpatient methadone programs and significantly less likely to do so in residential programs. The relationship was not significant for outpatient drug-free programs. Other characteristics showed even more inconsistent findings by modality.

Thus, factors related to length of stay in treatment for the most part differ by modality. This finding may account for some of the inconsistent results of prior research. With the exception of heavy alcohol use, which is a strong and consistent predictor across each of the modalities, factors related to longer stays in treatment are meaningful only within the context of a particular modality. For outpatient methadone clients, longer stays in treatment are characteristic of females, Hispanics, those with three or more prior drug abuse treatments, those who used only heroin, and those who were not heavy alcohol users. Among residential clients, lengthier stays were characteristic of older clients, those who were not currently married, criminal justice referrals, and those who were not depressed at entry to treatment. For outpatient drug-free clients, lengthier stays were characteristic of females, older clients, those with more than a high school education, criminal justice referrals, and those who were not heavy alcohol users.

It can be argued that clients who are satisfied with treatment are more likely to remain in treatment. To address this issue, the effect of a prospective measure of treatment satisfaction on time in treatment was tested using subsamples of clients who remained in treatment at least 1 month but less than 1 year. Across all modalities, the higher the level of satisfaction with treatment, the longer the subsequent time spent in treatment.

## Conclusions

The drug abuse treatment modalities serve a predominantly young adult, poorly educated, male clientele, but there are substantial differences in other client characteristics and behaviors across the three modalities. In contrast to clients in other modalities, outpatient methadone clients on average were older, were more likely to be black or Hispanic, and were more likely to be married or living as married. A majority were opioid abusers and had prior treatment admissions. Compared with other clients, residential clients were somewhat more likely to be male, had more diverse drug abuse patterns, and were more likely to have been criminally active and heavy alcohol users before entering treatment. In contrast, a majority of outpatient drug-free clients were white, were better educated, and had diverse drug abuse patterns. These differences in client populations suggest that the modalities be separately considered in analyses of drug abuse treatment effectiveness, as they are in this book.

Comparisons of these clients with those of prior studies indicates that major changes in the nature of the client population, most notably in the extent of multiple drug abuse, have occurred during the past decade. Clients are now more likely to be female, white, older and returning to treatment rather than entering treatment for the first time. Comparison of the early and later admission cohorts in this study suggests that these changes are continuing. Clients in the later cohorts were more likely to be multiple drug users and female, although they did not differ substantially on problem severity.

These findings suggest the need for the adaptability of drug abuse treatment to changes in client populations. Treatment regimens directed toward the abuser of specific drugs may not be effective for the multiple drug abuser; similarly, treatment approaches appropriate for the opioid abuser may not be as effective for the nonopioid abuser. Thus, treatment must be directed toward a heterogeneous group of clients, and a full range of settings is necessary to treat the variety of drug abuse patterns currently prevalent. The future success of the publicly funded drug abuse treatment system will depend in large part on how programs work with their state and local government agencies to meet the needs of future client populations. In addition to the continuing problems associated with drug abuse, the threat of Acquired Immune Deficiency Syndrome has introduced a greater sense of urgency in the effective treatment of intravenous drug abuse. Findings regarding time spent in treatment suggest that many clients are staying in treatment for substantial periods of time. Whether these periods are sufficient to generate lasting changes in drug abuse and other behaviors is investigated in subsequent chapters.

# 5. Reducing Drug Abuse

Eliminating or reducing drug abuse among clients remains the primary goal of drug abuse treatment. Numerous studies have concluded that treatment is effective in reaching that goal. A series of studies has documented the positive effects of therapeutic communities (DeLeon 1984; Holland 1982a; Smart 1976). Burt Associates (1977) found substantial reductions in opioid abuse after treatment and little evidence of drug substitution. Both clinical trial studies and epidemiological outcome research demonstrate that methadone treatment reduces heroin abuse (Cooper et al. 1983). Similar reductions in daily opioid use were reported for former Civil Addict Program clients (McGlothlin, Anglin, and Wilson 1977), though the authors caution that part of this reduction may be due to subsequent enrollment in methadone programs. The Drug Abuse Reporting Program (DARP) studies of clients entering treatment between 1969 and 1974 indicated significant reductions in drug abuse while clients were in treatment (Sells 1974; Sells and Simpson 1976), and improvements remained after leaving treatment (Simpson and Sells 1982). However, alcohol and marijuana use increased after treatment in all groups (Simpson and Lloyd 1977). Findings from the 12-year follow-up of DARP clients show that the decreases in drug abuse that were apparent for the first six years after treatment had stabilized by the twelfth year. Little change in drug abuse occurred between the sixth and twelfth years after treatment except for an increase in cocaine abuse (Simpson et al. 1986).

These existing studies of drug abuse treatment describe effectiveness for the clients and programs of the 1970s. However, significant changes have occurred over the past decades in the nature of drug abuse and related behaviors and the sociodemographic composition of treatment populations. A major question facing program administrators and policymakers is whether the three major modalities will continue to be effective for the clients in subsequent decades, particularly for the multiple drug abuser, the greater diversity of clients entering publicly funded programs, and the intravenous drug user who is a major link in the spread of the Human Immunodeficiency Virus (HIV) that causes Acquired Immune Deficiency Syndrome (AIDS).

This chapter describes the nature and extent of changes in drug abuse associated with participation in treatment. The extent of involvement in drug abuse is compared for the year before entering treatment, the time spent in treatment, and the years after leaving treatment. Because of clinical and policy interest in specific drugs of abuse, changes in use of heroin, cocaine, psychotherapeutic drugs, and marijuana are examined separately. We also key our analysis to a drug abuse pattern index (described in Chapter 2) that captures the multiple drug abuse typical of the client of the 1980s. By using this index, we can point to changes in drug abuse associated with treatment in terms of more or less serious patterns of abuse (Hubbard and Marsden 1986). We also consider changes in intravenous drug use, because of its role in the AIDS epidemic.

In this chapter, we first compare the prevalence of abuse of specific drugs and patterns of multiple drug abuse for selected periods before, during, and after treatment. We examine for each time point the prevalence of regular use, defined here as daily or weekly use of the specific drug or involvement in particular drug abuse patterns. We focus on regular use to distinguish sustained, abusive patterns of use from less frequent use or brief periods of relapse. We note for each specific drug or drug abuse pattern the direction and magnitude of change during and after treatment and discuss client characteristics and behaviors, aspects of treatment, and certain posttreatment experiences that are related to posttreatment abuse.

In addition to examining prevalence of drug abuse patterns at each of the time points, we calculate one-year abstinence rates and improvement rates for each of the specific drugs. These two rates are necessary to describe both realistic and ideal goals of treatment. The one-year period is chosen because it is congruent with many of the studies of effectiveness. Abstinence rates define the percentage of regular users of each specific drug in the year before treatment who did not use that drug with any frequency in the year after treatment. Improvement rates, on the other hand, define the percentage of regular users of a particular drug in the year before treatment who decreased their frequency of use or ceased use in the year after treatment. Abstinence is, of course, a more stringent requirement than improvement, and rates are correspondingly lower.

These three types of rates—prevalence, abstinence, and improvement—are necessary to describe changes in drug abuse. Prevalence figures provide an overview of the extent of drug abuse among clients before, during, and after treatment and indicate the magnitude of changes attributable to treatment. The figures, however, include not only those who continue to abuse the specific drug or are described by a particular drug abuse pattern throughout the time period under consideration, but also those who newly use the drug or change their drug use pattern compared to the year before treatment. In contrast, abstinence rates and improvement rates provide an indication of the extent of changes in drug abuse for specific individuals; these rates pertain only to those who were regular (daily or weekly) users of the specific drug or drug type in the year before treatment and the course of their use during and after treatment. In this chapter, discussion focuses on those in treatment for at least three months, in order to illustrate the potential impact of drug abuse treatment for those who remain in treatment for a sufficiently long period of time to bring about change in drug abuse. However, exact prevalence figures for those in treatment less than three months and three months or more are presented in Table A-2 in the Appendix.

Results of multivariate analyses that examine the factors associated with a lower risk of drug abuse after leaving treatment (Hubbard, Marsden, et al. 1988) are also described in this chapter. The multivariate analyses consider factors that predict the abuse of specific drugs in the year after treatment, with time in treatment and drug abuse in the year before treatment included as the major predictors. Log-odds ratios for the "time in treatment" categories in each modality are shown in Tables A-4, A-5, and A-6 in the Appendix. Additional predictors include client characteristics, such aspects of treatment as time spent in treatment and service intensity, and other client behaviors. As with other analyses presented elsewhere in this book, the course of drug abuse treatment is examined for clients in each modality. However, for some analyses we consider separately long-term methadone maintenance clients, who in fact remained in treatment throughout the entire time period in question. In the last month of the follow-up study, these clients were asked about their behavior and experience in the year before the interview. Coding specifications for major variables included in these analyses are presented in Chapter 2.

## Heroin Use

Since the 1950s drug abuse treatment has focused on opioid addiction, principally heroin addiction, because of its prevalence and causal association with massive social costs. Although problems with cocaine, marijuana, and other drugs of abuse rapidly escalated in the 1970s, the treatment of heroin abuse continues to be a major objective of most publicly funded drug abuse treatment programs. Indeed, heroin was commonly and frequently abused by clients entering treatment during the 1970s. Eighty-two percent of clients entering DARP programs in 1969–1974 had used heroin in the preceding 2 months; 73 percent had used it daily (Simpson et al. 1976). Similar daily use rates were reported by clients entering methadone maintenance and methadone-to-abstinence programs in New York City and a multimodality program in Washington, D.C. (Burt Associates 1977), a large therapeutic community between 1970 and 1971 (DeLeon 1984), and referrals to the California Civil Addict Program in 1970 (McGlothlin, Anglin, and Wilson 1977).

Despite this pervasiveness, heroin abuse appears to be abating in the drug abusing population. The percentage of heroin users among clients admitted to programs that were part of the Client Oriented Data Acquisition Process (CODAP) decreased from 61 percent in 1976 to 36 percent in 1981 (NIDA 1982). Similarly, DeLeon (1984) found that the proportion of clients in a large therapeutic community whose primary problem was heroin was much lower in 1974 than in 1970–1971 (41 percent compared with 84 percent). DesJarlais and Uppal (1980) found a steady decline in the number of new "intensive" users during the 1970s. Further, the character of heroin abuse has changed. More recent heroin abusers are more likely to abuse a variety of drugs in addition to heroin, notably cocaine, marijuana, and alcohol (Bray et al. 1982; Hubbard, Bray, Craddock, et al. 1986).

Drug abuse treatment has been shown in a variety of studies to be effective in reducing heroin abuse. Simpson and Savage (1980) found, for instance, that 63 percent of pretreatment daily opioid abusers reported any opioid use and 47 percent reported daily opioid use in the first years after DARP treatment. These reductions in abuse continued throughout the first 6-year follow-up period, when 42 percent reported any opioid use and one-fourth reported daily use. Simpson et al. (1986) found an overall trend toward stabilization 6 to 12 years after treatment, with 23 percent increasing their frequency of opioid use and an equal percentage stopping or decreasing use. Burt Associates (1977) found rates of daily heroin use decreased from about 70 percent before treatment to 12 percent immediately after treatment to less than 5 percent one to three years after treatment in methadone and residential programs. Similar low rates of opioid addiction were found by DeLeon (1984) for clients two years after leaving a large New York City therapeutic community.

*Heroin Use before, during, and after Treatment*

Heroin use declines dramatically during and after treatment. The prevalence of regular heroin use before, during, and after treatment in the three major modalities during the 1980s is illustrated in Figure 5-1. The figure demonstrates the substantial modality differences in the percentage of regular heroin users in the year before entering treatment, rare and infrequent heroin use during treatment in each of the modalities, a slight increase in the percentage of regular users immediately after leaving treatment, and a leveling off of the percentage of regular users in subsequent years to a percentage that is substantially lower than pretreatment levels, at least for outpatient methadone and residential programs. For those who stayed in treatment at least three months, about 63.5 percent of clients entering outpatient methadone treatment, 30.9 percent of those entering residential programs, and about 8.6 percent of those entering outpatient drug-free treatment were regular heroin users in the year before treatment. Three to five years after treatment, these figures were about 17.5 percent for outpatient methadone clients, 11.8 percent for residential clients, and 4.6 percent for outpatient drug-free clients. Reductions in prevalence were most dramatic for clients in outpatient methadone and residential programs, both of which had sizable percentages of regular heroin users entering treatment. A small but sustained reduction in the percentage of regular heroin users was also seen for outpatient drug-free programs, although these programs had a small proportion of heroin abusers. Despite these declines, regular heroin use is not eliminated by any type of drug abuse treatment.

These reductions in the prevalence of regular heroin use are perhaps better described by one-year abstinence and improvement rates. For those who were regular heroin users in the year before entering treatment and stayed in treatment at least three months, one-year abstinence rates show that over half of outpatient methadone clients and residential clients did not use heroin with any frequency in the year after treatment. Comparable one-year improvement rates show that fully 7 of every 10 outpatient methadone clients and residential clients decreased their level of use or ceased heroin use in the year after treatment. Abstinence and improvement rates were not calculated for clients in outpatient drug-free programs because of the small percentage of regular heroin users entering treatment in those programs. These abstinence and improvement rates suggest that although the modalities differ substantially in the percentage of regular heroin users entering treatment, they are effective approaches to decreasing heroin use.

*Factors Affecting Posttreatment Heroin Use*

A variety of factors influences the magnitude of impact of treatment on heroin use, including the severity of drug use and drug-related problems of clients upon entering treatment, client receptivity to change, time spent in treatment, the nature and intensity of treatment services received, and certain posttreatment experiences such as social support, aftercare, and reentry to drug abuse treatment. Of these characteristics,

time spent in treatment has been found to be perhaps the strongest predictor of treatment success (Cushman 1977; Hubbard et al. 1984; McLellan et al. 1986; Ogborne and Melotte 1977; Riordan et al. 1976; Simpson
1979, 1980, 1981b). In the DARP research, subsequent admissions (Simpson and Savage 1980) and employment (Simpson 1981a) were also found
to be associated with decreases in opioid use. McGlothlin, Anglin, and
Wilson (1977) found that clients enrolled in methadone programs after the

Figure 5-1 Changes in Prevalence of Regular Heroin Use (clients treated
three months or longer)

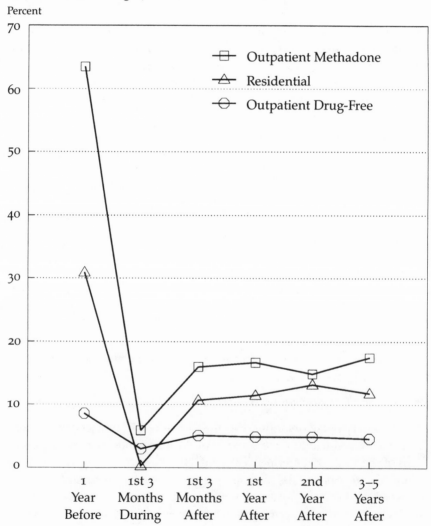

Civil Addict Program reported less heroin use. Few other strong predictors of successful outcomes have been found. Simpson et al. (1986) in fact found demographic and background factors to be relatively unimportant in explaining long-term treatment outcomes.

We conducted a series of log-linear regression analyses to examine the impact on posttreatment regular heroin use of client characteristics and pretreatment behaviors, aspects of treatment, and certain posttreatment experiences. The dependent variable was regular (weekly or daily) heroin use in the year after treatment, compared to infrequent use or no use. Across all these analyses, the most important predictors of posttreatment regular heroin use for clients in each of the modalities were pretreatment drug abuse pattern and time spent in treatment. Posttreatment heroin use was unrelated to demographic characteristics (age, sex, race) or the number of prior admissions to drug abuse treatment (an indicator of the stage of drug abuse) and was not strongly related to the intensity of services received during treatment. Included in the regressions, conducted separately for each modality, were only those clients who had histories of daily heroin use at some point in their lives. Pretreatment drug abuse was categorized in terms of the drug abuse pattern index, as heroin/ other opioids, heroin, other opioids, and former daily use (those who had histories of daily heroin use but not in the year prior to entering treatment). Sociodemographic characteristics included age, sex, race/ethnicity, source of referral, and number of prior admissions to treatment.

Across the three modalities, compared to clients who reported daily heroin use in the past, clients who used heroin regularly in the year before treatment were two to three times more likely to use heroin regularly in the year after treatment; other opioid abusers were about three times less likely to do so. Other types of pretreatment drug abuse were not significantly related to posttreatment heroin abuse. These findings indicate that relapse to heroin in the year after treatment is much more likely for those who were regular users in the year before treatment (rather than former daily users or other opioid abusers) and more likely among those who used heroin as their principal opioid rather than heroin in combination with other opioids. The latter may have been more likely to substitute other drugs for heroin. Thus, although there are substantial reductions in the prevalence of regular heroin use during and after treatment, for many the pattern of regular posttreatment heroin use is a continuation of drug abuse patterns prior to treatment.

Posttreatment regular heroin use was also strongly related to time spent in treatment, although the amount of time necessary to produce significant results differed across modalities. A significant reduction in the likelihood of posttreatment regular heroin use was evident for outpatient methadone clients and residential clients only after one year of treatment and for outpatient drug-free clients after six months of treatment. However, the small proportions of heroin users in outpatient drug-free programs precluded strong conclusions being drawn. The finding that relatively long stays in treatment are necessary to produce positive treatment outcomes contrasts markedly with the findings of prior research that shorter stays are sufficient (Simpson 1981b). This difference may reflect changes in the nature of client populations, the intensity of drug abuse, or the nature of treatment, but it bears further investigation.

Posttreatment regular heroin use was not directly or significantly related to the number and intensity of services received during treatment. Posttreatment use was less likely among clients who stayed in treatment shorter periods of time but received a greater number of services, compared with those staying in treatment longer periods of time but in less service-intense programs. Further, longer stays in treatment were required to effectively treat clients who were principally heroin abusers and seldom used other opioids (Hubbard et al. 1987). Heroin abusers who also used other opioids regularly before treatment may have been more likely to use other opioids in place of heroin after treatment. Although clients who are multiple opioid abusers may well reduce their abuse of heroin, they may nevertheless continue or increase their abuse of other drugs as substitutes for heroin.

## Cocaine Use

Cocaine has long been used by segments of the drug-abusing population and recently has increased significantly among the general population. According to the National Household Survey on Drug Abuse, positive responses to a question on use of cocaine during a particular month increased from 3.1 percent of persons 18 to 25 in 1974 to a peak of 9.3 percent in 1979 and leveled off to 7.6 percent in 1985 (NIDA 1988b). Among clients entering DARP programs between 1969 and 1974, over 33 percent had used cocaine in the two months before admission, and over 16 percent had used it weekly or more often (Spiegel 1974). In 1981, cocaine was the primary drug of abuse for 6 percent of clients admitted to the federally funded treatment programs reporting to the Client Oriented Data Acquisition Process (CODAP), the secondary drug for another 11 percent, and the tertiary drug for another 3 percent (NIDA 1982). Strug et al. (1985) reported that cocaine use among methadone clients doubled between 1970 and 1981. Thus, cocaine use has escalated in recent years, both in the general population and among drug abusers entering treatment.

Perhaps because of this increase in abuse, there has been a proliferation of studies focusing on cocaine use among drug abuse treatment populations. Most of these studies have focused on the nature of pretreatment drug abuse patterns. Gawin and Kleber (1985, 1986) argue that most cocaine abusers who seek treatment have progressed from a phase of continuous daily use to one of cyclic binges or relatively infrequent but highly concentrated episodes of use. Indeed, a series of studies supports the assertion that about half of those seeking treatment or in treatment for cocaine abuse had been daily users before treatment and the other half were probably infrequent heavy users (Helfrich et al. 1983; Hunt et al. 1984; Schnoll et al. 1985; Semlitz and Gold 1985; Washton, Gold, and Pottash 1985). Kleber and Gawin (1984) suggest that cocaine abusers seeking treatment may have more varied use patterns than those seeking treatment for the abuse of other types of drugs.

On average, abusers of cocaine first tried the drug five years prior to admission to treatment (Gawin and Kleber 1986; Helfrich et al. 1983). Studies differ as to the most common route of administration, some finding that inhalation is the most popular (Semlitz and Gold 1985; Washton, Gold, and Pottash 1985), others that intravenous injection is the most popular (Gawin and Kleber 1985; Washton and Tatarsky 1984). These differences in studies as to method of administration may however be associated with differences in populations studied—treatment population or general population, or populations that differ in sociodemographic composition.

There are relatively few studies about the effects of treatment on posttreatment cocaine abuse. From the DARP study, Simpson et al. (1986) reported that 38 percent of their sample of opioid users had used cocaine prior to treatment; only 18 to 22 percent used it one to six years after treatment, but 39 percent had used it in the twelfth year after treatment. This increase in the proportion of users may reflect the increased popularity of cocaine more than a decaying impact of treatment. Several studies found that outpatient treatment was less effective than residential treatment in reducing cocaine abuse (Burt Associates 1977; Kosten et al. 1986, 1987b). Siguel (1977) found that most cocaine abusers were treated in the drug-free modalities.

*Cocaine Use before, during, and after Treatment*

About one-fourth of all clients were regular cocaine users in the year before entering treatment, that is, they used it once a week or more often, and about 60 percent had used it during the year prior to treatment. Cocaine abuse was more likely among some types of clients. Over 70 percent of heroin abusers and over 80 percent of multiple nonopioid users had used cocaine with some frequency in the year before treatment, but use was less common among other types of drug abusers. Regular cocaine use was most common among multiple opioid abusers (52 percent) and heroin/no other opioid abusers (41 percent). However, cocaine was the pretreatment primary drug of abuse for only about 2 percent of methadone clients and about 8 percent of residential or outpatient drug-free clients. Thus, cocaine was used by many treatment clients but was rarely identified as the primary drug of abuse.

Most clients either inhaled cocaine or injected it, often in combination with heroin. About two-thirds of methadone clients reported that the primary route of administration was injection; among residential clients, three in five clients reported injecting and two in five reported inhaling; almost three-fourths of outpatient drug-free clients reported inhaling cocaine. Fewer than 2 percent in any of the modalities reported other routes of administration (including freebasing or smoking). These differences in route of administration among modalities probably reflect the fact that residential and outpatient drug-free clients were less likely than methadone clients to inject heroin or other drugs.

The prevalence of regular cocaine use among clients before, during, and after treatment is illustrated in Figure 5-2 for those who stayed at least three months in the three major modalities. About 26.4 percent of outpatient methadone and 27.6 percent of residential clients used cocaine regularly in the year before treatment, compared with about 13 percent of outpatient drug-free clients. Fewer than 1 in 10 clients in any of the modalities were regular users during treatment, and use was almost nonexistent among residential clients during treatment. The percentages of regular users were somewhat higher three months after treatment and moderated in the years following treatment. The slightly higher prevalence of regular users three to five years after treatment may reflect the current resurgence in the popularity of cocaine. In addition to clients who relapse, this prevalence rate may include those who initiate regular use after treatment. This finding is consistent with the DARP study, which also noted an increase in the prevalence of cocaine use twelve years after treatment. Three to five years after treatment, the percentage of regular cocaine users was 6 to 16 percent in any of the modalities, compared with 13 to 28 percent in the year before entering treatment.

These decreases in prevalence are reflected in the one-year abstinence rates and improvement rates calculated for those who were regular cocaine users in the year before entering treatment. One-year abstinence rates for those who stayed in treatment at least three months show that among regular cocaine users entering treatment in the three major modalities, 47 percent of residential clients were abstinent from cocaine in the year after treatment, 40 percent among outpatient methadone clients, and 42 percent among outpatient drug-free clients. Thus, one-year abstinence rates were slightly higher for residential clients than for clients in

Figure 5-2 Changes in Prevalence of Regular Cocaine Use (clients treated three months or longer)

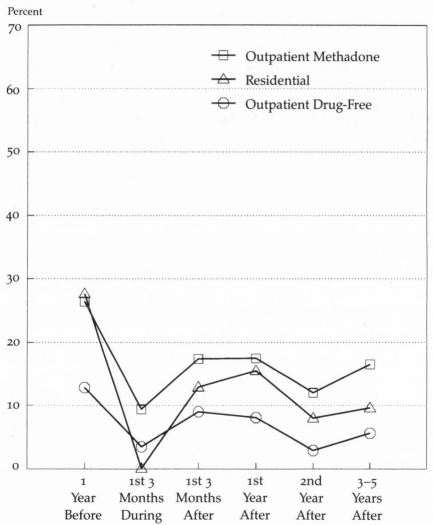

other modalities. However, of those who stayed in treatment at least three months, clients in outpatient drug-free programs had slightly higher one-year improvement rates (77 percent of regular cocaine users in the year before treatment reduced or ceased cocaine use in the year after treatment), than outpatient methadone clients (70 percent) and residential clients (68 percent). Judging by one-year abstinence rates, then, residential programs are somewhat more effective in reducing cocaine abuse than outpatient methadone or outpatient drug-free programs. On the other hand, judging by one-year improvement rates, outpatient drug-free programs are the most effective in reducing regular cocaine use.

These overall comparisons do not, however, control for modality differences in client populations that may result in differential effectiveness rates. For instance, the lower proportion of heroin abusers in outpatient drug-free programs compared with other modalities suggests a client population that is less involved in intravenous drug use or in abuse of opioids. These sorts of factors may mean that the client population of outpatient drug-free programs is somewhat more amenable to change in cocaine abuse and that this propensity is reflected in higher improvement rates. Changes in use of a particular drug may also be tied to changes in use of other drugs. For instance, reductions in heroin use may be associated with increases in cocaine use, as cocaine is substituted for heroin. Conversely, cessation of heroin use as a result of treatment may help suppress cocaine use, especially among clients who injected heroin and cocaine concurrently.

*Factors Affecting Posttreatment Cocaine Use*

A number of factors may affect changes in the frequency or character of cocaine abuse. A major factor is certainly the character of the treatment itself—the modality, number of months spent in treatment, and the nature and intensity of services received. The number of prior admissions may reflect the client's stage in a drug abuse history and his or her readiness for change. Sociodemographic characteristics such as sex, age, and race/ethnicity may also characterize clients who are likely to reduce cocaine abuse. The effect of each of these factors on the likelihood of using cocaine regularly in the year after treatment was examined in logistic regression analyses, conducted separately for each modality. Only those clients who were regular cocaine users in the year before treatment were included in the analyses. Independent variables included age, sex, race/ethnicity, number of prior treatment episodes, source of referral, and time spent in treatment.

Posttreatment regular cocaine use was not significantly related to time spent in treatment for clients in any of the modalities, and few other factors approached statistical significance. These findings reveal that posttreatment regular cocaine abuse is not easily predicted from client behaviors or treatment experience. For some clients, posttreatment regular cocaine use is a continuation of pretreatment use. For others, however, cocaine use may be substituted for other drugs or its use a reflection of the increasing popularity of the drug in recent years.

A major concern about cocaine abuse after treatment is that intravenous use will facilitate the transmission of HIV infection. The question of which types of drug abusers continue or initiate intravenous cocaine use can suggest where education and treatment resources to prevent AIDS need to be employed. The results of this study include that clients who currently use or formerly used heroin are the most likely to use cocaine intravenously after treatment. Only 1 in 10 clients reporting intravenous cocaine use in the year after treatment did *not* have a history of heroin use, and only 2 in 10 were not currently injecting heroin. The remaining 70 percent of intravenous cocaine users were injecting cocaine and heroin. The drug abuse pattern prior to treatment was also a major predictor of the route of cocaine use. Only 2 in 10 cocaine users without a history of heroin abuse reported using cocaine intravenously. This rate contrasts with the reported preference for intravenous use by 8 of 10 heroin abusers, and two-thirds of former daily heroin users and multiple opioid abusers.

These results suggest two major thrusts for AIDS prevention. First, outreach efforts need to focus on intravenous cocaine users as well as heroin addicts. Second, programs that treat heroin addiction must include a component to treat cocaine abuse among those clients abusing both drugs. Although treatment for heroin shows impressive gains in reducing intravenous heroin abuse, unless specifically addressed in treatment, the intravenous abuse of cocaine will continue to contribute to the spread of HIV infection.

## Nonmedical Use of Psychotherapeutic Drugs

Psychotherapeutic drugs include amphetamines, tranquilizers, barbiturates, and other sedatives and hypnotics. They may be medically prescribed and used for legitimate medical purposes or they may be obtained illegitimately and used for nonmedical purposes. The National Household Survey on Drug Abuse has documented the pervasiveness of nonmedical use of these drugs among members of the general population. In 1979, about 6.2 percent of persons 18 to 25 had engaged in nonmedical use of any psychotherapeutic drug in the past month; the comparable figure for 1982 was 7.0 percent; and for 1985, 6.3 percent (NIDA 1988b). Lau and Benvenuto (1978) estimate that about two million adults in the United States have abused nonopioid drugs (including prescribed psychotherapeutics). They suggest that this total may be four times the number of heroin abusers and the social costs may exceed those of opioid abuse.

Little detailed information exists about the nonmedical use of psychotherapeutic drugs among clients entering drug abuse treatment. Much of the existing literature concerns nonopioid abuse not separating psychotherapeutic drugs from other nonopioids such as cocaine and marijuana. Among clients entering DARP from 1969 to 1973, for instance, 58 percent used nonopioids (including cocaine) and 13 percent used them daily in the two months before entering treatment. DARP clients who had used only nonopioids before treatment were concentrated in outpatient drug-free programs (41 percent of clients), followed by residential programs (17 percent), and methadone maintenance programs (1 percent) (Simpson 1981b). Among clients who entered or were discharged from federally funded drug abuse treatment programs in 1981, 16 percent reported psychotherapeutic drugs as their primary drugs of abuse, including barbiturates (3 percent), amphetamines (8 percent), tranquilizers (2 percent), and other sedatives or hypnotics (3 percent) (NIDA 1982). Hunt (1978) reported that 67 percent of a national sample of clients were nonmedical users of barbiturates/sedatives; 52 percent, of amphetamines; 45 percent, of psychotropics; and 39 percent, of hallucinogens before or during treatment. Barbiturates were the drug of choice for 21 percent, amphetamines for 15 percent, hallucinogens for 8 percent, and psychotropics for 9 percent.

Few studies have examined the effect of treatment on abuse of psychotherapeutic drugs. The few existing studies concur that such use declines during the year before to the year after treatment. Simpson (1981b) included nonopioid use as part of a composite index of treatment outcome and examined factors producing positive outcomes. In a four- to six-year follow-up of DARP clients, time in treatment and type of termination (quit or expelled, completed) both affected the composite outcome measure. Positive outcomes were associated with longer treatment tenure and satisfactory completion of treatment. These findings, however, held true only for residential and outpatient drug-free clients, not for methadone maintenance clients. In a 12-year follow-up of DARP clients, Simpson et al. (1986) reported that use of nonopioids (including cocaine as well as psychotherapeutic drugs) dropped from 55 percent before treatment to 39 percent one year after treatment. In years two, three, and six after treatment, about 35 percent were using nonopioids, but in the twelfth year after treatment as many as 47 percent reported using nonopioids. The authors attribute this increase to an increase in the use of cocaine. In fact, they report that use of each of the other nonopioids had decreased over time. McLellan et al. (1986, 1982) also reported reductions in the use of stimulants and/or depressants before or after treatment in samples of clients and military veterans in outpatient and residential programs. Clients in the treatment sample reduced their days of stimulant use by 85 percent and days of depressant use by 60 percent. In the sample of veterans, stimulant use was reduced by 50 percent.

*Nonmedical Use of Psychotherapeutic Drugs before, during, and after Treatment*

Over three-fourths of clients entering treatment engaged in the nonmedical use of psychotherapeutic drugs in the year before treatment. Half used these drugs regularly (weekly or daily) not under prescription or doctor's direction. Regular nonmedical use was most common among residential clients (49.9 percent), followed by outpatient drug-free clients (35.7 percent), and outpatient methadone clients (30.3 percent). Minor tranquilizers were the psychotherapeutic drug abused most often: regular use was reported by one in five clients. Amphetamines had been used by 36 percent of all clients, as had barbiturates/sedatives. Two in 10 clients had used amphetamines weekly or daily; 1 in 10 had used barbiturates or sedatives other than barbiturates regularly.

Despite the prevalence of nonmedical use, psychotherapeutic drugs were not often reported as the primary drug of abuse. They were the primary problem for 22.8 percent of outpatient drug-free clients, 20.2 percent of residential clients, and 1.9 percent of outpatient methadone clients. About 1 of every 10 residential and outpatient drug-free clients reported amphetamines to be their primary problem drug, followed by sedatives, minor tranquilizers, and barbiturates.

The prevalence of regular (weekly or daily) nonmedical psychotherapeutic drug use before, during, and after treatment in the three major modalities is illustrated in Figure 5-3. Although the prevalence of regular use was substantially higher among residential clients in the year before treatment (about 50 percent for residential compared with 30 percent for outpatient methadone and 36 percent for outpatient drug-free), abuse in all modalities declined precipitously during treatment, increased immediately after treatment, but again declined until three to five years after treatment, when levels of regular use were only 4 to 10 percent in the three modalities.

One-year abstinence and improvement rates are also instructive about the magnitude of change in regular use of these drugs. One-year abstinence rates for those in treatment at least three months show that residential programs are somewhat more effective than other modalities in bringing about a cessation of abuse of prescription drugs. Abstinence rates were 62 percent for residential clients, 45 percent for outpatient methadone clients, and 49 percent for outpatient drug-free clients. Com-

Figure 5-3 Changes in Prevalence of Regular Nonmedical
Psychotherapeutic Use (clients treated three months or longer)

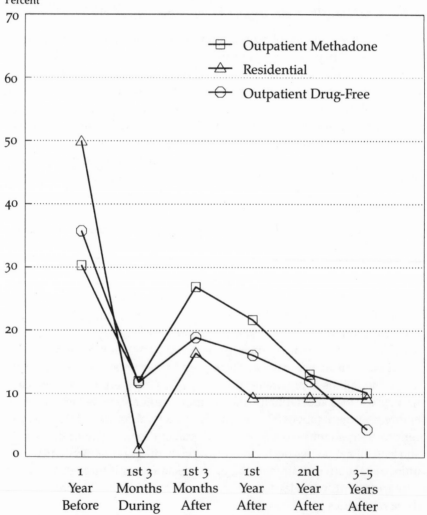

paring one-year improvement rates for those in treatment in the three modalities at least three months also suggests that residential programs were somewhat more effective (79 percent of those who were regular users in the year before treatment reduced or ceased use) than outpatient drug-free programs (69 percent) or outpatient methadone programs (70 percent). These findings reveal that, across the three modalities, almost one-half of regular users were abstinent in the year after treatment and another 25 percent decreased their frequency of use.

*Factors Affecting Posttreatment Nonmedical Use of Psychotherapeutic Drugs*

Among clients in this study, regular posttreatment nonmedical use of psychotherapeutic drugs was associated with time spent in treatment, type of drug use in the year before treatment, and age. Significant reductions in the likelihood of nonmedical use were evident for residential clients only after one year in treatment and for outpatient drug-free clients after six months in treatment; no significant effects for time in treatment were found for methadone clients. These findings are consistent with those of Simpson (1981b), who found significant time-in-treatment effects only for residential and outpatient drug-free clients.

Posttreatment psychotherapeutic drug abuse among TOPS clients was also related to drug abuse pattern in the year before treatment, although the nature of the relationship varied by modality. Among methadone clients, the risk of such drug abuse was significantly higher among other opioid abusers compared to heroin/other opioid abusers. Among residential clients, the risk was significantly lower among heroin, multiple nonopioid, single nonopioid, and alcohol/marijuana abusers. Among outpatient drug-free clients, the risk was significantly lower among alcohol/marijuana and minimal users. The risk of posttreatment abuse was also negatively associated with age, although effects were significant only for residential and outpatient drug-free clients. Younger clients (those age 20 or younger) were more than twice as likely as older clients (those over 30) to abuse psychotherapeutics after treatment.

These findings suggest that drug abuse treatment is associated with substantial decreases in nonmedical abuse of psychotherapeutic drugs, even in programs not specifically oriented toward decreasing dependence on psychotherapeutic drugs. Improvement rates were among the highest for any type of drug. However, a substantial proportion of psychotherapeutic drug abusers continue regular use after treatment and many increase their use. For these clients, psychotherapeutics may be a substitute for other drugs during and after treatment.

## Marijuana Use

Marijuana is the most widely abused illicit drug, both among the general population and among drug abuse treatment clients. A series of national surveys has shown that current and lifetime use of marijuana increased markedly since the 1960s, with a recent decrease in use. The percentage of young adults (aged 18 to 25) using marijuana within the past month increased from 34.2 percent in 1974 to a rate of 46.9 percent in 1979 but decreased to 36.9 percent in 1985 (NIDA 1988b). In 1985, 9 percent of the population were current marijuana users; that is, they had used it during the past month (Clayton 1987). Similar trends are observed among high school seniors, surveyed since 1975. Findings indicate a steady decline in use during the 1980s. In 1987, 50.2 percent of high school seniors had ever used marijuana and 21.0 percent used it during the past year (Johnston, O'Malley, and Bachman 1988). These figures suggest 18.2 million citizens age 12 and over use marijuana each month.

Marijuana abuse was even more widespread among drug abuse treatment clients. For instance, in the two months prior to entering a DARP program between 1969 and 1973, 52 percent had used marijuana and 36 percent had used it weekly or more often (Simpson et al. 1976). Thus, marijuana abuse has been pervasive among drug abuse treatment clients. Indeed, there has been a recent controversy over whether the continuation of marijuana use (or alcohol use) during and after treatment is a sign of treatment failure or success, if use of other more serious drugs of abuse declines.

### Marijuana Use before, during, and after Treatment

Marijuana was the drug most commonly used by clients in the year before entering treatment and remained the most commonly used drug despite substantial reductions during and after treatment. As shown in Figure 5-4, among those who stayed in treatment at least three months, 55.0 percent of outpatient methadone clients, 64.4 percent of residential clients, and 61.5 percent of outpatient drug-free clients were regular marijuana users in the year before entering their current program. Regular marijuana use was common among all types of drug abusers, although most common among multiple nonopioid abusers and less common among heroin and other opioid abusers. Comparison with DARP clients indicated that marijuana abuse had increased between the 1970s and 1980s; 15 percent of DARP clients and 35 percent of TOPS clients were daily marijuana users before entering treatment.

The percentage of regular marijuana users decreased to about 47 percent among outpatient methadone and outpatient drug-free clients and 5.1 percent among residential clients in the first three months of treatment. In the first three months after treatment, use was slightly lower among outpatient methadone and outpatient drug-free clients compared to the first three months in treatment, and levels of use for residential clients increased to 47.0 percent. Thus, in contrast to the immediate post-treatment increases for other drugs, the prevalence of regular marijuana use actually declined slightly. However, the intreatment decreases tended to be less dramatic than for other drugs (except for residential clients). Regular marijuana use remained relatively stable to one year after treatment, when use began to decrease slightly. By three to five years after treatment, 36.4 percent of outpatient methadone clients, 38.8 percent of residential clients, and 31.0 percent of outpatient drug-free clients were regular marijuana users. These prevalence figures were substantially higher than for any other drug three to five years after treatment.

One-year abstinence rates and improvement rates were also computed to illustrate the magnitude of change in regular marijuana use. Both the one-year abstinence rates and one-year improvement rates show that marijuana use is more resistant to change than any of the other drugs. Of those who were regular marijuana users in the year before treatment and stayed in treatment at least three months, only 2 of 10 residential and outpatient methadone clients, and 1 of 10 outpatient drug-free clients were abstinent from marijuana in the year after treatment; only half of residential clients and one-third of outpatient methadone and outpatient drug-free clients either decreased the frequency of marijuana use or ceased use in the year after treatment. These findings show that many clients continue to engage in regular marijuana use during and after treatment.

*Factors Affecting Posttreatment Marijuana Use*

In our analyses of the effectiveness of treatment in decreasing regular marijuana use among clients, we used logistic regression models to examine the independent effect of selected sociodemographic and other factors on the likelihood of using marijuana regularly in the year after treatment. Three regression analyses, one for each modality, were used to describe the effect of each of the variables on the odds of being a weekly or daily marijuana user in the year after treatment. The independent variables included sex, age, race, prior admissions, source of referral, pretreatment drug abuse pattern, and time in treatment.

Time in treatment, age, and sex were important predictors of post-treatment regular marijuana use, but not consistently across each of the modalities. The likelihood of regular posttreatment use was significantly lower for residential clients who stayed in treatment more than a year and for outpatient drug-free clients who stayed in treatment at least six months; time in treatment was not significantly related to posttreatment use for outpatient methadone clients. Females in each of the modalities had a significantly lower likelihood of posttreatment use than did males, and younger clients (those under 30) had significantly higher likelihoods

Figure 5-4 Changes in Prevalence of Regular Marijuana Use (clients treated three months or longer)

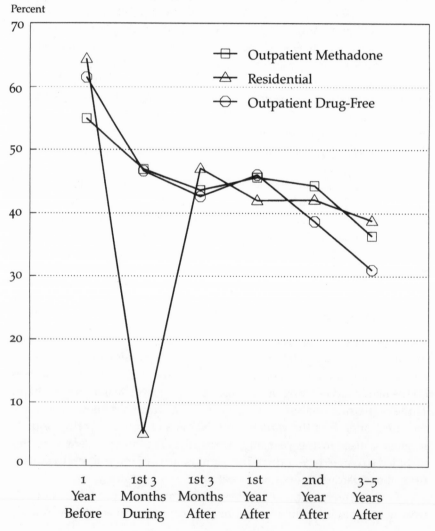

than older clients (those 30 and over). Other factors, such as pretreatment drug abuse pattern, number of prior treatments, and race/ethnicity, were not strong or consistent predictors. Thus, posttreatment regular marijuana use was in general more likely among males and younger clients and less likely among those with fairly lengthy stays in treatment.

## Multiple Drug Use

Analyses described so far in this chapter have examined each of the major drugs of abuse separately: heroin, cocaine, psychotherapeutics, and marijuana. Although these analyses are informative, they do not take into account the multiple drug abuse of most clients today. Many heroin abusers, for instance, abuse other drugs as well; many who primarily abuse a particular drug before treatment may continue or initiate abuse of one or more secondary drugs in the year after treatment, as use of the primary drug declines. The nature of drug abuse may thus be more effectively described in terms of a pattern of abuse of two or more drugs and of new patterns of abuse in the posttreatment period. For these reasons, analyses described in this section are based on an index that describes client drug abuse before, during, and after treatment in terms of patterns of abuse rather than abuse of single drugs. This issue is also investigated in Hubbard and Marsden (1986).

Many have noted that drug abusers who enter treatment have abused a wide variety of drugs (Clayton 1987; Hubbard, Bray, Craddock, et al. 1986; Kleinman et al. 1986; Robins 1974; Simpson and Sells 1974; Wesson et al. 1978). Simultaneous multiple drug abuse may serve several functions, to enhance the effects of another drug, counteract the effects of another drug, substitute for preferred drugs that are not available, or conform to normative ways of using drugs (Hubbard, Bray, Craddock, et al. 1986). The National Drug/Alcohol Collaborative Project (NDACP) conducted from 1974 to 1978 (Wesson et al. 1978) found that certain drugs were used to alter, enhance, or counteract the effect of other drugs. Marijuana served these functions for abusers of alcohol or hallucinogens; cocaine and marijuana for heroin abusers; heroin and alcohol for methadone abusers; and alcohol for abusers of most other drugs.

Despite awareness of the multiple drug abuse patterns of clients, many prior studies have focused on the daily use of a single drug, generally heroin or other opioids. Implicit in these studies was the belief that heroin was the most serious drug of abuse and the primary reason for treatment. However, over the past decades, the drugs abused by clients entering treatment have become more diverse, the number of nonopioid abusers has increased, and multiple drug abuse has become common. Among clients participating in this study, for instance, a majority of clients in all modalities had used two or more drugs at least weekly in the year before treatment, and one-third of outpatient methadone clients, 40 percent of residential clients, and 20 percent of outpatient drug-free clients had used four or more drugs at least weekly in the year before treatment (see Chapter 4). Half to two-thirds of the clients in each modality regularly used alcohol or marijuana in addition to other drugs. These changes in the nature of abuse necessitate the consideration of the multiple drug abuse patterns of clients.

*Patterns of Multiple Drug Use before, during, and after Treatment*

In order to describe the multiple drug abuse patterns of this generation of clients, an index of multiple drug abuse was developed by Bray et al. (1982), as described in Chapter 2. The distribution of clients among these seven drug abuse patterns upon entering treatment was described in Chapter 4. As noted earlier, clients entering outpatient methadone programs were primarily opioid abusers, residential clients were a mix of opioid and nonopioid abusers, and outpatient drug-free clients were primarily nonopioid abusers. The percentage distributions of clients in the residential modality across the drug abuse patterns is presented in Table 5-1 for time periods before, during, and after treatment. For the sake of greater simplicity, the two nonopioid patterns are combined to yield six

Table 5-1  Changes in Drug Abuse Patterns among Residential Clients

| | Time Period | | | | | |
|---|---|---|---|---|---|---|
| Pattern | One Year Before | First 3 Months During | First 3 Months After | First Year After | Second Year After | 3–5 Years After |
| | % | % | % | % | % | % |
| Heroin/other opioids | 13.2 | 0.1 | 1.9 | 4.1 | 7.6 | 1.0 |
| Heroin | 20.1 | 0.2 | 9.4 | 7.2 | 5.6 | 10.8 |
| Other opioids | 17.1 | 1.0 | 9.6 | 6.7 | 2.9 | 6.6 |
| Nonopioids | 26.4 | 0.7 | 13.5 | 13.0 | 6.0 | 12.3 |
| Alcohol/marijuana | 14.4 | 2.1 | 43.8 | 35.4 | 43.6 | 42.4 |
| Minimal | 8.8 | 95.9 | 21.8 | 33.5 | 34.3 | 26.8 |
| Total | 100.0 | 100.0 | 100.0 | 100.0 | 100.0 | 100.0 |

*Note:* Percentages are column percentages.

patterns. These are regular users of heroin and other opioids, heroin as the principal opioid, other opioids, nonopioids, alcohol/marijuana, and minimal users of any drug. As with other analyses described in this book, figures are reported separately for each modality and for those in treatment at least three months. However, for the sake of brevity in the text, we report below only the drug abuse patterns of residential clients before, during, and after treatment. Findings are similar for outpatient methadone and outpatient drug-free clients and are not presented here.

The drug abuse patterns of clients before, during, and after treatment show that, for residential clients, the percentage with more serious patterns of use such as heroin/other opioids and heroin tends to be lower at each time point after treatment. Correspondingly higher percentages of clients indicating less extensive patterns of abuse such as alcohol/marijuana and minimal levels of use of any drug are seen at each time point after treatment. Thus, based on these prevalence figures, there is a steady decline in the severity of drug abuse during and after treatment. From pretreatment patterns of abuse in which almost one-third used heroin/other opioids or heroin as the only opioid, virtually all residential clients (96 percent) and over half of outpatient methadone and outpatient drug-free clients were minimal drug users during treatment. By three to five years after treatment, 26.8 percent of residential clients, 32.5 percent of outpatient methadone clients, and 29.3 percent of outpatient drug-free clients were minimal drug users. These figures compare with pretreatment levels of minimal drug use of less than ten percent in the three modalities.

*Changes in Drug Use Patterns*

These changes in drug abuse patterns with treatment are perhaps better illustrated by the cross-tabulation of drug abuse pattern in the year before treatment and the year after treatment that is presented in Table 5-2. This table presents drug abuse patterns for residential clients who remained in treatment at least three months. Findings are similar for outpatient methadone and outpatient drug-free clients and are not presented here. Of clients with more extensive patterns of abuse in the year before treatment (heroin/other opioids, heroin, other opioids or nonopioids), fully three-fourths shifted to a less complex pattern of abuse. This shift is illustrated by the percentage of abusers in the year after treatment who had a posttreatment pattern of lesser complexity. Of these four types of user, about one-half to three-fourths were alcohol/marijuana or minimal users in the year after treatment. Thus, as with findings for specific drugs, these figures demonstrate a substantial degree of improvement in drug abuse after treatment. However, changes in the drug abuse pattern indicate the shift to patterns of involvement with fewer drugs. These findings suggest that treatment is effective for the multiple drug abuser, encouraging a shift to less serious drugs and less complex patterns of abuse.

## Intravenous Drug Use

Interest in drug abuse treatment has recently increased, partly because of its potential role in combating AIDS. Drug abuse treatment may be an effective strategy against further spread of AIDS because, on a general level, it decreases the drug abuse that weakens the immune system and, on a more specific level, it may reduce the number of intravenous drug users (Hubbard, Marsden, et al. 1988). Intravenous drug users rank second only to male homosexuals among the high risk groups for contracting AIDS (Watkins et al. 1988). Regardless of sexual orientation, past or present intravenous drug users represent about one-fourth of AIDS cases and are at risk because they share or have shared hypodermic needles. This practice facilitates the transmission of the Human Immunodeficiency Virus (HIV) that is associated with AIDS (DesJarlais and Friedman 1988; Osborn 1986; Turner, Miller, and Moses 1989). Intravenous drug users may further pass the virus to their female sexual part-

Table 5-2  Changes in Drug Abuse Patterns from the Year before to the Year after Treatment for Residential Clients

| | Pattern Before | | | | | |
|---|---|---|---|---|---|---|
| Pattern After | Heroin/ Other Opioids | Heroin | Other Opioids | Non- opioids | Alcohol/ Marijuana | Minimal |
| | % | % | % | % | % | % |
| Heroin/other opioids | 23.5 | 2.5 | 3.7 | 0.6 | 0.0 | 1.9 |
| Heroin | 9.6 | 16.6 | 2.5 | 3.8 | 1.8 | 8.8 |
| Other opioids | 5.9 | 0.0 | 25.2 | 5.1 | 1.8 | 2.8 |
| Nonopioids | 1.2 | 6.7 | 17.0 | 16.9 | 21.4 | 11.0 |
| Alcohol/marijuana | 31.8 | 42.7 | 33.1 | 35.8 | 35.2 | 22.2 |
| Minimal | 27.9 | 31.5 | 18.6 | 37.9 | 39.9 | 53.3 |
| Total | 100.0 | 100.0 | 100.0 | 100.0 | 100.0 | 100.0 |

ners, who in turn may pass the virus to unborn children. Further, prostitutes who use intravenous drugs are another link in the spread of HIV from drug abusers to the general heterosexual population. Thus, intravenous drug users are directly at risk of contracting AIDS and may act as a link in the further spread of HIV infection.

Intravenous drug users seem to be almost universally aware of the risks involved in needle-sharing and have accordingly reduced their incidence of this practice (DesJarlais and Friedman 1988). However, the nature of changes in drug abuse and route of administration following treatment and the effectiveness of treatment in combating the spread of HIV have not been adequately studied. Here we examine changes in the prevalence of intravenous drug use, the shift to alternative routes of administration, and broader changes in drug abuse with treatment. In addition, we examine changes in drug use for abusers who participated in treatment before and after awareness of AIDS. These changes are examined for all three admission cohorts (1979, 1980, and 1981).

In the year before admission, about 65 to 70 percent of clients in all three admission cohorts were regular intravenous drug users and approximately 25 to 30 percent were intravenous users in the varying time periods after treatment. These declines in intravenous drug use were similar for the three cohorts, regardless of whether they occurred before or after widespread awareness of AIDS, about 1982. Thus, there is no evidence of a dramatic decline in intravenous drug use that would have occurred if the observed changes were associated with awareness of AIDS and fear of exposure to the virus from intravenous drug use. Because changes in intravenous drug use appear to be similar across the admission cohorts before and after the spread of AIDS, observed reductions appear to have been associated with participation in treatment programs, not with fear of AIDS and awareness of the risk behaviors. Those who stop intravenous drug use appear to do so as the result of treatment and not in reaction to the threat of AIDS.

This substantial decline in the percentages of intravenous drug users after treatment may be the result of two types of behavioral changes. The decline may be the result of changes in the frequency of drug use or in the route of administration between admission and follow-up. That is, the observed decline may be the result of a decrease in the percentage of regular drug users per se or in the percentage of intravenous drug users among regular users. These alternatives were investigated by examining changes in the percentage of regular drug users and the percentage of regular drug users who were intravenous users. Substantial declines between admission and follow-up were seen in the percentages of clients

who were regular drug users, but among regular drug users the percentage of intravenous drug users was relatively stable. These findings suggest a sizable treatment effect in terms of the reduction in regular drug
users. However, regular drug users who remain regular users even after
treatment do not appear to be changing their route of administration in
response to the threat of AIDS.

Multivariate regression analyses were conducted to examine factors
related to change in intravenous drug use, both discontinuing such use or
decreasing its frequency. These analyses yielded few significant predictors among sociodemographic, treatment, and background factors.

These findings suggest that drug abuse treatment is an effective
means of reducing the risk of exposure to HIV infection. Treatment
appears to result in a substantial decrease in the percentage of regular
drug users and thereby in a decrease in intravenous drug users. Those
intravenous drug users who remain regular drug users after treatment
appear to be relatively resistant to changing their route of administration.
This finding suggests that many who do not enter treatment are likely to
continue regular intravenous drug use, perhaps regardless of the intensity of educational efforts about the risk factors for HIV infection. The
substantial reductions in regular drug use and the associated reductions
in intravenous drug use suggest that further attention should be
addressed to drug abuse treatment as a means to help control the AIDS
epidemic.

## Conclusions

Eliminating or reducing drug abuse and associated consequences is
the primary goal of drug abuse treatment. Findings from the Treatment
Outcome Prospective Study show that treatment results in substantial
decreases in the abuse of both opioid and nonopioid drugs but that the
goal of abstinence is achieved for relatively few.

Changes in the prevalence of regular (weekly or daily) abuse of specific drugs such as heroin, cocaine, and psychotherapeutics before, during, and after treatment show similar patterns of change. Pretreatment
levels of drug use decline dramatically during treatment, increase slightly
immediately after treatment relative to intreatment levels, and again
decline in subsequent periods after treatment. The prevalence of regular
cocaine use increased slightly three to five years after treatment, while
use of most other drugs continued to decline. In contrast, declines in the
prevalence of regular marijuana use were less dramatic. Indeed, one-year
abstinence and improvement rates for marijuana were the lowest for any

drug. Three to five years after treatment, less than 20 percent of clients in any modality were regular users of any drug except marijuana, which about one-third of former clients used regularly.

These trends in use were apparent for clients in each of the three major modalities. In fact, although methadone, residential, and outpatient drug-free programs treated client populations with very different levels of use and problems, one-year abstinence and improvement rates were not substantially different across the modalities for heroin, cocaine, and nonmedical psychotherapeutic drug use. Abstinence rates averaged about 40 to 50 percent and improvement rates 70 to 80 percent for each of the three drugs other than marijuana. For marijuana, abstinence rates averaged about 20 percent and improvement rates about 40 percent.

Time spent in treatment was among the most important predictors of posttreatment drug abuse for all types of drugs. It was a particularly strong predictor of posttreatment regular heroin abuse and psychotherapeutic drug abuse. In contrast to prior studies, however, we found the time in treatment necessary to produce positive outcomes was relatively long: 6 to 12 months. This difference from prior studies may be accounted for by differences in the client populations in the studies or by changes in the nature of drug abuse treatment. The multiple drug abuser, for instance, may be more resistant to change. Posttreatment cocaine use was not well predicted by time in treatment or client characteristics and behaviors. This finding may be more related to the growth in cocaine abuse during this study than to characteristics of treatment or clients.

Findings regarding changes in intravenous drug use associated with participation in treatment indicate that treatment can be an effective strategy in slowing the spread of AIDS. The percentage of clients who were regular intravenous drug users decreased during and after treatment, apparently primarily as the result of treatment participation rather than fear of contracting AIDS.

These findings reveal substantial reductions in drug abuse after treatment, reductions that continue even three to five years after a specific episode of treatment. Thus, the three major modalities are effective approaches to the problem of drug abuse and also to the AIDS crisis. However, the analyses reported here are not an exhaustive investigation of the factors responsible for producing change. Client motivation to enter and remain in treatment through its course, social support systems, and the nature of treatment itself are factors that require further investigation in the study of treatment effects.

# 6. Building Productive Lives

In addition to reducing drug abuse, many programs also seek to build productive lives by decreasing involvement in criminal activity, increasing employment and productivity, and improving psychological well-being. To accomplish these goals, treatment programs must either begin habilitation for addicts lacking basic skills, provide rehabilitation for clients to restore skills destroyed by drug abuse, or maintain the productivity of those clients who have remained socially productive despite their addiction. To these ends, many programs provide psychological counseling, family support, vocational rehabilitation, and other services directed toward changing behaviors other than drug abuse. The range and intensity of ancillary services provided, however, may vary greatly from program to program.

Progress toward the development of productive lives during and after treatment is investigated in this chapter. We examine the course of involvement in criminal activity, employment, alcohol use, and symptoms of depression before, during, and after treatment. For each of these outcomes we describe changes for those who remained in treatment at least three months, in order to provide a view of the impact of treatment on clients who had stayed in treatment periods of time sufficient to foster meaningful changes. However, we present in Table A-3 in the Appendix the percentages of clients remaining in treatment less than three months and three months or more who engaged in each behavior at the various time points. One-year abstinence rates and one-year improvement rates for several of the outcomes are also presented for those who remained in treatment at least three months to provide a more complete picture of the magnitude of change in behavior. As in the previous chapter, we assess for each outcome the factors affecting posttreatment involvement in the year after treatment. Odds ratios for each time-in-treatment category for each modality are shown in Tables A-4, A-5, and A-6 in the Appendix. In addition, we consider readmissions to drug abuse treatment after leaving the program examined in this study and factors affecting return to treatment in the year after a given treatment episode. We also consider the special case of the effectiveness of treatment for the client referred to treatment by the criminal justice system or those who were either on probation or parole at the time they entered treatment.

## Criminal Activity

The strong relationship between drug abuse and criminal behavior is a major justification for public provision of drug abuse treatment. Despite disagreement about the nature and extent of the causal relationship of drug abuse and crime (see Moore 1977; Panel on Drug Abuse 1976; Peterson and Braiker 1980), it has been assumed that if drug abuse were reduced, there would be a concomitant reduction in drug-related crime. This effect of treatment is thought to be most pronounced for income-generating crime.

Previous research is consistent in showing that drug abusers reduce their criminal involvement while they remain in treatment (Dole and Joseph 1978; Gorsuch, Abbamonte, and Sells 1976; McGlothlin, Anglin, and Wilson 1977; Nash 1976). Evidence regarding posttreatment effects is less clear. Findings from the Drug Abuse Reporting Program (DARP) study, for instance, suggest that the capacity of treatment to bring about changes in posttreatment criminal activity is limited. Posttreatment arrest rates were found to be lower only for clients in methadone maintenance and residential programs, and only the declines for methadone maintenance clients were statistically significant (Simpson et al. 1978). Nash (1976), however, reviewed findings from 12 studies and concluded that the weight of evidence supports the finding that drug abuse treatment does reduce criminal activity. The review by Lukoff and Kleinman (1977) of the same studies, on the other hand, is less supportive of the assertion because of methodological problems with the studies.

We investigate these issues for clients in the three major modalities. We examine the prevalence of criminal activity before, during, and after treatment by focusing on self-reported involvement in predatory crimes (robbery, burglary, larceny, etc., as described in Chapter 2). Crimes more directly related to drug use such as drug dealing and prostitution were not included as predatory crimes for these analyses. This allows us to focus on types of criminal activity that would not necessarily decline because drug use is reduced. As with analyses reported in Chapter 5, we present figures for those clients who remained in treatment at least three months. We also examine one-year abstinence rates. Factors associated with involvement in predatory crimes in the year after treatment are also discussed. For these analyses we have chosen self-reported criminal offenses rather than arrests because the former, despite problems of validity discussed in Chapter 2, is a more inclusive indicator of criminal activity. Number of arrests may underestimate actual criminal activity since offenders are not always caught or prosecuted. Analyses of changes in predatory criminal activity before, during, and after treatment and factors related to posttreatment criminal activity are described more fully in Collins et al. (1983, 1988).

*Criminal Activity before, during, and after Treatment*

About 60 percent of residential clients and about one-third of outpatient methadone and outpatient drug-free clients had committed one or more predatory crimes in the year before entering the TOPS program. The substantially higher percentage of residential clients who reported predatory criminal activity in the year before entering treatment may be a reflection of the fact that about one-third of residential clients were referrals from the criminal justice system. However, about one-third of the clients in outpatient drug-free programs were as well. Despite these pretreatment differences in criminal activity, during treatment the proportion of clients committing predatory crimes decreased to ten percent or less in all three modalities; for residential clients, only 3.1 percent reported committing predatory crimes during treatment.

In the three months after leaving treatment, the percentage of clients in all three modalities who committed predatory crimes increased, particularly for residential clients. Criminal activity continued to increase slightly for residential clients during the first year after treatment but again decreased slightly during the second year after treatment, and further decreases were found three to five years after treatment. Posttreatment criminal activity was lower among outpatient methadone and outpatient drug-free clients than among residential clients at every time point except during treatment, at which time residential clients had lower crime rates. After increases in criminal activity immediately after treatment, clients tended to show a long-term decline in criminal activity. These changes in criminal activity for all three modalities are illustrated in Figure 6-1. Three to five years after leaving treatment, 16.2 percent of outpatient methadone clients, 19.8 percent of residential clients, and 7.6 percent of outpatient drug-free clients reported involvement in predatory crimes. Thus, three to five years after leaving treatment, the proportion of clients who were involved in predatory crimes was one-third to one-half the pretreatment proportion in each of the modalities.

These changes in the prevalence of criminal activity are reflected in the one-year abstinence rates for changes in the percentage of clients criminally involved. One-year abstinence rates were similar for each of the modalities: about two-thirds of the clients who reported predatory criminal activity in the year before treatment had ceased involvement in the year after treatment.

*Factors Affecting Posttreatment Criminal Activity*

Three logistic regression analyses, one for each modality, were conducted to examine the factors predicting the likelihood of involvement in predatory crimes in the year after treatment. Variables that were included in the model include pretreatment commission of predatory crime, time spent in treatment, number of services received in treatment, pretreatment drug abuse pattern, sociodemographic characteristics (age, sex,

Figure 6-1 Changes in Prevalence of Predatory Crime (clients treated three months or longer)

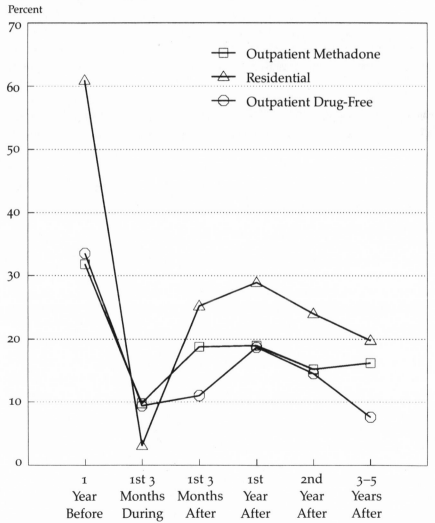

Percent

race/ethnicity), number of prior treatments, and source of referral. Across all three models the strongest predictor of posttreatment predatory criminal activity was pretreatment criminal activity, particularly commission of more than 10 offenses. Pretreatment drug abuse pattern and sociodemographic characteristics were not strong predictors. In contrast to findings for posttreatment drug abuse, time spent in treatment was a significant predictor of posttreatment criminal activity only among residential clients. Significant benefits in terms of reduction in the likelihood of posttreatment criminal activity were observed after only three months of residential treatment.

Thus, although substantial decreases in criminal activity were observed after participation in drug abuse treatment, aspects of treatment measured here, such as number of services received or time spent in treatment (except for residential clients), were not strong predictors of posttreatment criminal activity. The finding that staying in treatment three months or more is associated with lower criminal involvement for residential clients suggests that in order to foster improved levels of treatment effectiveness, greater efforts need to be addressed to retaining clients in treatment. Even though clients can be coerced to stay in treatment, they may not comply with treatment regimens or become actively involved in the treatment process. Further, criminal activity may not be reduced by merely meeting the attendance requirements of outpatient drug-free programs (Collins and Allison 1983).

### Criminal Justice Clients

Many clients were either directly referred to treatment by the criminal justice system as a diversion from incarceration or were on probation or parole at the time they entered treatment. These clients present special problems for drug abuse treatment programs because of their involvement in the criminal justice system as well as their history of criminal behavior. Although many are under the supervision of the criminal justice system, and the conditions of probation or parole may require successful completion of a course of treatment, they may not be willing participants in the treatment process. Indeed, Collins and Allison (1983) have reviewed research on the impact of coercion on treatment outcomes, and several authors have documented the fact that legal pressure is positively related to treatment retention (Dunham and Mauss 1982; Friedman, Horvat, and Levinson 1982) but have not found evidence that improved treatment effectiveness necessarily follows.

Analyses of treatment effectiveness for the criminal justice client use two measures of criminal justice involvement—any criminal justice involvement upon entering the TOPS program and participation in Treatment Alternatives to Street Crime (TASC) programs. Criminal justice involvement refers here to any stage in the criminal justice process (probation, parole, bail, jail or prison, or referral to treatment by an agent of the criminal justice system). This definition is, thus, broader than criminal justice referral; criminal justice clients include both those who were formally referred to treatment and those who were in some stage of the judicial process at the time of entering treatment. TASC programs refer to those funded under the Drug Abuse Office and Treatment Act of 1972. These programs were federally funded and locally administered and were intended to become institutionalized under state or local auspices at the expiration of their federal grants. The goals of the TASC programs were to identify drug users who came into contact with the criminal justice system, refer those who were eligible to appropriate treatment, monitor clients' progress, and return violators to the criminal justice system. These programs provided drug-abusing offenders with alternatives to incarceration and created a linkage between the criminal justice system and the drug abuse treatment system. Thus, TASC clients were a subset of criminal justice clients.

We examine here in what ways criminal justice clients differ from other clients in terms of treatment needs, to what degree programs were successful in retaining criminal justice system clients in treatment, and the behavior of these clients during and after treatment. Formal referral programs such as TASC may increase the number of drug abusers in the criminal justice system who are treated. Drug abusers in the criminal justice system are thought to be more unlikely than other drug abusers to seek treatment of their own accord. Nonvolunteer clients, however, may be more difficult to treat than clients who seek treatment on their own. Because the TASC programs operated in only five of the cities with programs participating in this study and only in outpatient drug-free and residential programs in those cities, analyses reported here and described more fully elsewhere (Collins et al. 1988; Hubbard, Collins, et al. 1988; Marsden and Collins 1987) are based on this limited sample of cities and modalities.

Systematic differences in type of criminal justice involvement were found between the three categories of clients entering treatment in the outpatient drug-free and residential modalities. About one-half of TASC clients in residential programs and non-TASC criminal justice clients in both outpatient drug-free programs and residential programs were on probation at the time of admission to treatment. Half of the TASC clients in outpatient drug-free programs were on bail, indicating pretrial or presentencing diversion. These findings indicate that TASC and non-TASC criminal justice clients were referred to the two drug abuse treatment modalities at different stages of the judicial process.

The treatment histories of clients with different criminal justice involvement categories differed by modality but not by type of criminal justice involvement. Residential clients were far more likely than outpatient drug-free clients to have been in drug abuse treatment before (about 50 percent in each criminal justice system involvement category) and to have had three or more previous treatment episodes (21 to 25 percent). Within modalities there was little difference in the prior treatment histories of the three categories of clients.

Multivariate regression analysis showed that clients who were involved in the criminal justice system when entering treatment were more likely than those not involved to be male, young, have no prior drug abuse treatment episodes, have less serious drug abuse patterns (not heroin abuse) and, not surprisingly, to be more criminally active. Compared with other criminal justice clients, TASC clients were somewhat more likely to have a high school education and to have fewer arrests. These differences in client characteristics indicate that although the criminal justice client was more criminally active than those with no involvement, the criminal justice client may have had lower problem severity on other measures such as pattern of abuse and treatment histories. Thus, certain formal or informal selection criteria that would affect the relative chance of treatment success for clients with and without criminal justice system involvement and for types of criminal justice client may have been operating.

Consistent with the findings of prior research, the criminal justice client, particularly the TASC client, stayed in treatment longer than the client with no criminal justice involvement. In multivariate regression analyses, TASC and non-TASC criminal justice statuses were significant predictors of the length of time spent in treatment for both residential and outpatient drug-free clients. After controlling for the other variables in the regression model, outpatient drug-free TASC clients stayed 45 days longer, and other criminal justice clients stayed 17 days longer than clients with no involvement. TASC and other criminal justice residential clients were estimated to stay about 50 days longer than clients with no involvement.

In other regression analyses, TASC and non-TASC criminal justice involvement were not significant predictors of posttreatment predatory criminal activity but were for posttreatment arrest (outpatient drug-free clients only). Clients referred from the criminal justice system were significantly less likely to report weekly or daily use of their primary problem drug in the year after treatment. Relatively worse outcomes for criminal justice referrals were found for depression, employment, or other behaviors.

The results of these analyses support the conclusion that criminal justice clients do as well or better than other clients in drug abuse treatment. TASC programs and other formal or informal criminal justice system mechanisms appear to refer individuals who had not previously been treated and many who were not yet heavily involved in drug abuse. This early interruption of the criminal and drug abuse careers may have important long-term benefits in reducing both crime and drug abuse among treated offenders. Criminal justice system involvement also helps retain clients in treatment. The estimated six to seven additional weeks of time in treatment for TASC referrals provided programs with considerably more time for rehabilitation efforts. There also seemed to be more substantial changes in behavior during treatment for TASC clients compared with other types of criminal justice clients. These findings support efforts to continue to expand criminal justice programs such as TASC. Other results suggest the need for careful assessment of how TASC and other criminal justice programs might be improved.

TASC programs have a broad mandate to identify and refer drug abusers in the criminal justice system to treatment. It is clear, however, that many individuals entering treatment are involved with the criminal justice system but not a TASC program. Whether these individuals were not identified by TASC, were not considered to be eligible by TASC, were not allowed to enroll for other reasons (such as the decision of a judge or prosecutor), or chose not to participate in TASC needs to be studied. These data do not indicate the structure and process of formal criminal justice programs and referral processes other than TASC. Further studies are needed to identify these mechanisms and to determine how they complement the TASC programs.

One major finding in this research is that few TASC clients and other criminal justice clients enter outpatient methadone programs. The reasons for the low numbers in methadone programs need to be explored. There appear to be many heroin addicts in the criminal justice system who could benefit from methadone treatment to reduce their criminal behavior.

Although criminal justice status was not a significant predictor of posttreatment criminal activity, the criminal activity for those with a criminal justice status decreased substantially while in drug abuse treatment. Further, the tendency of those with criminal justice status to stay in treatment longer encourages positive treatment outcomes. Thus, there is no reason to expect that those who are referred to treatment by the criminal justice system or whose treatment participation results from a desire to avoid or minimize criminal justice status will do less well than those who seek treatment under less coercive circumstances. That criminal activity is substantially reduced for the criminal justice client during and after treatment argues for the use of drug abuse treatment as an alternative crime control technique.

## Employment

An issue closely related to the criminal activity of clients is their involvement in the legitimate economy, in that those who are criminally active may not be participating in the work force. Despite this relationship, there are few systematic data about the employment and earnings of drug abusers (see reviews of the substance abuse literature by Brewington et al. 1987, and Hubbard, Harwood, and Cruze 1977). Neither are there any data to investigate the assumption that as drug abusers decrease their abuse after participation in treatment, there are corresponding decreases in criminal activity and increases in involvement in legitimate activity. We investigate these issues by considering the extent of involvement of clients in employment before, during, and after treatment. In contrast to the limited number of prior studies of the employment and earnings of drug abusers, this study uses standard labor force concepts and measurements.

For our analysis of employment we have chosen as the basic measure full-time employment in specific time periods before, during, and after treatment. The criterion for full-time employment is working 35 or more hours per week for at least three-quarters of the weeks in the three months or twelve months before the interview was conducted. This is a stringent measure of employment and signals a return to full functioning in society.

### Employment before, during, and after Treatment

In comparison with other outcomes, relatively small changes in the employment of clients are associated with participation in drug abuse treatment. The percentages of clients employed full-time in the time periods prior to the intake interview and during and after treatment are presented in Figure 6-2. Each modality shows a net increase in the percentage of clients employed full time, comparing the year before treatment with the second year after treatment, but the changes across the time periods are not fully consistent with this long-term gain. The most consistent pattern of increase in employment is seen for outpatient drug-free clients, who show a steady increase in the proportion employed full time from 27.1 percent in the year before treatment to 36.0 percent during treatment, 39.4 percent in the second year after treatment, and 49.7 percent three to five years after treatment. These clients had the highest levels of pretreatment as well as posttreatment employment, perhaps an indication of lesser problem severity and better functioning in society relative to clients in

Figure 6-2 Changes in Prevalence of Full-Time Employment (clients treated three months or longer)

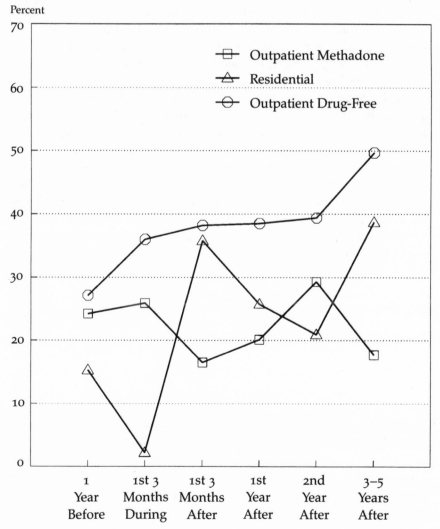

other modalities. For outpatient drug-free clients, then, treatment is associated with a steady improvement in employment.

Outpatient methadone clients were slightly less likely than outpatient drug-free clients to be employed full time in the year before treatment (24.2 percent). Their employment levels remained relatively stable during treatment but declined slightly after treatment, to increase to 29.3 percent by the second year after treatment. Thus, although there was a net increase in the percentage of outpatient methadone clients employed full time, from 24.2 percent to 29.3 percent by the second year after treatment, the change in employment was not as steady as among outpatient drug-free clients. However, the percentage employed full time dropped to 17.7 percent three to five years after treatment, similar to pretreatment levels.

Residential clients were least likely to be employed full time in the year before treatment (15.3 percent) but increased their employment dramatically to 35.8 percent in the first three months after treatment. This increase in the immediate posttreatment period was perhaps the result of assistance from program personnel with securing employment. However, in the first and second years after treatment, employment levels declined from these immediate posttreatment increases. By the second year after treatment, 20.9 percent of residential clients were employed full time, a slight increase over pretreatment levels. By three to five years after treatment, however, 38.7 percent of residential clients indicated full-time employment, equal to the rate immediately after treatment and more than double pretreatment levels.

These changes in the prevalence of full-time employment are further illustrated in one-year improvement rates. Among those who were not fully employed in the year before treatment, 18 percent of outpatient methadone, 40 percent of residential, and 35 percent of outpatient drug-free clients had more weeks of full-time employment in the year after treatment. Although these improvement rates are not as high as those for other outcomes, they do mark substantial improvement in the year after treatment.

Thus, overall the treatment experience appears to be associated with an increase in employment, but the increases are not consistent across the time period, nor are they large compared with other outcomes. These analyses, however, represent an average experience for all the cohorts across the time periods and do not control for relevant background factors. Nor do they consider the fact that although employment and legal earnings tend to increase only slightly after treatment, illegal earnings decrease significantly as criminal activity declines (Harwood et al. 1987). Thus, drug abuse treatment is associated with a substantial decrease in criminal activity but not a corresponding large increase in productive activities. Many former clients remain dependent on public assistance as they decrease their illegal activities. This finding suggests that greater emphasis be placed on the provision of employment and training services for clients to reduce their dependence on society for support and to increase their productivity and employment as their drug abuse is reduced.

## Factors Affecting Posttreatment Employment

To examine the effect of selected client characteristics, treatment factors, and other client behaviors on posttreatment employment, three logistic regression analyses were conducted, one for each modality. The dependent variable was full-time employment in the year after treatment, while the independent variables included pretreatment full-time employment, age, sex, race/ethnicity, number of prior treatment episodes, source of referral, and time spent in treatment.

As in most previous research, employment before treatment is a major predictor of employment after treatment. In outpatient drug-free and methadone programs, clients who were fully employed in the year prior to treatment were six to eight times more likely to be fully employed in the first year after treatment. Employment history was much less important for residential clients.

Even after accounting for the large effects of pretreatment employment, other factors also played a significant role in success in finding and holding a full-time job after treatment. Sex was a strong predictor of full-time employment after treatment. Males from outpatient modalities were more likely to have full-time work, but female residential clients were more likely to hold full-time jobs. Previous treatment also had opposite effects for residential and outpatient clients. No prior treatment appeared to be a detriment to residential clients but was beneficial to methadone and outpatient drug-free clients. The apparent inconsistency in the relationship of these variables between residential and outpatient modalities may be accounted for, in part, by the stronger emphasis on vocational services in residential programs. These services may help residential clients surmount obstacles to employment such as sex bias and a history of drug abuse treatment.

Although the overall changes in employment observed before, during, and after treatment were small, the effect of long-term treatment on employment was strongly illustrated in the results of the multivariate analysis. Those clients who remained in treatment for one year or more in residential treatment or at least six months in outpatient drug-free treatment were about twice as likely to hold full-time jobs as were clients who remained less than one week. Similar positive, although less impressive, effects were also found for clients in methadone treatment for at least one year. These findings indicate that treatment can increase the chances of returning to a fully productive life after addiction.

## Alcohol Use

Alcohol use is widespread among clients before, during, and after treatment. Estimates of the extent of alcohol use among clients vary, depending on the specific treatment population and the definition of alcohol use employed. In a review of prior research on this issue, Stimmel et al. (1983) report rates of alcoholism among methadone clients to vary between 5 and 45 percent; Hunt et al. (1986) cite rates of 20 to 53 percent for alcohol abuse among those entering drug abuse treatment; Belenko (1979) estimates that 20 to 30 percent of heroin addicts have a past or current drinking problem. Thus, clients—particularly those in methadone programs—have higher rates of alcohol abuse than those in the general population (Brown et al. 1973).

Alcohol use may predate drug use, be concurrent with drug use, or addicts may alternate periods of drug use and alcohol use. Schut, File, and Wohlmuth (1973) find that for about one-half of clients, the period of greatest alcohol use coincides with or predates experimentation with drug use; many others use alcohol most heavily just before daily opioid use. For all clients alcohol use tends to decline as drug use increases or increase as clients begin to withdraw from methadone or other drugs (see also Brown et al. 1973). Alcohol may thus act as a substitute for drug use, as in periods during or after treatment (Barr and Cohen 1979; Hunt et al. 1986; Joseph and Appel 1985). Thus, alcohol use may be expected to increase for clients as they decrease their drug use.

Clients' use of alcohol and the role of alcohol in the treatment process suggest that services are needed for alcohol abuse as well as drug abuse (Simpson and Lloyd 1981; Stimmel et al. 1983). Further, the fact that dual addiction is more frequent among younger clients suggests that alcohol abuse will be an increasingly important problem for drug abuse treatment programs (Winston et al. 1986).

We investigate here the extent of involvement of clients in heavy alcohol use (defined in Chapter 2) before, during, and after treatment and factors affecting posttreatment involvement. We concentrate on heavy alcohol use because of the pervasive use of alcohol and the fact that heavy alcohol use may better approximate abusive levels of use. A more complete description of changes in alcohol use among clients is presented in Marsden, Hubbard, and Schlenger (1984, 1987).

*Alcohol Use before, during, and after Treatment*

The majority of clients drank in the year before entering drug abuse treatment and about one-third were heavy drinkers. Among those who were to stay in treatment at least three months, residential (35.4 percent) and outpatient drug-free clients (33.4 percent) were more likely than outpatient methadone clients (25.2 percent) to be heavy drinkers in the year before treatment. The percentage of heavy drinkers decreased substantially during the first three months of treatment in outpatient programs as well as in the restricted environments of residential programs. In the first three months after treatment, the percentage of heavy drinkers rose, close to pretreatment levels. After this immediate posttreatment period, however, the percentage of heavy drinkers decreased steadily until three to five years after treatment. Then the percentage of heavy drinkers among those who had stayed in treatment at least three months was about 6 to 8 percentage points less than in the year before treatment (Figure 6-3). These findings suggest that drug abuse treatment has a moderating effect on heavy alcohol use. Although the effect extends at least until three to five years after treatment, it is not strong.

These prevalence figures are informative as to the extent of alcohol use before, during, and after treatment. However, they do not provide information about the course of alcohol use for individual clients. Comparison of levels of alcohol use in the year before and the year after treatment revealed that most clients continued their pretreatment level of alcohol use in the year after treatment. In contrast to prior studies that suggest that drug abusers increase their pretreatment levels of alcohol use as drug use decreases, these findings suggest that alcohol use after treatment is simply a continuation of pretreatment drinking patterns. Further evidence for this assertion is provided by examination of the nature of changes in alcohol use that accompany changes in drug abuse. Clients who reduce the severity of their drug abuse in the year after treatment relative to the year before treatment are no more likely to increase their alcohol use than other clients whose drug abuse remains similar to pretreatment patterns or intensifies. Those who reduced the severity of their drug abuse were most likely to continue their moderate to heavy pretreatment patterns of alcohol use (Marsden, Hubbard, and Schlenger 1987). This finding further suggests that alcohol use is not substituted for drug use after treatment, but that pretreatment patterns of alcohol use are simply continued.

This tendency to continue pretreatment patterns of alcohol use is further demonstrated by the one-year abstinence rates among those who were heavy drinkers in the year before entering drug abuse treatment. These abstinence rates were among the lowest of any drug, second only to marijuana. Of pretreatment heavy users, only 22 percent of outpatient methadone clients, 25 percent of residential clients, and 19 percent of outpatient drug-free clients were abstinent from alcohol in the year after treatment.

Figure 6-3 Changes in Prevalence of Heavy Alcohol Use (clients treated three months or longer)

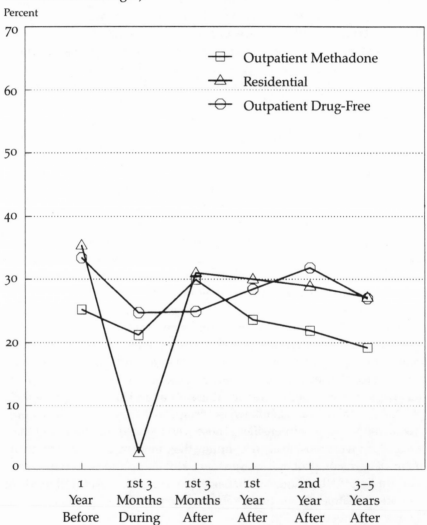

Examination of one-year improvement rates for those who were heavy alcohol users in the year before treatment shows some decrease in alcohol use after treatment. As with abstinence rates, improvement rates were lower than for any drug other than marijuana—55 percent of outpatient methadone, 59 percent of residential, and 45 percent of outpatient drug-free clients who remained in treatment at least three months reduced or ceased alcohol use in the year after treatment. However, most of this improvement was from heavy use to moderate use, rather than less serious levels of use. Further, there was little change in the prevalence of heavy alcohol use. These findings are consistent with a number of prior studies that find that changes in alcohol use during or after treatment are not large (Barr and Cohen 1979; Brown et al. 1973; Joseph and Appel 1985; Simpson and Lloyd 1977, 1981).

These findings, however, contrast with other studies. The results of the DARP follow-up (Simpson et al. 1978) show, for instance, that as both opioid and nonopioid abuse decreased after treatment, alcohol use increased. The findings from our study also contrast with research by Judson et al. (1980) in a five-year follow-up of methadone clients and in a study of those withdrawing from methadone (Schut, File, and Wohlmuth 1973).

*Factors Affecting Posttreatment Heavy Alcohol Use*

A number of studies have examined the impact of the nature of drug abuse treatment (including time spent in treatment, modality, and satisfactory completion of treatment) on posttreatment levels of alcohol use. Research findings are not, however, consistent regarding the impact of these factors. Barr and Cohen (1979), for instance, find that methadone clients but not residential clients decreased their alcohol consumption after treatment, while Simpson and Lloyd (1981) argued that treatment modality had no effect on posttreatment alcohol use. The latter study found that for residential and outpatient drug-free clients, favorable treatment termination was related to a decrease in alcohol use. Barr and Cohen (1979), Barr, Ottenberg, and Rosen (1973), McLellan et al. (1986), and Simpson (1981b) find that longer times in treatment foster a decrease in alcohol use, while Maddux and Elliott (1975) and Simpson and Lloyd (1977) find that there is no effect. Other studies find heavy alcohol use among clients with multiple drug use patterns (Jackson and Richman 1973; Simpson 1974; Simpson and Lloyd 1977).

For these clients, we examined with logistic regression analyses the impact of selected treatment factors, pretreatment drug use, and sociodemographic characteristics on the likelihood of heavy alcohol use in the three-month posttreatment period. Three log-linear regression models, one for each modality, were used to describe the effect of these factors on the odds of being a heavy drinker in this posttreatment period. Posttreatment heavy alcohol use was not strongly related to time spent in treatment, pretreatment drug abuse pattern, or most sociodemographic characteristics. The strongest predictor of heavy posttreatment alcohol use was pretreatment heavy drinking. Being a heavy drinker before treatment increased the odds of posttreatment heavy drinking by 4.27 for outpatient methadone clients, 2.43 for residential clients and 3.01 for outpatient drug-free clients, all significant at the .01 level.

More specifically, heavy posttreatment alcohol use was unrelated to time in treatment for residential and outpatient drug-free clients, and significantly related only for long-term methadone clients. Being in treatment at least three months and receiving intensive services (at least two types of services) significantly reduced the odds of posttreatment alcohol use for outpatient drug-free clients but not for clients in other modalities. Returning to drug abuse treatment for a substantial part of the year after leaving treatment also reduced the odds of being a heavy drinker for outpatient drug-free and residential clients. Posttreatment heavy drinking was unrelated to pretreatment drug abuse patterns. Significant effects were found for race/ethnicity, but the effects were not significant across modalities. Posttreatment heavy drinking was unrelated to other sociodemographic characteristics.

These findings further indicate that posttreatment alcohol use patterns are largely a continuation of pretreatment patterns. Drug abuse treatment has little impact on posttreatment alcohol use except perhaps in the case of lengthy stays in treatment with highly intense services. Alcohol use is common among treatment clients before, during, and after treatment and far more common than among DARP clients of ten years before. One-year improvement rates were lower than for any of the other drugs. These findings suggest that greater attention should be paid to the alcohol use patterns of drug abuse treatment clients and the role of alcohol use in interfering with drug abuse treatment effectiveness.

## Depressive and Suicidal Indicators

Depression is common among clients and may impede the treatment process. According to the results of a number of studies, 30 to 50 percent of clients entering drug abuse treatment programs could be diagnosed as at least moderately depressed (DeLeon 1974, 1984; Frederick, Resnick, and Wittlin 1973; Harris, Lynn, and Hunter 1979; Uhde et al. 1982;

Weissman et al. 1976; Zuckerman et al. 1975). These percentages compare with estimates that 14 to 20 percent of the general population experience symptoms of depression at any given time (Midanik 1981; President's Commission on Mental Health 1978) and 4 to 7 percent may be diagnosable as having clinical depression (Weissman, Myers, and Harding 1978). From the Epidemiological Catchment Area (ECA) surveys, 1 to 4 percent of the general population indicate a six-month prevalence of a major depressive episode (Myers et al. 1984). In addition, Miles (1977) has estimated that 10 percent or more of opioid addicts will die by suicide. Thus, depression, whether cause or effect of drug abuse, is certainly a strong correlate.

The effects of drug abuse treatment on depression are unclear. Dorus and Senay (1980), for instance, found in a long-term study of drug abusers that scores on depression scales decreased substantially regardless of the type of substance abuse or duration of treatment. Woody and Blaine (1979) also reported that the high levels of depression at intake decreased over time, although suicide attempts were more common during the withdrawal phases of treatment. Thus, there should be further investigation of the course of depressive symptoms during and after treatment and particular consideration of the course of both depression and suicidal indicators.

As noted in Chapters 2 and 4, we have considered in this research three indicators of depression: one general indicator of depression, one measure of suicidal thoughts, and one measure of suicidal attempts. For some analyses we have considered all three indicators together; for other analyses, such as those reported here, we have chosen to examine a more stringent indicator that includes only that the client has experienced suicidal thoughts or has attempted suicide. As with other measures of treatment outcome, we examine the persistence of these symptoms before, during, and after treatment for clients who stayed in treatment at least three months. In addition, we examine factors associated with posttreatment suicidal symptoms, including client characteristics, the nature of treatment received, and selected posttreatment experiences. More complete analyses of the correlates of depression and suicidal symptoms and their course during and after treatment are reported in Allison, Hubbard, and Ginzburg (1985) and Magruder-Habib, Hubbard, and Ginzburg (1988).

*Suicidal Symptoms before, during, and after Treatment*

The frequency of suicidal thoughts and attempts decreased dramatically during and after drug abuse treatment, as shown in Figure 6-4. Suicidal thoughts or attempts were common among outpatient drug-free clients (45.0 percent) and residential clients (42.6 percent) in the year before treatment, and somewhat less common among outpatient methadone clients (32.5 percent). Suicidal symptoms decreased substantially in the first three months of treatment. Only 1 in 10 residential and methadone clients and 2 in 10 outpatient drug-free clients reported suicidal thoughts or attempts. In contrast to most other treatment outcomes, this low rate was maintained in the first three months after treatment. Symptoms increased slightly in the first year after treatment. Despite small

Figure 6-4 Changes in Prevalence of Suicidal Indicators (clients treated three months or longer)

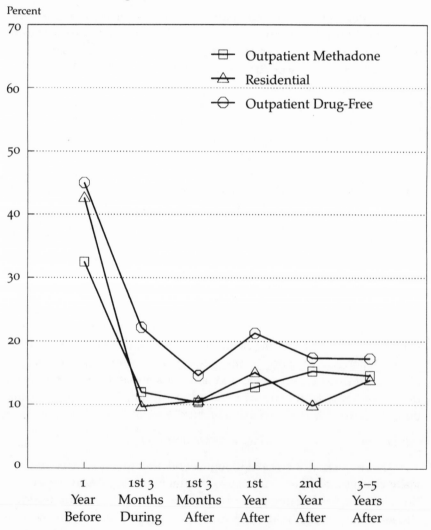

Percent

increases and decreases throughout the posttreatment period, by three to five years after treatment the prevalence of these suicidal symptoms was similar to intreatment levels and one-half to one-third pretreatment levels. The prevalence of suicidal thoughts and attempts was higher among outpatient drug-free clients than other clients at each time period before, during, and after treatment.

These changes in suicidal symptoms are reflected in one-year abstinence and one-year improvement rates. Among those who reported suicidal thoughts or attempts in the year before treatment, one-year abstinence rates indicate the percentage who reported no symptoms of depression (either depressive symptoms or suicidal symptoms) in the year after treatment. That is, they no longer indicated that they were depressed. These abstinence rates were quite high relative to other treatment outcomes, ranging from 63 percent for residential clients to 51 percent for outpatient drug-free clients and 52 percent for outpatient methadone clients. One-year improvement rates were also high; these rates reflect the percentage of those who indicated suicidal thoughts or attempts in the year before treatment and who indicated either no symptoms of depression in the year after treatment or a less severe symptom. One-year improvement rates ranged from 79 percent for residential clients and 79 percent for outpatient methadone clients to 61 percent for outpatient drug-free clients. Thus, in terms of reduction or elimination of reported suicidal symptoms in the year after treatment, residential programs have the highest effectiveness rates of any of the major modalities, but outpatient methadone and outpatient drug-free programs are almost as effective.

*Factors Affecting Posttreatment Suicidal Symptoms*

The likelihood of posttreatment suicidal symptoms was related only to having experienced suicidal symptoms before treatment and to race, number of prior drug abuse treatment episodes, and posttreatment readmission, according to the results of logistic regression analyses conducted separately for each modality. It was not significantly related to pretreatment drug abuse pattern, time spent in treatment, service intensity, or other sociodemographic characteristics (age, sex, source of referral). In general, posttreatment suicidal symptoms were more likely among those with pretreatment suicidal symptoms, whites (for residential clients, whites were less likely to indicate posttreatment suicidal symptoms), those with three or more prior drug abuse treatments, or those who reentered drug abuse treatment in the year after leaving the program included in this study.

The prevalence of depression and suicidal symptoms among clients before, during, and after treatment indicates the need for thorough evaluation of clients at admission and provision of appropriate services during treatment directed toward identification and treatment of suicide potential. Although suicidal symptoms declined dramatically during and after treatment, depression is a strong correlate of drug abuse and should be closely monitored. Findings regarding the correlates of posttreatment suicidal symptoms indicate that clients who return to drug abuse treatment are prone to depressive and suicidal symptoms; these clients in particular should be closely evaluated and counseled.

## Return to Treatment

Drug abuse treatment, as drug abuse, is for many a recurrent phenomenon. The life history of drug abusers is often marked by numerous episodes of abuse and treatment. There is, however, little research that documents the nature of treatment histories or the role of treatment histories in the effectiveness of any specific treatment episode or on the long-term prognosis for recovery from drug abuse.

Much of what is known about the treatment histories of drug abusers comes from the Drug Abuse Reporting Program. Joe and Gent (1978) find, for instance, that before entering the DARP program 39 percent had been admitted to drug abuse treatment; in the first six years after leaving the DARP program, about 61 percent had a subsequent treatment experience. The percentage of DARP clients in drug abuse treatment during each of the posttreatment years ranged from 39 to 40 percent in years one, two, three, and six and was 31 percent 12 years after DARP (Simpson et al. 1986).

Several client characteristics and treatment factors have been found to be related to the return to drug abuse treatment. Although sociodemographic characteristics in general have not been found to be strongly linked to the likelihood of returning to treatment (Savage and Simpson 1978; Simpson and Savage 1978), the number of prior admissions has been found to be a strong predictor. The greater the number of prior admissions, the greater the likelihood of readmission (Siguel and Spillane 1978; Simpson and Savage 1978). Clients in residential programs and outpatient drug-free programs are less likely to return to treatment than outpatient methadone clients (Bracy and Simpson 1982–83; Joe and Gent 1978; Simpson and Savage 1978, 1980). Longer stays in treatment and completion of treatment are associated with a lower likelihood of return (Simpson and Savage 1978).

In analyses reported here, we examine the return to treatment in the year after leaving the treatment program included in this study and factors related to the return. Prior to examining subsequent treatment episodes, however, we describe the often lengthy treatment histories of clients. Fuller descriptions of treatment histories are presented in Marsden, Hubbard, and Bailey (1988), which also describes the factors affecting the timing of the return to treatment in the first year after treatment.

## Treatment Histories of Drug Abusers

On average, clients entered drug abuse treatment for the first time at age 24, having begun regular drug use about age 16. Thus, most clients had engaged in regular drug use for approximately 8 years before entering treatment. Women on average entered treatment only slightly earlier than men, although men began regular drug use at earlier ages. Whites entered treatment at earlier ages than blacks and Hispanics. These findings regarding the average age of entering treatment for the first time and demographic patterns of entering treatment are consistent with findings of prior research (Cuskey, Ipsen, and Premkumar 1973; Sells and Simpson 1977; Spiegel 1974).

Comparing the average age at entry to treatment for clients in different age cohorts suggests that the average age of beginning regular drug use and entering treatment for the first time is decreasing. Younger clients, those born in 1960 or later, began regular drug use on average at age 14 and first entered treatment at age 17. Older clients, those born in previous decades, began drug abuse and first entered treatment at progressively older ages. Although these groups may not be representative of all drug abuse treatment clients, these trends are indicative of an increasingly younger client at entry to treatment and a younger treatment population.

About two in five clients had a drug abuse treatment episode prior to entering the program included in this study, 21.5 percent had received treatment for alcohol abuse, and about 24.1 percent had received treatment for a mental health or emotional problem. Thus, the drug abuse treatment population is a multiple problem population (see descriptions in this chapter and Chapter 4) and a high user of social services.

The drug abuse treatment histories of many clients are lengthy, characterized by multiple episodes in several modalities and perhaps years spent in treatment. To examine the nature of treatment histories, we considered the total number of drug abuse treatment admissions before entering the program included in this study, the TOPS episode, and any admissions in the year after leaving the TOPS program. Including detoxification and treatment in the three major modalities, clients on average had almost four treatment episodes during this period. Excluding detoxification and including only the three major modalities, there were an average of 2.4 episodes of drug abuse treatment within the same time period. Males had a slightly higher number of treatment episodes than females, blacks and Hispanics had a greater number of episodes than whites, and those who had ever used heroin had a substantially greater number of episodes than those without histories of heroin abuse. If we consider the experience of clients aged 30 and over to represent the experience of a drug abuser who may be near completion of the drug abuse and drug abuse treatment history, abusers may in their lifetimes expect to have five treatment episodes and about 70 weeks spent in treatment, including detoxification. Excluding detoxification, there are likely to be three episodes, and 63 weeks are likely to be spent in treatment.

These lifetime measures of drug abuse treatment suggest that drug abuse and drug abuse treatment are recurrent phenomena for many. Although any specific treatment episode may result in lengthy periods of abstinence, for many the episode results only in improvement, not cure. There is a real possibility of relapse to drug use and a subsequent return to treatment. These findings suggest that substantial public expenditures may be necessary over the life of a typical drug abuser to provide treatment for recurrent problems.

### Readmission to Treatment

Almost one-third of clients returned to treatment in the year after leaving the program included in this study; the average interval between leaving treatment and returning was 12 weeks. Outpatient methadone clients were substantially more likely to continue or return to treatment in the year after leaving treatment than were residential and outpatient drug-free clients.

Figure 6-5 presents the prevalence of readmission to treatment for clients who remained in treatment for at least three months. These data indicate the percentage of clients who at each time point report having entered treatment in the preceding year (for the first three months after treatment, the percentage who reenter treatment during the three months after treatment). For clients treated in methadone programs, the likelihood of readmission actually increases after leaving treatment. Between 50 and 60 percent report being treated in the years after enrollment in the program included in this study. This suggests methadone clients need to remain in contact with treatment for long periods. For residential clients, the rate of readmission to treatment declines steadily after the first year

out of treatment. About one in five long-term residential clients is readmitted to treatment during the periods two or more years after leaving
treatment. The proportion of outpatient drug-free clients admitted to treatment is relatively constant over the periods before and after treatment.
Between 10 and 20 percent are readmitted to treatment in a given year.

Older clients, married or once married, and Hispanics were more
likely than their counterparts to return to treatment. Two types of regres-

Figure 6-5 Changes in Prevalence of Admission to Drug Abuse
Treatment (clients treated three months or longer)

Percent

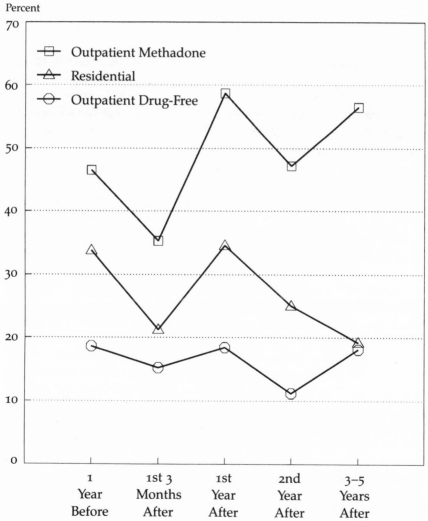

sion analyses were conducted to examine the likelihood of returning to treatment (logistic regression in which the dependent variable was any readmission in the year after treatment) and the timing of returning (multivariate regression analyses in which the dependent variable was the number of weeks to return to treatment for those who returned in the year after treatment). Both the likelihood of returning and the timing of return were unrelated to how quickly the client returned to drug abuse and were not strongly related to sociodemographic characteristics or pretreatment drug abuse pattern. The likelihood of a return to treatment for those who spent longer times in treatment is, perhaps, indicative of the fact that, for many, drug abuse treatment is a recurrent, chronic phenomenon.

## Conclusions

Corresponding to the substantial declines in the abuse of specific drugs and in overall drug abuse severity, as well as abstinence for many clients during and after treatment, is an improvement in other behaviors associated with drug abuse. Substantial declines were observed for criminal activity and suicidal symptoms, while heavy alcohol use was stable in the years after treatment. Indeed, one-year abstinence rates for criminal activity were the highest for any treatment outcome measure, while the low abstinence rates for alcohol use were second only to marijuana use. Indications are that pretreatment levels of heavy alcohol use are simply maintained. Thus, there is a substantial improvement in many of the negative behaviors associated with drug dependency, but the findings for the relative stability of employment indicate that drug abuse treatment does not necessarily guarantee a return to or entry into productive activity. Further, many clients return to drug abuse treatment in the years after leaving a particular treatment episode.

Although time spent in treatment was among the strongest predictors of posttreatment drug abuse, it was not a good predictor for many of the other behaviors examined here. Staying in residential treatment at least one year and in outpatient drug-free treatment for at least six months doubled the likelihood of full-time employment in the year after treatment. Time in treatment was a significant predictor only for posttreatment criminal activity among residential clients and for heavy alcohol use among long-term methadone clients, but not for clients in other modalities or for other behaviors. Indeed, time spent in treatment was positively related to the return to treatment; the longer clients spent in treatment, the more likely were they to return to treatment in the year after treatment. This latter finding is perhaps indicative of the recurrent nature of treatment for many drug abusers and the need for services that will help prevent relapse. These treatment outcomes other than drug abuse were not strongly related to sociodemographic characteristics or pretreatment behaviors.

Findings regarding the effectiveness of treatment for the criminal justice client suggest that treatment can be an effective alternative to incarceration for many criminally active drug abusers. The criminal justice client fares no worse in treatment than other clients and indeed substantial decreases in criminal activity are found.

These findings indicate the substantial improvements in criminal activity and suicidal symptoms as drug use declines during and after treatment. However, the relative stability of alcohol use and irregular patterns of employment indicate the need for intensified treatment services directed toward improvement in these areas. Although treatment results in reductions in drug abuse and criminal activity, it does not result in consistent increases in employment or productivity. Indeed, the continuing heavy alcohol use of many clients may interfere with future progress or precipitate relapse.

# 7. Costs and Benefits of Drug Abuse Treatment

A major question facing public officials and program managers is the cost-effectiveness of drug abuse treatment, or the economic returns to public expenditures for drug abuse treatment. In 1980, approximately $1.2 billion was spent by local, state, and federal governments for drug abuse treatment. An additional $243 million was spent for other health support services, including education, prevention, and research. Significantly more substantial than these direct expenditures for treatment services were public expenditures for the crime-related costs of drug abuse. Law enforcement and private protection costs included $537 million for federal drug traffic control, $4.5 billion for other public criminal justice expenditures, and $1.3 billion in private police protection services. Additional losses to society included the losses of potential legitimate productivity due to the crime careers and incarcerations of criminally active drug abusers ($10.2 billion), losses to victims from property damage, and lost productivity and homicide ($1.8 billion). A total of $28.6 billion in costs of drug abuse not related to crime includes the costs of drug abuse treatment and other health expenditures noted above, but is largely accounted for by reduced productivity of drug abusers in the work force ($25.7 billion). Thus, in 1980 the economic costs of drug abuse to the nation were estimated to be $46.9 billion and in 1983, $59.7 billion (Harwood et al. 1984). Of this total, crime-related costs accounted for 39.1 percent.

The $60 billion estimate is a conservative one. The figure excludes expenditures on illegal drugs and the value of property stolen by drug abusers. Estimates of the retail value of illegal drugs consumed in 1979 range from $21 billion to $65 billion (U.S. Department of the Treasury 1983). Perhaps $1.5 billion of the $7.3 billion that was stolen from individuals in 1980 (U.S. Department of Justice 1983b) could be attributed to thefts by drug addicts (Harwood et al. 1984). This latter amount is excluded from the total to avoid a potential problem with double counting. The $60 billion estimate is also conservative in that it excludes those costs of crime that can not be measured in monetary terms. These costs include the pain and suffering of victims or losses that exceed the market price of a stolen good.

A major justification for drug abuse treatment is its impact for crime reduction. It is argued that if drug abuse is reduced by treatment, the motivation for committing crimes will be correspondingly reduced. In analyses of declines in criminal behavior described in Chapter 6, significant reductions in predatory crime were recorded during and after treatment. In this chapter we estimate the economic benefits of these intreatment and posttreatment reductions of criminal activity of drug abusers. Specifically, we compare the costs of drug abuse treatment to the savings associated with lower crime rates of drug abusers during and after treatment. Some analyses compare the cost savings of clients referred to drug abuse treatment by the criminal justice system to those referred by other sources. Descriptive and multivariate analyses are discussed. Most analyses rest on the one-year follow-up sample, although some analyses of the two- and three- to five-year follow-up samples were also conducted as described elsewhere (Harwood et al. 1987, 1988).

Note that the analyses described in this chapter estimate the economic benefits of drug abuse treatment in terms of crime reduction. Although the savings associated with crime reduction are expected to be a large part of the benefits of treatment, we do not estimate the savings associated with improvements in other behaviors during and after treatment. For instance, economic benefits may be derived from increases in the legitimate productivity of drug abusers in treatment who were not criminally active or from decreased need for other community services. Furthermore, prior studies have seldom considered health-related benefits of treatment. These benefits would result in increased productivity and decreased health care utilization. Further, treatment can dramatically increase the returns from expenditures for the treatment through the prevention of AIDS among intravenous drug abusers, their sexual partners, and their newborn children.

## Calculation of Crime-Related Costs of Drug Abusers

Analyses of the cost savings associated with drug abuse treatment described in this chapter are based on the cost-of-illness framework adapted by Harwood et al. (1984) to estimate the costs to the nation of alcohol and drug abuse and mental illness. In that methodology the costs are the tangible consequences of those three disorders that can be assigned dollar values. In the case of the crime-related costs of drug abuse under examination here, four values were estimated for the crime-related consequences of drug abuse: costs to victims, costs for criminal justice, crime career/productivity costs, and losses from theft. Each of these valuations estimates the loss of resources to victims or to society at large. The victim's costs include the expense of medical treatment, the value of personal property damaged or destroyed in the crime, and reduced productivity at work or at home because of injury or inconvenience occasioned by the crime. Costs for criminal justice include expenditures for police services, adjudication, and incarceration. Crime career/productivity costs occur when drug abusers are removed from the productive economy, such as when they are involved in illegal pursuits at the expense of legitimate activities or when incarcerated. The costs of theft, incurred by the victim, are estimated separately because of the method of calculation of two summary measures of the costs of crime, one that includes and one that excludes the cost of theft. These two alternative summary measures are the costs to society and the costs to law-abiding citizens. The cost to society includes costs to victims, criminal justice costs and crime career/productivity costs but excludes losses to theft, which are borne directly by victims. The cost to law-abiding citizens includes costs to victims, criminal justice costs, and losses to theft but excludes the crime career/productivity costs, which are borne by law-breaking citizens and their families. These calculations exclude certain additional costs, such as income subsidies received by drug abusers and their families or taxes, fines, or restitution paid by drug abusers. They, however, provide an overview of the magnitude of crime-related costs of drug abuse borne by the nation. Analyses described in this chapter concentrate on the two summary measures, although some information is provided about the components of these summary measures.

Costs to victims include the medical expenses, property damage, and employment-related costs incurred by victims of offenses. Average costs to victims per offense were estimated for aggravated assault, robbery, burglary, theft, and auto theft, based on the 1979 National Victimization Survey (U.S. Department of Justice 1984). The value of property stolen (theft) was separately estimated from the same source. Criminal justice costs were estimated from information about government expenditures for police services, adjudication, and incarceration (U.S. Department of Justice 1983a). Crime career/productivity costs were estimated for each drug abuser by calculating the difference between the person's self-reported legitimate earnings and the national average for persons of the same age and sex. Virtually all drug abusers in this sample of clients had actual earnings substantially below the national average both before and after treatment. Also included in this cost were estimates of the losses of expected fringe benefits and household productivity.

## Economic Costs before, during, and after Treatment

Economic costs were estimated for the year before treatment and one, two, and three to five years after treatment. Costs were also estimated for clients in each of the modalities for the entire length of time spent in treatment by each client. Discussion focuses here on the year before and after treatment and the time spent in treatment, although summary measures for the two- and three- to five-year follow-ups are also noted. The samples analyzed and additional details about the calculation of costs are discussed in Harwood et al. (1987).

Information about the economic impact of drug abuse in the year before and year after treatment is presented in Table 7-1. Costs are presented for each of the four categories described above, the two summary measures of crime-related costs, and for selected other costs that are not included in the summary measures. These other costs are further indications of the magnitude of the burden of drug abuse on the nation. Legal earnings are presented for the sake of comparison with the magnitude of illegal income and to illustrate the posttreatment changes in productivity.

Virtually all economic measures show that the burden of crime and other economic consequences of drug abuse are lower after treatment than before. Overall, the costs of drug abuse to law-abiding citizens fell from $9,190 per drug abuser in the year before treatment to $7,379 per addict in the year after treatment, a decrease of about 20 percent. Comparable costs to society declined from $15,262 to $14,089, a decrease of about 8 percent. Costs to victims declined by about 30 percent, criminal

Table 7-1  Economic Impacts of Drug Abusers One Year before Treatment and One Year after Leaving Treatment

| Impact Category | Before Treatment | After Treatment |
|---|---|---|
| Crime-related costs | | |
|    1. Costs to victims | $1,802 | $1,236 |
|    2. Criminal justice | 3,926 | 3,049 |
|    3. Crime career/productivity | 9,534 | 9,804 |
|    4. Theft | 3,462 | 3,094 |
| Costs to law-abiding citizens[a] | 9,190 | 7,379 |
| Costs to society[b] | 15,262 | 14,089 |
| Other costs | | |
|    Drug expenditures | 6,854 | 2,687 |
|    Illegal income | 6,937 | 2,546 |
|    Legal earnings | 3,437 | 3,858 |

a. Sum of 1, 2, and 4.
b. Sum of 1, 2, and 3.

justice costs by about 24 percent, and the cost of theft by about 11 percent. Partially offsetting these decreases was a slight increase in crime career/productivity losses and little improvement in legal earnings. Note, however, the substantial decreases in illegal income, from $6,937 in the year before treatment to $2,546 in the year after treatment, and also the close correspondence between drug expenditures and illegal income in both periods.

These decreases in the crime-related costs of drug abuse after treatment are consistent with the decreases in criminal activity among clients in the year after treatment relative to the year before treatment (see Chapter 6 and Collins et al. 1987). They are also consistent with the observation by several authors that criminal activity is lower during periods of nonaddiction (Ball et al. 1981; Collins, Hubbard, and Rachal 1985; Johnson et al. 1985). That is, as drug abuse decreases in severity after treatment (Hubbard and Marsden 1986), criminal activity also decreases and the crime-related costs of drug abuse correspondingly decline.

Findings for the second year after treatment are consistent with the declines seen for the one-year period, but in the three to five years after treatment there appears to be a reversal of the favorable trend. By three to five years after treatment there was a return to pretreatment levels of costs. Drug expenditures and illegal income, however, continued to mirror the immediate posttreatment declines, while legal earnings increased little in each of the follow-up periods. Thus, although clients decreased their criminal activity immediately after treatment, they did little to improve their integration into the legitimate economy.

Comparisons of the pretreatment and posttreatment costs of clients referred from the criminal justice system to those who were referred from other sources showed the distinctiveness of criminal justice clients (see Chapter 6). The clients referred by the criminal justice system incurred greater crime-related costs than self-referred criminally active clients in the year before admission. However, they also demonstrated larger absolute and proportional reductions in costs between the pretreatment and posttreatment periods. These findings were apparent for both the costs to law-abiding citizens and costs to society. Both groups showed only modest increases in legal earnings during the year after treatment.

The summary measures for all clients reveal substantial declines in costs in the year after treatment compared to the year before treatment, but they are not instructive about which modalities produce such changes. To examine this issue, average daily costs to law-abiding citizens and to society were calculated for each modality for the year before, the period spent in treatment, and the year after treatment. These figures enable comparison with the average daily costs of treatment to determine the benefits of treatment expenditures. Estimates of the costs to law-abiding citizens and to society for the year before treatment, the intreatment period, and the year after treatment are presented in Table 7-2 for each modality. Note that the values for the intreatment period are averages of the costs based on all intreatment interviews through 12 months in treatment. Because the modalities differ substantially in client populations, treatment effectiveness, and average daily costs, their separate consideration is necessary.

The costs to law-abiding citizens and to society differ substantially among the modalities in the year before treatment, as shown in Table 7-2. Residential clients have the highest costs to law-abiding citizens and to society, an indication of their higher rates of criminal activity in the year before treatment and of the higher proportion of criminal justice referrals (Chapters 3 and 6 of this volume; Collins et al. 1987). Outpatient methadone clients have intermediate levels of costs, and outpatient drug-free clients the lowest in the year before treatment.

The costs to law-abiding citizens and to society decreased substantially during treatment for clients in each of the modalities. The restrictive nature of residential treatment resulted in particularly low crime-related costs to law-abiding citizens during treatment of $0.65 per day. These costs may have been from thefts from other clients, from program staff members, or while working temporarily in the community. The somewhat higher intreatment costs of outpatient methadone clients and outpatient drug-free clients is probably a function of their less restricted environments. Costs to society among residential clients were also substantially lower, about $20 lower, during treatment compared to the year before

Table 7-2 Average Economic Impacts of Drug Abusers One Year before, during, and One Year after Treatment, by Modality (in dollars per person per day)

| Modality | Costs to Law-abiding Citizens Treatment Period | | | Costs to Society Treatment Period | | |
|---|---|---|---|---|---|---|
| | Before | During | After | Before | During | After |
| Outpatient methadone | $18.16 | $7.57 | $23.57 | $46.54 | $39.25 | $43.04 |
| Residential | 43.17 | 0.65 | 25.01 | 53.18 | 33.13 | 44.61 |
| Outpatient drug-free | 12.84 | 5.00 | 12.46 | 27.95 | 19.51 | 26.33 |

treatment. These costs nevertheless remained substantial because the clients could not work and, therefore, had productivity losses while in treatment. Reductions in the costs to society during treatment were less marked for outpatient modalities, $10 or less per day. However, as noted in the next section, although the cost reductions of residential treatment are substantially higher than for outpatient methadone or outpatient drug-free clients, the costs of providing residential treatment are also substantially higher.

In the year after treatment, the costs to law-abiding citizens and costs to society were lower than pretreatment costs for residential clients, about $18 and $9 respectively. However, for outpatient methadone clients and outpatient drug-free clients posttreatment costs were similar in value to pretreatment costs. In fact, posttreatment costs for methadone clients were higher than pretreatment costs. This increase may, however, be an artifact of the high rate of nonresponse for methadone clients in the pretreatment period (Harwood et al. 1987). The increase may also be related to the fact that many methadone clients were in other restrictive environments in the year before entering the TOPS program, environments that limited their ability to incur crime-related costs in the year before treatment but less so in the year after treatment.

Thus, for all modalities and for both measures of costs, the crime-related costs of drug abuse are substantially lower during treatment than costs before or after treatment. Posttreatment costs are lower than pretreatment costs for residential clients, but for other modalities posttreatment costs are almost as large as, or exceed, pretreatment costs. The examination of the benefits of drug abuse treatment, however, rests with comparisons with the costs of providing treatment, as discussed in the next section. Further, regression analyses were utilized to develop estimates of the average daily returns to drug abuse treatment in terms of reductions in crime-related costs in the year after treatment. These estimates contrast with the simpler estimates presented above, which do not control for variation in certain pretreatment characteristics.

## Summary of Costs and Benefits of Drug Abuse Treatment

The simple comparisons of costs before and after treatment erroneously suggest that there are only meager economic benefits following discharge from treatment. These figures do not adequately portray results for those quitting treatment early or those remaining in treatment for periods of time considered necessary to gain therapeutic benefits from treatment. Length of stay in treatment is one of the primary determinants of outcome, and this is true when economic measures of outcome are used as well.

To examine the role of length of stay in determining economic benefits, a regression analysis was performed. Posttreatment costs were attributed to clients as a function of their time spent in treatment, type of treatment, prior treatment experiences, costs imposed on society in the year before admission to treatment, and other characteristics including sociodemographic characteristics, pretreatment drug abuse pattern, and prior work history.

The economic benefits of one day in treatment were estimated using this technique. In contrast to the simple pre- and posttreatment comparisons of costs, there were found to be meaningful positive returns to time spent in treatment. The results of the regression analysis are used to produce average daily estimates and per episode estimates of benefits to law-abiding citizens and to society.

The average daily cost of providing drug abuse treatment in residential facilities is approximately $18.50, almost three times the $6.00 cost of providing treatment in outpatient methadone programs or outpatient drug-free programs (Allison, Hubbard, and Rachal 1985). The average benefit per day while in treatment was estimated for the average economic impacts by modality. The intreatment benefits were calculated by averaging the differences between pretreatment and intreatment costs, and between intreatment and posttreatment costs. Estimates were developed in this manner for each of the modalities and for costs to law-abiding citizens and to society, separately. Finally, the average benefit per day in the year after treatment was estimated by regression analyses in which length of stay was the primary independent variable.

Residential treatment has the greatest returns per day spent in treatment, both for the intreatment period and the year after treatment. Each day in residential treatment results in an average benefit of $33.44 for the intreatment period compared to $13.30 for outpatient methadone and $7.65 for outpatient drug-free in terms of costs to law-abiding citizens. In terms of costs to society, comparable figures were $15.77 for residential treatment, $5.54 for outpatient methadone, and $7.63 for outpatient drug-free. These intreatment cost reductions were similar to the costs of providing treatment. Thus, the costs of providing drug abuse treatment were almost entirely recouped during the intreatment period. However, there were important posttreatment gains as well, which reflected the clients' continued reduction in criminal activity and thus in crime-related costs. These posttreatment benefits were $37.62 for residential clients, $10.96 for outpatient methadone clients, and $16.40 for outpatient drug-free clients in terms of costs to law-abiding citizens. In terms of costs to society, comparable figures were $21.40, $9.95, and $18.06, respectively.

The large differences between the posttreatment benefits to law-abiding citizens and to society for residential clients indicate that most of the economic benefits from residential clients come from reduced criminal activity rather than from increases in productivity. That is, the major difference between the two cost estimates is that the costs to law-abiding citizens includes the costs of theft, which are substantially reduced in the posttreatment period. There is also strong evidence that clients referred by the criminal justice system benefit from longer stays in residential treatment. In results not presented here, the returns per day of treatment were substantially greater for criminal justice clients; their higher post-treatment costs suggest that they must stay in treatment longer than self-referrals to have the same expected level of posttreatment costs. In addition, results from the regression analyses indicate that methadone maintenance clients with greater pretreatment criminal activity had lower returns per day of treatment than those who were less criminally active.

Weighing the costs and benefits for a specific treatment episode is perhaps more instructive about the overall value of treatment. These figures for costs to law-abiding citizens and costs to society are shown in Table 7-3. Average lengths of stay are 159 days for residential treatment, 267 for outpatient methadone treatment, and 101 for outpatient drug-free treatment. These lengths of stay yield total average treatment costs for a single treatment episode of $2,942 for residential, $1,602 for outpatient methadone, and $606 for outpatient drug-free clients. Summing the intreatment and posttreatment benefits yields a favorable ratio of benefits to costs, for both costs to law-abiding citizens and to society. In most cases the benefits of providing treatment are substantially higher than the costs.

These findings indicate that there are significant economic benefits

Table 7-3 Crime Reduction in the First Year after Treatment: Ratio of Benefits to Costs of Treatment

| | Modality | | |
|---|---|---|---|
| Impact Category | Outpatient Methadone | Residential | Outpatient Drug-Free |
| Costs to law-abiding citizens | 4.04 | 3.84 | 1.28 |
| Costs to society | 0.92 | 2.10 | 4.28 |

associated with drug abuse treatment. These benefits appear to be at least as large as the cost of providing treatment, and much of the cost is captured during the treatment. Posttreatment gains are virtually an economic bonus. Note, however, that analyses described here do not examine the longer-term impact of treatment, nor do they control for differences in client populations across the modalities. However, these analyses suggest that there are real returns to law-abiding citizens and to society from the impact on crime reduction of drug abuse treatment.

## Conclusions

Analyses presented in this chapter have demonstrated the substantial crime-related and other costs to the nation of drug abusers prior to entering treatment and the substantial reductions in these costs both during and following participation in treatment. This reduction appears to be at least as large as the cost of providing treatment and much of the expenditure is recovered during the time the drug abuser is in treatment. Thus, the return on investment is sizable and continues at least one year after leaving treatment and potentially even longer. Indeed, in that substantial benefits are to be gained during the treatment period in terms of reductions in criminal activity and associated costs to the nation, long-term drug abuse treatment appears to be an effective mechanism to limit the burden of drug abusers on the nation.

The costs of drug abusers to the nation were estimated in two ways, in terms of the costs to society (excludes losses to theft, which are borne by the victim) and costs to law-abiding citizens (excludes losses resulting from reduced productivity of drug abusers involved in crime and their families). Although the measure of costs to law-abiding citizens yields a lower estimate of total costs than does the measure of costs to society, both illustrate the sizable burden to society posed by drug abusers. The crime career/productivity costs are by far the largest component of crime-related costs. The economic impacts of drug abuse decline substantially during and after treatment, as indicated by both measures. Relative to the costs of treatment, great benefits resulted from treatment in each of the three modalities.

Thus, substantial benefits to the nation occur from public investment in drug abuse treatment. Although only the benefits associated with crime-reduction have been estimated here, drug abuse treatment results in substantial improvements in other negative behaviors, which may further reduce the costs incurred by the nation. For instance, productivity gains may be made by those who are not criminally involved, and treatment will most likely result in lower demand for social services by this population. A major economic benefit in the future will likely be from the prevention of AIDS among intravenous drug abusers and their sex partners. Thus, while drug abuse treatment has been shown to be a good return on investment simply in terms of crime reduction, the returns may be substantially greater than those estimated here.

The fact that there are substantial returns even during treatment and that outcomes in general are more positive for longer stays in treatment argues for long-term treatment of drug abusers. Thus, investigation of factors related to longer stays in treatment and successful completion of the course of treatment are critical undertakings.

# 8. Strengthening Drug Abuse Treatment

In the preceding chapters, we have used data collected from a national sample of 10,000 clients to establish that publicly funded treatment programs are effective in reducing drug abuse and that long-term treatment helps addicts to become more productive members of society. These benefits of reduced drug abuse and increased productivity justify the tax dollars expended on outpatient methadone, residential, and outpatient drug-free programs. Indeed, the costs of drug abuse treatment are substantially recovered during the time a client is in treatment, and the savings to society after a client has left treatment represent further returns on the investment. By serving as an alternative to incarceration, treatment can be particularly beneficial for drug abusers identified in jails or prisons, and it can play a central role in combating the spread of Acquired Immune Deficiency Syndrome (AIDS) by reducing the intravenous use of heroin and other drugs. Although abstinence is difficult to achieve because of the variety of problems suffered by clients, their long histories of deviant and debilitating lifestyles, and a lack of support in the community, publicly funded drug abuse treatment is essential to our national effort to reduce the demand for drugs and the related social and economic costs.

To insure that clients receive maximum benefits from the publicly funded system and can progress toward the difficult long-term goals of drug-free lives and full productivity, programs need to be strengthened. But the already overburdened and poorly supported treatment system faces new challenges from the AIDS epidemic and the increase in cocaine abuse. The Presidential Commission on the Human Immunodeficiency Virus Epidemic has called for a doubling of treatment capacity for intravenous drug abusers, and the Anti–Drug Abuse Act of 1988 promises hundreds of millions of additional dollars to increase the availability and quality of treatment services for drug abusers generally. To meet these expectations of policymakers and taxpayers, the publicly funded drug abuse treatment system must expand and improve. A firm foundation of knowledge based on 20 years of research and experience can contribute to this effort.

## Effectiveness of the Major Modalities

What is the overall effectiveness of drug abuse treatment? We considered this question both from the standpoint of reducing drug abuse and from the standpoint of building more productive lives (decreasing criminal activity, alcohol use, and depression, and increasing employment). Our most dramatic finding is that drug abuse treatment has been notably effective in reducing drug abuse up to five years after a single treatment episode. The major modalities have had more limited success in rebuilding the lives of drug abusers and reintegrating them into society.

### Reduced Drug Abuse and Increased Productivity

Substantial decreases in heroin abuse, reductions in cocaine abuse, less nonmedical use of psychotherapeutic drugs, and diminished overall severity of drug abuse were apparent during and after treatment for clients treated over a period of at least three months. The prevalence of regular heroin use for methadone clients in the first year after treatment (17 percent) was one-fourth of the pretreatment rate; the prevalence of regular cocaine use was cut in half, and regular nonmedical psychotherapeutic use was cut by one-third. In the case of residential clients, the posttreatment prevalence of regular heroin use (12 percent) was one-third of the rate prior to treatment, and nonmedical psychotherapeutic drug use (9 percent) was one-fifth of the rate prior to treatment; regular use of cocaine declined by half to 16 percent in the posttreatment period. And in the case of outpatient drug-free clients, reductions in prevalence of regular use were one-half for heroin and nonmedical psychotherapeutic use and one-third for cocaine. Except while clients lived in the restricted environment of residential programs, relatively little change in regular marijuana use or abuse of alcohol was found in any modality. Although relapse was not uncommon within the five years after treatment, in any given year less than 20 percent of former clients in any modality were regular users of any drug other than marijuana or alcohol.

The evidence of positive changes in productivity in the years after leaving treatment was mixed. There were reductions in criminal activity and indicators of depression, but little overall increase in employment. The pretreatment proportions of clients involved in criminal activity and reporting suicidal tendencies were reduced by at least 50 percent after treatment in all modalities. For these behaviors, a pattern similar to that for drug abuse was evident: dramatic improvement during treatment, some deterioration immediately after leaving a program, and a leveling off in the years after treatment. This marked improvement over pretreatment levels was maintained up to five years after treatment.

*Contribution of Long-term Treatment*

A variety of analyses confirmed that the time spent in the program was the single most important factor contributing to the improvement observed after treatment. Residential clients staying in treatment more than one year were significantly less likely than other clients to report regular use of heroin, marijuana, or psychotherapeutics. In addition, the likelihood of their being employed full time and not engaging in crime was almost three times greater than for clients remaining in treatment less than three months. The results for outpatient drug-free clients staying in programs for at least six months showed a similar pattern. Compared with those who were in treatment for a shorter time, these clients were twice as likely to be fully employed and to stop committing predatory crimes. A statistically significant reduction in drug abuse for long-term outpatient drug-free clients, however, was found only for regular non-medical use of psychotherapeutics.

The statistically significant effects of duration of methadone treatment were found in the case of clients who were maintained on methadone continuously for at least two to three years. Compared with those leaving treatment within a year, the maintained clients were four times less likely to use heroin regularly, three times less likely to commit predatory crimes, and two times less likely to use alcohol heavily. There was also a significantly decreased likelihood of regular heroin use for clients who stayed in methadone treatment at least one year compared to those leaving after less than one year. This reduced likelihood, however, was not as great as for clients maintained on methadone. Consistent with other studies (Ball, Corty, et al. 1988; Ball, Lange, et al. 1988; Milby 1988), the results of this analysis support the concept of continued maintenance as the most efficacious in sustaining a reduction in heroin abuse for methadone clients.

Combined with results from other research, our findings provide comprehensive and convincing evidence that long-term treatment does work. Few alternative explanations for the observed effects are plausible. Some may attribute these differences to client motivation to remain in treatment rather than treatment itself. Several studies, however, including experiments with random assignment (Newman and Whitehill 1979) and evaluation of abrupt closures of methadone programs (McGlothlin and Anglin 1981) provide evidence that programs do produce effects independent of client motivation to remain in treatment. Further, the multivariate analyses and the research design used in our study carefully considered and took into account potential indicators of client motivation including previous treatment and reasons for entering treatment.

Perhaps the most impressive evidence of treatment effectiveness is the consistent replication of the findings in this study among modalities, in multiple years, for different types of clients, and across various programs. Previous research (Kosten, Rounsaville, and Kleber 1987a; Simpson and Sells 1982) also bears out our conclusions. The multiple confirmation of findings, combined with the reasoned rejection of alternative explanations, is compelling evidence that retention of at least six months in treatment is responsible for the changes in behavior observed after treatment.

## Return on Investment

The second major question that we asked at the beginning of this study concerns the return on investment in drug abuse treatment. The modest investment of $5,000 for a year of outpatient drug-free or methadone treatment and $15,000–20,000 a year for residents of therapeutic communities will produce benefits that far outweigh the costs. It is also more prudent to invest in treatment rather than pay the $10,000–25,000 annual costs of incarceration or the $80,000 in medical costs for each AIDS patient.

### Comparison of Costs and Benefits

Our analyses of the costs and benefits of each modality found that there was a substantial return on investment simply in terms of reducing crime. Using a cost-of-illness framework, we estimated the crime-related economic costs of drug abuse before, during, and after treatment. Regardless of the summary measure used, or the modality, the benefits matched or exceeded the costs of treatment within the first year after a typical client terminated a program. By this time, the return on the investment of tax dollars for law-abiding citizens was four to one for both methadone and residential programs. The crime-reduction impact estimated here, however, represents only a portion of the potential savings attributable to drug abuse treatment. Significant returns can also be gained by changes in employment and productivity independent of criminal activity and in terms of the contributions of treatment to reducing the tremendous social and economic costs related to AIDS.

*Treatment as an Alternative to Incarceration*

Our analyses also show that drug abuse treatment can be an effective alternative to incarceration for criminally active drug abusers. Many drug abusers either are directly referred to treatment by the criminal justice system prior to trial or are on probation or parole at the time they enter treatment. Although these clients had committed many crimes, criminal justice involvement was not a significant predictor of most outcomes, even criminal activity, and clients referred from the courts and corrections agencies have outcomes that are at least as positive as clients entering on their own or those referred by other sources. The criminal justice client did tend to stay in programs longer than other clients, perhaps contributing to more positive outcomes than otherwise would have been possible. Furthermore, close supervision of clients by probation or parole officers during and after treatment may contribute to the maintenance of gains occasioned by treatment. These findings indicate that drug abuse treatment can be an important component of the overall strategy of reducing crime as well as drug abuse.

*Prevention of AIDS*

Because drug abuse treatment has had considerable success in reducing intravenous drug use, it can be viewed as an effective means of inhibiting the spread of Human Immunodeficiency Virus (HIV) infection (Turner, Miller, and Moses 1989; Day et al. 1988). It has to be said, though, that the reduction is largely attributable to a substantial decline in regular heroin use rather than a change in the route of administration. Among heroin addicts who remained regular drug users after treatment, relatively few had ceased intravenous use. Indeed, many reported continued intravenous use of cocaine. The changes in intravenous usage did not appear to be affected by the increasing knowledge of AIDS and the risk of sharing needles. In findings described here, drug abusers reported the same rates of intravenous drug use in 1982 (before awareness of AIDS became widespread) as in 1985, after the risk of sharing needles became well known.

Whether or not addicts decrease their exposure to risk of infection because of awareness of AIDS or because of an overall decrease in intravenous use, drug abuse treatment can play an important role in reducing the spread of HIV infection. Indeed, the potential contribution of drug abuse treatment in stemming the AIDS epidemic is now well recognized (Turner, Miller, and Moses 1989; Watkins et al. 1988). However, given the increasing rates of intravenous cocaine consumption and the limited effects of traditional modalities on cocaine abuse, there is an urgent need to treat all forms of intravenous use.

## Improving Publicly Funded Treatment

The third major question that we posed concerns the improvement of effectiveness. Despite their demonstrated efficacy, publicly funded programs can and should be substantially improved. Some of the gaps in services can be closed within the constraints of existing funding; others will necessitate the prudent investment of additional monies.

### Outreach and Recruitment

Recruiting more abusers into treatment is one way to further reduce drug abuse. This is the approach envisioned by the Presidential Commission on the Human Immunodeficiency Virus Epidemic and the Congress in the Anti–Drug Abuse Act of 1988. However, at most 10 percent of the estimated 1.5 million intravenous drug abusers in the United States enter treatment in any given year (Butynski and Canova 1988). Outreach programs have recently been implemented to attract intravenous drug abusers into treatment (DesJarlais and Friedman 1988), and the role of compulsory treatment for drug abuse has been reexamined (Leukefeld and Tims 1988).

Recent research suggests that aggressive outreach and strong incentives can help recruit those who would not otherwise seek treatment (DesJarlais and Friedman 1988). Denial of dependence and misunderstanding of treatment are often cited as important reasons for not entering treatment. For example, interviews with a group of untreated addicts (Rounsaville and Kleber 1985) indicated that most did not seek treatment because they felt they were in control of their drug use and because they feared dependence on methadone.

One key to recruitment is the immediate access to attractive and effective treatment. In many locales, long waiting lists, fees for services, and poor-quality services have made treatment unattractive or unavailable for many abusers. If the effects of treatment are to be broadened to a larger population of drug abusers, affordable treatment of good quality must be provided. Whether the previously untreated drug abusers recruited by aggressive outreach techniques will fare as well as those abusers who have traditionally sought treatment is a critical question.

### Assessment and Treatment Planning

Federal and state regulations and accepted clinical practice require treatment plans that outline the services clients need in order to achieve mutually acceptable goals. Adequate treatment planning should be based on a comprehensive assessment of a client's drug abuse patterns, treatment history, and other problems including psychopathology. Few programs in this study made such comprehensive assessments, and clients were often unaware of their treatment plans.

Treatment programs in the 1970s and 1980s often limited their focus to the one primary drug of abuse, although even then most clients abused multiple drugs. Drugs other than the primary drug have often been ignored or overlooked in client assessments (Gordis 1988; Zweben and Smith 1986). Now, however, protocols to assess multiple drug abuse patterns (Bray et al. 1982; Hubbard, Bray, Craddock, et al. 1986) and dependence (Rounsaville, Kosten, Williams, et al. 1987; Skinner and Goldberg 1986) for the full range of drugs and alcohol are available. Their use can help identify the need for combined or supplementary therapies for alcohol abuse and other secondary drugs of abuse.

Perhaps the most important point to bear in mind about chronic abusers of drugs is that they also suffer from a variety of serious medical and mental health problems, family disruption, and poor employment histories. These "addiction-related" problems can be gleaned from standard assessment instruments, such as the Addiction Severity Index (McLellan et al. 1985), and information about these problems can be useful in matching clients with treatments and in predicting optimal length of stay and treatment response. To maximize the gains experienced during treatment, programs must assess a variety of client needs and provide services to meet those needs effectively (Allison, Hubbard, and Rachal 1985). Our analyses indicate that clients in each of the three modalities had different patterns of problems—and problems of differing severity—that they themselves attributed to their drug abuse (Hubbard, Bray, Cavanaugh, et al. 1986). Compared to outpatient methadone clients, residential clients and outpatient drug-free clients typically suffered from a larger number of drug-related problems, which tended to be more severe.

Our analyses also show that many clients have lengthy histories of drug abuse and treatment and that they are intense users of other social services as well. A substantial proportion of these clients previously had been in drug abuse treatment or received treatment for alcohol or mental health problems. Many reenter treatment after the treatment episode studied in this research. At the same time, many clients are on public assistance and use other community-based services. For that reason, treatment plans need to build on the treatment histories of clients.

Surprisingly, clients had limited information on their treatment plans despite the fact that almost all had signed plans in their case records. It seems advisable, then, that treatment staff be more direct in discussing those plans with the clients, and they should explain in detail the activities, goals, expectations, purposes, and optimal length of treatment. To the extent that success is dependent on motivation (Havassy and Tschann 1983; Metzger and Platt 1987; Wilson 1987; Wheeler, Biase, and Sullivan 1986), the clients' involvement in and compliance with the contents of the treatment plan are important.

*Counseling and Services*

The treatment regimen provided in most programs includes a combination of counseling and an array of habilitation and rehabilitation services. Counseling is the cornerstone of treatment (McLellan et al. 1988; Nurco et al. 1988), and the primary counselor typically sees to it that the client follows the treatment plan and receives the needed services.

In general, the counselors in the late 1970s were experienced, and— regardless of their backgrounds in the treatment of addiction—they had college degrees and professional training. Residential programs were oriented toward group counseling, supplemented by weekly individual sessions. Counselors in outpatient programs typically handled between 20 and 35 cases at a time, but with usually less than one hour per week of direct contact with each client. More recent data from methadone programs in the Northeast (Ball and Corty 1988) suggest that the amount of counselor-client contact declined between 1981 and 1986. On average, about 80 minutes a month was spent in counseling with each client in 1985–86, much less than the minimum of two hours per month we found in 1979–81.

There was also evidence of discontinuity in the therapeutic process. In methadone clinics there was a troubling turnover in primary counselors: clients often had two or three in the course of treatment. Various therapeutic approaches were used even within a particular outpatient drug-free program with little attempt to match client and counselor. If programs are to improve outcomes, more coordinated and intensive counseling is required. The use of paraprofessional counselors or case managers should be reconsidered to help reduce caseloads within budget constraints as well as provide job opportunities for program graduates. Paraprofessional counselors have yielded outcomes as positive as professional counselors (Aiken et al. 1984), and program graduates have long formed the core counseling staff within therapeutic communities.

It is clear that programs provide different levels of services (Corty and Ball 1987) and cannot provide the full array of services necessary for complete habilitation or rehabilitation for all clients. In virtually all clinics in all three modalities, we found substantially higher percentages of clients who needed services of various types, particularly psychological and family services, than had received them. One way that many programs increased the diversity of services was through referral arrangements and interagency cooperation. Few clients, however, reported referrals, and barriers to working with other agencies in the community still exist (Brewington et al. 1987). Another way to provide services may be to affiliate smaller treatment programs with larger, multifaceted programs that address not only drug abuse but physical and mental health, financial, educational, and employment problems as well.

These general considerations should also be seen in relation to specialized needs of certain types of clients. Although publicly funded drug abuse treatment primarily serves a young adult male population, it also serves many youth and women, as well as criminal justice clients and intravenous drug users. Effective treatment of these diverse client populations requires an understanding of their specific needs and perhaps the provision of specialized services. For example, in order to attract and retain female clients in treatment, programs may have to intensify their child care and family services (Anglin, Hser, and Booth 1987; Beschner, Reed, and Mondanaro 1981; Beschner and Thompson 1981; Rosenbaum and Murphy 1987). In the case of many adolescent clients, treatment must be directed at a complex array of drug abuse, alcohol use, delinquency, and mental health problems, and these younger clients must be kept in treatment a sufficiently long period of time to bring about lasting changes in their behavior and lifestyles (Friedman and Beschner 1985; Hubbard et al. 1985; Sells and Simpson 1979). As noted before, because of the role of intravenous drug use in the AIDS epidemic, there is an urgent need to eliminate or reduce the sharing of needles among addicts and to educate them in the risks they and their sexual partners face (DesJarlais and Friedman 1988). And with the inclusion of criminally active clients in treatment, there is a need for close supervision (Hubbard, Collins, et al. 1988).

*Retention and Continuity of Treatment*

Because long-term treatment has been shown to be the major predictor of positive outcome, an important means of increasing effectiveness is insuring that clients spend sufficient amounts of time in treatment. However, because many clients drop out of treatment after a few days or at least before they have completed a planned stay, programs should make increased efforts to retain clients. If clients can be retained for at least three months, half can be expected to successfully complete the program.

Increased retention, though desirable, produces a dilemma. The longer a client remains in treatment, the longer another drug abuser must wait to be admitted to the program. One remedy would be to have different levels of services for long-term clients and for newly enrolled clients. A reallocation rather than an expansion of staff and resources may be feasible. Some limited basic services, such as relapse prevention (McAuliffe and Ch'ien 1986; McAuliffe et al. 1985; Sorensen et al. 1987), should be provided to clients who demonstrate that they have been abstinent and productive after a specified length of time. All clients would have access to appropriate levels of counseling and any services necessary to sustain their recovery. Such an approach would help increase treatment effectiveness by directing more resources to intensive services for clients as they enter programs.

Our findings also suggest that greater emphasis be placed on reintegrating clients to society once their addiction is controlled, through meaningful vocational and employment services, posttreatment support groups, and family counseling. Although all drug abuse treatment programs attempt to reduce drug abuse, they may vary in the extent to which they can help to build productive lives. Many programs may not be sufficiently large to include a full range of services, including mental health services, family counseling, and vocational programs. Furthermore, clients may not remain in a single treatment episode for a sufficient period of time to engender the attitudinal and behavioral changes necessary to become abstinent, law-abiding, productive citizens.

A number of recent studies have also pointed to posttreatment experiences such as stressful events and the availability of social resources as critical factors in impeding or sustaining recovery (Billings and Moos 1983; Cronkite and Moos 1980; Finney, Moos, and Mewborn 1980). Though many clients show substantial improvement during treatment, the gains they have made tend to ebb in the months following treatment as supervision, support, and restrictions on behavior decrease. Maintaining those gains is a major challenge confronting treatment programs.

Few clients, however, received any type of continuing services after they left treatment. Although methadone programs reported the availability of such services, commonly referred to as aftercare, only about one-third of the clinic records for former clients indicated that any aftercare was provided. Except for clients in one program, few former residents of therapeutic communities had a record of aftercare services. Aftercare services were not commonly reported in outpatient drug-free program records. Most of the program directors stated that they regard reintegration with society at large as an important and achievable goal of treatment, and aftercare seems essential to the accomplishment of this goal. It appears, though, that few programs are successfully focusing on the key transition between program completion and reentry into the community. The need for transitional and aftercare services should not be neglected.

## Challenges for the Future

The findings in this book should be applicable to the three major publicly funded modalities for the foreseeable future. The basic characteristics of the client population have not changed (NIDA 1988a), and the therapeutic approaches in methadone, residential, and outpatient drug-free programs have become institutionalized. However, major changes in the drug abuse treatment system and in the problems experienced by the client population are occurring. Although the majority of clients in publicly funded programs will continue to be young adult males from poor socioeconomic backgrounds, they are likely to suffer from more complex drug abuse and behavioral problems, which will require new and more intensive therapies. Further, these clients and programs are being joined by a broader array of individuals with the resources to pay for treatment in private settings.

### The Drug-Abusing Population

Over the past decade, large numbers of youth and young adults used an increasingly varied assortment of illicit drugs. But of all the drugs commonly used, cocaine has rapidly become the focus of most concern, and it is now dealt with in all modalities. The admissions of cocaine abusers to publicly funded programs doubled from 40,000 in 1985 to 84,000 in 1987 (Butynski and Canova 1988), and this rate of increase is expected to continue. Cocaine abusers are also seeking treatment in short-term inpatient programs that have traditionally focused on alcohol abuse (Blume 1987). These clients represent a type of abuser who has not previously been treated in the publicly funded system.

Because the funding for public health and social services has been cut back in the past decade, clients now entering treatment may need help for an even greater array and greater severity of problems, particularly psychological problems. It has become clear that the severity of a client's psychological problems affects the outcome of treatment (Rounsaville, Dolinsky, et al. 1987). Those who are free of serious psychological difficulties stand a much better chance of successfully completing treatment. Although our study has provided information about the prevalence of psychological problems among clients, the in-depth psychiatric assessment necessary to address questions about their prevalence and effects has not been undertaken in the publicly funded system.

A major result of the reduced support for drug abuse treatment in the 1980s is the evolution of a two-tiered system. Although treatment is readily available for abusers with health insurance or other resources to pay for services, not even half of those entering treatment in 1979–81 were covered by any type of health insurance and only one in five had private coverage. Because most people seeking treatment are poor, and because publicly funded programs tend to have relatively few openings at any one time, long waiting lists for treatment exist in many communities. The differential access to treatment may affect motivation to enter treatment, as well as the outcome, when a client is eventually admitted. The implications of limited access have been recognized for intravenous drug abusers (Watkins et al. 1988), but the full effect on all types of drug abusers is still unknown.

*The Treatment System*

Concerns have been raised that changes in the organization of the drug abuse treatment system may affect the way services are delivered and may ultimately influence treatment efficiency and effectiveness (D'Aunno and Price 1985). States, rather than the federal government, now fund and administer programs (Tims 1984), and a broad spectrum of private programs has been established (Jaffe 1984). Programs in the traditional modalities are using professionally trained staff (Carroll and Sobell 1986), and treatment is being provided by private physicians (Novick et al. 1988) in a broader variety of medical and mental health institutions outside the traditional modalities. These changes could jeopardize the fundamental orientation toward peer-supported recovery that has characterized community-based treatment (DeLeon 1985, 1986; O'Brien and Biase 1984).

An increased concern for cost containment of publicly delivered services may further threaten the effectiveness of treatment. We have already noted that many publicly funded programs have long waiting lists and limited access to treatment, and some depend on client fees to support services. Cost issues were also raised when fixed costs for an episode of alcohol and drug abuse treatment were proposed in the Medicare system. The example set by Medicare could be followed by other public programs and private insurance policies. The emphasis on the containment of costs raises many concerns about the quality of treatment that may be available in the future (Mezochow et al. 1987). Although longer stays are related to more successful outcomes (DeLeon 1984; Hubbard, Marsden, et al. 1988; Simpson and Sells 1982), cost constraints and client preference for short-term chemical dependency and alcohol treatment programs may pressure traditional programs to consider shorter treatment and more effective aftercare and relapse prevention efforts in place of long-term retention (Tims and Leukefeld 1986).

Even though concern for the effective matching of types of clients and particular treatments has been expressed (Finney and Moos 1986; Glaser 1980; Jaffe 1984; McLellan et al. 1983; Rounsaville, Dolinsky, et al. 1987), there has been little direct research on the issue, particularly for publicly funded programs. The appropriateness of any given type of treatment for a particular client depends on such factors as the effective match between client problems and the attributes of therapists, the goals and therapeutic approaches of particular treatment programs, and the provision of needed ancillary services that foster overall recovery. For example, drawing on the work of McLellan and others, Jaffe (1984) argues that some opioid clients, particularly those with severe psychological problems, do poorly in the confrontational environment of a therapeutic community and do better in methadone maintenance programs. Although the matching issue is a critical one, the question of what treatment works best for what type of client still needs adequate investigation.

*Responses to the Challenges*

During the past decade, in response to declining public support and escalating problems within the client population, many programs have had to innovate to maintain their viability. DeLeon (1986), for example, has described the increasing entrepreneurship of therapeutic communities, and many outpatient programs have turned to client fees to make up for lost public funding (Rosenbaum, Murphy, and Beck 1987).

Pressing clinical problems have also prompted efforts to integrate new elements into therapeutic regimens. Alcohol abuse has been recognized as a major problem in both therapeutic communities (Zweben and Smith 1986) and methadone programs (Gordis 1988; Stimmel et al. 1983), and attempts have been made to accommodate the philosophy and approach of the 12 Steps of Alcoholics Anonymous in methadone programs (Gordis 1988; Obuchowsky and Zweben 1987). New knowledge about treatment for cocaine (Gawin and Ellinwood 1988; Siegel 1985; Smith 1986; Zweben 1986) has been developed and is being implemented in some programs. A critical question is when the therapy for a secondary drug such as alcohol or cocaine should be initiated for particular types of abusers. Differential effects may be obtained with concurrent compared to sequential approaches. Limited current information is available to inform programs about effective approaches to treatment of multiple drug abuse (Wesson et al. 1978) or secondary drugs of abuse.

Other efforts have been made to introduce cost-effective therapies within traditional modalities and in new settings (Ashery 1985). The therapeutic community model has been established in correctional settings for prisoners with drug abuse problems (Wexler 1986; Wexler and Williams 1986). The efforts to obtain knowledge and improve treatment are now being vigorously supported by the National Institute on Drug Abuse through major long-term multimillion-dollar research initiatives. These include grants to demonstrate the effectiveness of new treatment approaches and funds to develop outreach efforts to attract more abusers into treatment as well as to continue the support of basic research. The Anti–Drug Abuse Act of 1988 also mandates the collection of systematic information on clients and services in treatment programs receiving public funds. This renewal of interest and support offers the opportunity to make major advances in our capability to effectively treat drug abuse.

## Development of New Knowledge

While there is no question that treatment works, not enough is known about how and why it works. In general, outcomes have not been linked to the nature of the treatment that clients have received. Variables in the "black box" that is drug abuse treatment need to be better specified and their role in producing positive outcomes better understood (DeLeon 1986; DeLeon and Rosenthal 1979; Meyer 1983; Sells 1979). Much needs to be learned from a careful examination of the reasons for seeking treatment, as well as the readiness or motivation for being in treatment in order to design more appropriate assessments and treatment plans. In addition, a better understanding of how counselors and clients interact could lead to more efficient therapy, as could a greater specification of the social and psychological changes that occur during treatment. More current information is clearly needed about the nature, quality, and quantity of services rendered in the traditional modalities as well as new alternatives for treatment. To increase retention and foster participation in a support system after treatment, further insight is needed into the critical phases of the treatment process and the cognitive or behavioral changes that occur as a client progresses through treatment.

Drug abuse treatment has often been investigated as if it were differentiated only by modality. More detailed analyses of the effectiveness of particular treatment approaches for particular client types are needed. For example, can we reallocate methadone maintenance resources within programs to enroll more clients? How can cocaine abuse be treated within current modalities? In which modalities are nonopioid abusers most effectively treated? Can more intensive services or aftercare be substituted for longer durations of treatment? The nature of elements such as program services, therapeutic approaches, and aftercare associated with effective drug abuse treatment similarly should receive greater attention. Finally, greater recognition should be given to the fact that multiple treatment episodes are often required before treatment has an impact on the lives of drug abusers.

Cost-benefit studies of drug abuse treatment are needed to meet the increasing concerns about cost containment in both the public and private sector. Most current cost-benefit studies are limited to the cost-effectiveness of alcohol abuse treatment and merely calculate the difference between treatment costs and the savings in health care expenditures following treatment (Holder 1985; Jones and Vischi 1979). But to date no study has rigorously assessed all economic benefits from drug abuse treatment. In addition to reduced health costs, the savings earned by changes in factors associated with drug problems such as increased employment and productivity, decreased expenditures on drugs, and decreased intentional and unintentional injuries will need to be considered in the calculations. Further, the impact of drug abuse treatment on the social costs associated with AIDS requires investigation.

These new questions will require the coordination of new comprehensive community-based outcome evaluations with other studies based on controlled experimental designs, as well as detailed case histories of individual programs and clients. A broad research agenda is needed to further clarify and specify factors that may affect the level of posttreatment functioning, such as client backgrounds, the nature of treatment received, and posttreatment experiences. Outcomes should be examined in terms of specific types of clients and approaches rather than simply across major modalities. Although treatment duration and a number of other factors have been shown to be important determinants of treatment outcome, a vital question remains unanswered: How do these factors interact to influence treatment outcome?

The answers to these new questions can build upon the findings from the Treatment Outcome Prospective Study. This research has demonstrated that treatment delivered in the major modalities has been effective and cost-effective and has met the needs of the variety of clients who have participated in publicly funded programs. Future research should investigate the efficacy of new methods to help drug abuse treatment achieve its full potential in reducing this nation's destructive demand for drugs and guiding clients on the road back to fully productive lives.

# Appendix

Table A-1 Number of Clients Interviewed at Admission and Sampled for Follow-up, by Modality and Year of Admission

| | Admission Cohort | | | |
| Modality | 1979 | 1980 | 1981 | Total |
|---|---|---|---|---|
| **Outpatient methadone** | | | | |
| Population at admission = $N$ | 1,135 | 1,563 | 1,486 | 4,184 |
| Sample for follow-up = $(n)$ | (323) | (841) | (375) | (1,539) |
| **Residential** | | | | |
| Population at admission = $N$ | 944 | 929 | 1,018 | 2,891 |
| Sample for follow-up = $(n)$ | (421) | (556) | (305) | (1,282) |
| **Outpatient drug-free** | | | | |
| Population at admission = $N$ | 906 | 1,134 | 874 | 2,914 |
| Sample for follow-up = $(n)$ | (415) | (714) | (320) | (1,449) |
| **Total** | | | | |
| Population at admission = $N$ | 2,985 | 3,626 | 3,378 | 9,989 |
| Sample for follow-up = $(n)$ | (1,159) | (2,111) | (1,000) | (4,270) |

Table A-2  Changes in Drug Abuse, by Modality and Treatment Duration

| | Outpatient Methadone | | Residential | | Outpatient Drug-Free | |
|---|---|---|---|---|---|---|
| | <3 Months | >3 Months | <3 Months | >3 Months | <3 Months | >3 Months |
| | % | % | % | % | % | % |
| **Regular heroin use** | | | | | | |
| 1 year before | 65.0 | 63.5 | 30.5 | 30.9 | 11.5 | 8.6 |
| 3 months in treatment | — | 5.9 | — | 0.3 | — | 3.0 |
| 3-month follow-up | 25.3 | 16.0 | 14.2 | 10.7 | 7.7 | 5.1 |
| 1-year follow-up | 31.2 | 16.7 | 16.8 | 11.5 | 9.1 | 4.9 |
| 2-year follow-up | 21.7 | 14.9 | 7.8 | 13.2 | 4.5 | 4.9 |
| 3- to 5-year follow-up | 24.9 | 17.5 | 12.2 | 11.8 | 5.2 | 4.6 |
| **Regular cocaine use** | | | | | | |
| 1 year before | 30.2 | 26.4 | 29.4 | 27.6 | 17.0 | 12.8 |
| 3 months in treatment | — | 9.4 | — | 0.1 | — | 3.5 |
| 3-month follow-up | 23.2 | 17.4 | 16.5 | 12.9 | 13.6 | 9.0 |
| 1-year follow-up | 19.3 | 17.5 | 19.1 | 15.5 | 10.8 | 8.1 |
| 2-year follow-up | 15.8 | 12.0 | 10.0 | 8.0 | 7.3 | 2.9 |
| 3- to 5-year follow-up | 9.3 | 16.5 | 21.8 | 9.6 | 12.5 | 5.6 |
| **Regular nonmedical psychotherapeutic use** | | | | | | |
| 1 year before | 35.3 | 30.3 | 52.2 | 49.9 | 41.1 | 35.7 |
| 3 months in treatment | — | 12.0 | — | 1.3 | — | 11.8 |
| 3-month follow-up | 24.7 | 26.9 | 29.7 | 16.4 | 27.3 | 18.9 |
| 1-year follow-up | 22.1 | 21.7 | 31.4 | 9.4 | 27.1 | 16.1 |
| 2-year follow-up | 15.3 | 13.1 | 19.6 | 9.4 | 23.5 | 12.0 |
| 3- to 5-year follow-up | 11.4 | 10.2 | 14.9 | 9.3 | 11.9 | 4.4 |
| **Regular marijuana use** | | | | | | |
| 1 year before | 62.4 | 55.0 | 67.1 | 64.4 | 70.9 | 61.5 |
| 3 months in treatment | — | 46.9 | — | 5.1 | — | 46.6 |
| 3-month follow-up | 52.3 | 43.6 | 52.0 | 47.0 | 57.8 | 42.6 |
| 1-year follow-up | 50.1 | 45.6 | 54.4 | 42.0 | 57.5 | 46.0 |
| 2-year follow-up | 40.4 | 44.3 | 48.4 | 42.1 | 45.5 | 38.7 |
| 3- to 5-year follow-up | 33.5 | 36.4 | 38.5 | 38.8 | 45.5 | 31.0 |

Table A-3  Changes in Concomitant Behaviors, by Modality and Treatment Duration

| | Outpatient Methadone | | Residential | | Outpatient Drug-Free | |
|---|---|---|---|---|---|---|
| | <3 Months | >3 Months | <3 Months | >3 Months | <3 Months | >3 Months |
| | % | % | % | % | % | % |
| Serious predatory illegal acts | | | | | | |
| 1 year before | 24.7 | 31.8 | 43.9 | 60.9 | 31.6 | 33.5 |
| 3 months in treatment | — | 9.8 | — | 3.1 | — | 9.4 |
| 3-month follow-up | 24.2 | 18.8 | 34.2 | 25.2 | 23.3 | 11.0 |
| 1-year follow-up | 29.1 | 19.0 | 44.4 | 28.9 | 25.7 | 18.7 |
| 2-year follow-up | 19.3 | 15.2 | 29.4 | 24.0 | 19.2 | 14.5 |
| 3- to 5-year follow-up | 22.8 | 16.2 | 23.9 | 19.8 | 14.8 | 7.6 |
| Worked full time | | | | | | |
| 1 year before | 23.0 | 24.2 | 13.3 | 15.3 | 24.2 | 27.1 |
| 3 months in treatment | — | 25.9 | — | 2.2 | — | 36.0 |
| 3-month follow-up | 27.7 | 16.5 | 23.9 | 35.8 | 33.4 | 38.2 |
| 1-year follow-up | 17.2 | 20.1 | 14.5 | 25.7 | 27.1 | 38.5 |
| 2-year follow-up | 17.8 | 29.3 | 15.2 | 20.9 | 27.4 | 39.4 |
| 3- to 5-year follow-up | 15.1 | 17.7 | 18.2 | 38.7 | 38.3 | 49.7 |
| Heavy alcohol use | | | | | | |
| 1 year before | 29.1 | 25.2 | 43.7 | 35.4 | 38.5 | 33.4 |
| 3 months in treatment | — | 21.2 | — | 2.6 | — | 24.7 |
| 3-month follow-up | 37.0 | 29.9 | 43.2 | 31.0 | 43.7 | 24.9 |
| 1-year follow-up | 29.0 | 23.6 | 38.6 | 30.0 | 37.2 | 28.4 |
| 2-year follow-up | 14.4 | 21.9 | 28.4 | 28.9 | 33.6 | 31.8 |
| 3- to 5-year follow-up | 18.0 | 19.2 | 34.3 | 27.1 | 19.9 | 26.9 |
| Suicidal thoughts or attempts | | | | | | |
| 1 year before | 28.0 | 32.5 | 44.3 | 42.6 | 48.6 | 45.0 |
| 3 months in treatment | — | 12.0 | — | 9.7 | — | 22.2 |
| 3-month follow-up | 17.8 | 10.4 | 21.0 | 10.6 | 29.7 | 14.6 |
| 1-year follow-up | 12.7 | 12.8 | 21.3 | 15.1 | 25.7 | 21.3 |
| 2-year follow-up | 8.1 | 15.3 | 24.1 | 9.9 | 21.6 | 17.4 |
| 3- to 5-year follow-up | 6.5 | 14.6 | 14.1 | 13.9 | 16.5 | 17.3 |
| Treatment admissions | | | | | | |
| 1 year before | 51.4 | 46.5 | 37.1 | 33.8 | 18.2 | 18.6 |
| 3 months in treatment | NA | NA | NA | NA | NA | NA |
| 3-month follow-up | 30.3 | 35.5 | 21.6 | 21.2 | 19.5 | 15.2 |
| 1-year follow-up | 37.7 | 58.7 | 28.7 | 34.6 | 24.8 | 18.4 |
| 2-year follow-up | 34.9 | 47.2 | 17.6 | 25.0 | 19.8 | 11.2 |
| 3- to 5-year follow-up | 46.2 | 56.5 | 14.9 | 19.2 | 19.9 | 18.1 |

Table A-4  Odds Ratios for Treatment Duration for Posttreatment Outcomes in the First Year after Methadone Treatment ($n=835$)

| Outcome | (Comparison Group: Less Than 1 Week) ($n=86$) | 1–13 Weeks ($n=161$) | 14–52 Weeks ($n=268$) | More Than 52 Weeks and Discharged ($n=137$) | Long-term Maintenance ($n=183$) |
|---|---|---|---|---|---|
| Regular heroin use | (1.00) | 1.16 | .83 | .47[a] | .23[c] |
| Regular cocaine use | (1.00) | 1.20 | 1.05 | .59 | 1.11 |
| Regular marijuana use | (1.00) | .62 | .82 | .59 | .85 |
| Regular nonmedical psychotherapeutic use | (1.00) | .82 | 1.12 | .60 | .78 |
| Regular consumption of 5 or more drinks in one sitting | (1.00) | .81 | .78 | .71 | .46[b] |
| Suicidal thoughts or attempts | (1.00) | 1.93 | 1.83 | 1.51 | 1.39 |
| Involvement in predatory illegal acts | (1.00) | .81 | .81 | .59 | .36[c] |
| Full-time employment | (1.00) | .70 | 1.13 | 1.74 | 1.44 |

a. $p < .05$
b. $p < .01$
c. $p < .001$

Table A-5  Odds Ratios for Treatment Duration for Posttreatment
Outcomes in the First Year after Residential Treatment ($n=731$)

| Outcome | Time in Treatment | | | | |
| --- | --- | --- | --- | --- | --- |
| | (Comparison Group: Less Than 1 Week) ($n=60$) | 1–13 Weeks ($n=325$) | 14–26 Weeks ($n=137$) | 27–52 Weeks ($n=95$) | More Than 52 Weeks ($n=114$) |
| Regular heroin use | (1.00) | .69 | .43 | .52 | .28[a] |
| Regular cocaine use | (1.00) | .98 | 1.04 | .85 | .38 |
| Regular marijuana use | (1.00) | 1.16 | 1.04 | .56 | .40[b] |
| Regular nonmedical psychotherapeutic use | (1.00) | 1.32 | 1.02 | .43 | .30[b] |
| Regular consumption of 5 or more drinks in one sitting | (1.00) | 1.14 | .82 | .96 | .89 |
| Suicidal thoughts or attempts | (1.00) | 1.28 | .93 | 1.09 | .44 |
| Involvement in predatory illegal acts | (1.00) | 1.07 | .61 | .43[a] | .29[c] |
| Full-time employment | (1.00) | .57 | .87 | .90 | 2.65[b] |

a. $p<.05$
b. $p<.01$
c. $p<.001$

Table A-6  Odds Ratios for Treatment Duration for Posttreatment
Outcomes in the First Year after Outpatient Drug-Free Treatment ($n=854$)

| Outcome | Time in Treatment | | | |
|---|---|---|---|---|
| | (Comparison Group: Less Than 1 Week) ($n=183$) | 1–13 Weeks ($n=344$) | 14–26 Weeks ($n=165$) | More Than 26 Weeks ($n=162$) |
| Regular heroin use | (1.00) | 1.03 | 1.43 | .35 |
| Regular cocaine use | (1.00) | 1.14 | 1.15 | .76 |
| Regular marijuana use | (1.00) | .98 | .58[a] | .70 |
| Regular nonmedical psychotherapeutic use | (1.00) | .83 | .69 | .44[a] |
| Regular consumption of 5 or more drinks in one sitting | (1.00) | 1.06 | .80 | .69 |
| Suicidal thoughts or attempts | (1.00) | 1.07 | 1.15 | .67 |
| Involvement in predatory illegal acts | (1.00) | .73 | .63[a] | .47[b] |
| Full-time employment | (1.00) | .90 | 1.35 | 1.95[a] |

a. $p < .05$
b. $p < .01$

184

# References

Aiken, Leona S., Leonard S. LoSciuto, Mary Ann Ausetts, and Barry S. Brown. 1984. Paraprofessional versus professional drug counselors: The progress of clients in treatment. *The International Journal of the Addictions* 19:383–401.

Allison, Margaret, and Robert L. Hubbard. 1985. Drug abuse treatment process: A review of the literature. *International Journal of the Addictions* 20:1321–45.

Allison, Margaret, Robert L. Hubbard, and Harold M. Ginzburg. 1985. *Indicators of suicide and depression among drug abusers.* Treatment Research Monograph. Rockville, Md.: National Institute on Drug Abuse. DHHS Publication No. ADM 85-1411.

Allison, Margaret, Robert L. Hubbard, Harold M. Ginzburg, and J. Valley Rachal. 1986. Validation of a three-item depression indicator scale for drug abuse clients. *Hospital and Community Psychiatry* 37:738–40.

Allison, Margaret, Robert L. Hubbard, and J. Valley Rachal. 1985. *Treatment process in methadone, residential, and outpatient drug free programs.* Treatment Research Monograph. Rockville, Md.: National Institute on Drug Abuse. DHHS Publication No. ADM 85-1388.

Anglin, M. Douglas, Yih-ing Hser, and Mary W. Booth. 1987. Sex differences in addict careers: Treatment. *American Journal of Drug and Alcohol Abuse* 13:253–80.

Armor, David J., J. Michael Polich, and Harold B. Stambul. 1978. *Alcoholism and treatment.* New York: John Wiley.

Ashery, Rebecca S., ed. 1985. *Progress in the development of cost-effective treatment for drug abusers.* Research Monograph Series 58. Rockville, Md.: National Institute on Drug Abuse. DHHS Publication No. ADM 85-1401.

Austin, Gregory A., Bruce D. Johnson, Eleanor E. Carroll, and Daniel J. Lettieri, eds. 1977. *Drugs and minorities.* Research Issues 21. Rockville, Md.: National Institute on Drug Abuse. DHEW Publication No. ADM 78-507.

Babst, Dean V., Carl D. Chambers, and Alan Warner. 1971. Patient characteristics associated with retention in a methadone maintenance program. *British Journal of Addiction* 66:195–204.

Bale, Richard N., William W. Van Stone, John M. Kuldau, Thomas M. J. Engelsing, Robert M. Elashoff, and Vincent P. Zarcone. 1980. Therapeutic communities vs. methadone maintenance. A prospective controlled study of narcotic addiction treatment: Design and one year followup results. *Archives of General Psychiatry* 37:179–93.

Ball, John C. 1967. The reliability and validity of interview data obtained from 59 narcotic drug addicts. *American Journal of Sociology* 72:650–54.

Ball, John C., and Eric Corty. 1988. Basic issues pertaining to the effectiveness of methadone maintenance treatment. In Carl G. Leukefeld and Frank M. Tims, eds., *Compulsory treatment of drug abuse: Research and clinical practice*. Research Monograph Series 86. Rockville, Md.: National Institute on Drug Abuse. DHHS Publication No. ADM 88-1578.

Ball, John C., Eric Corty, C. Patrick Myers, Henrietta Bond, Anthony Tommasello, Joanne Golden, and Teri Baker. 1987. *Patient characteristics, services provided and treatment outcome in methadone maintenance programs in three cities, 1985 and 1986*. Baltimore, Md.: The University of Maryland, School of Medicine.

Ball, John C., Eric Corty, C. Patrick Myers, and Anthony Tommasello. 1988. *The reduction of intravenous heroin use, non-opiate abuse and crime during methadone maintenance treatment: Further findings*. Research Monograph Series 81. Rockville, Md.: National Institute on Drug Abuse. DHHS Publication No. ADM 88-1564.

Ball, John C., W. Robert Lange, C. Patrick Myers, and Samuel R. Friedman. 1988. Reducing the risk of AIDS through methadone maintenance treatment. *Journal of Health and Social Behavior* 29:214–26.

Ball, John C., Lawrence Rosen, John A. Flueck, and David N. Nurco. 1981. The criminality of heroin addicts when addicted and when off opiates. In James A. Inciardi, ed., *Drugs-Crime Connection*. Beverly Hills, Calif.: Sage Publications, 39–65.

Baltes, Paul B. 1968. Longitudinal and cross-sectional sequences in the study of age and generation effects. *Human Development* 11:147–71.

Barr, Harriet L., and Arie Cohen. 1979. *The problem-drinking drug addict*. Services Research Reports and Monograph Series. Rockville, Md.: National Institute on Drug Abuse. DHEW Publication No. ADM 79-893.

Barr, Harriet L., Donald J. Ottenberg, and Alvin Rosen. 1973. Two-year follow-up study of 724 drug addicts and alcoholics treated together in an abstinence therapeutic community. *Proceedings of the Fifth National Conference on Methadone Treatment*. Vol. 1. New York: National Association for the Prevention of Addiction to Narcotics, 296–305.

Belenko, Steven. 1979. Alcohol abuse by heroin addicts: Review of research findings and issues. *International Journal of the Addictions* 14:965–75.

Benvenuto, John, and Peter G. Bourne. 1975. The federal polydrug abuse project: Initial report. *Journal of Psychedelic Drugs* 7:115–20.

Berk, Richard A., Robert F. Boruch, David L. Chambers, Peter H. Rossi, and Ann D. Witte. 1987. Social policy experimentation: A position paper. In C. S. Cordray and Mark Lipsey, eds., *Evaluation Studies Review Annual*. Vol. 11. Beverly Hills, Calif.: Sage, 630–72.

Beschner, George M., Beth G. Reed, and Josette Mondanaro. 1981. *Treatment services for drug dependent women*. Vol. 1. Treatment Research Monograph Series. Rockville, Md.: National Institute on Drug Abuse.

Beschner, George M., and Peggy Thompson. 1981. *Women and drug abuse treatment: Needs and services*. Services Research Monograph. Washington, D.C.: U.S. Government Printing Office. DHHS Publication No. ADM 81-1057.

Bihari, Bernard. 1973. Alcoholism in MMTP patients: Etiological factors and treatment approaches. *Proceedings of the Fifth National Conference on Methadone Treatment.* Vol. 1. New York: National Association for the Prevention of Addiction to Narcotics, 288–95.

Billings, Ann G., and Rudolf H. Moos. 1983. Psychosocial processes of recovery among alcoholics and their families: Implications for clinicians and program evaluators. *Addictive Behaviors* 8:205–18.

Blume, Sheila B. 1987. Alcohol problems in cocaine abusers. In Arnold, M. Washton and Mark S. Gold, eds., *Cocaine: A Clinician's Handbook.* New York: Guilford, 202–7.

Bonito, Arthur M., David N. Nurco, and John W. Shaffer. 1976. The veridicality of addicts' self-reports in social research. *International Journal of the Addictions* 11:719–24.

Bookbinder, S. M. 1975. Educational goals and schooling in a therapeutic community. *Harvard Educational Review* 45:71–94.

Bourne, Peter G., and Ann S. Ramsey. 1975. The therapeutic community phenomenon. *Journal of Psychedelic Drugs* 7:203–7.

Bracy, Steven A., and D. Dwayne Simpson. 1982–83. Status of opioid addicts 5 years after admission to drug abuse treatment. *American Journal of Drug and Alcohol Abuse* 9:115–27.

Braucht, G. Nicholas, Michael W. Kirby, and G. James Berry. 1978. Psychological correlates of empirical types of multiple drug abusers. *Journal of Consulting and Clinical Psychology* 46:1463–75.

Bray, Robert M., William E. Schlenger, S. Gail Craddock, Robert L. Hubbard, and J. Valley Rachal. 1982. *Approaches to the assessment of drug use in the Treatment Outcome Prospective Study* (RTI/1901/01-05S). Research Triangle Park, N.C.: Research Triangle Institute.

Brewington, Vincent, Lorinda Arella, Sherry Deren, and Joan Randell. 1987. Obstacles to the utilization of vocational services: An analysis of the literature. *The International Journal of the Addictions* 22:1091–118.

Brill, Leon. 1981. *The clinical treatment of substance abusers.* New York: The Free Press.

Brook, Robert C., and Paul C. Whitehead. 1980. *Drug-free therapeutic community.* New York: Human Sciences Press.

Brown, Barry S., ed. 1979. *Addicts and aftercare: Community integration of the former drug user.* Sage Annual Reviews of Drug and Alcohol Abuse. Vol. 3. Beverly Hills, Calif.: Sage.

Brown, Barry S., and Rebecca S. Ashery. 1979. Aftercare in drug abuse programming. In Robert L. DuPont, Avram Goldstein, and John O'Donnell, eds., *Handbook on drug abuse.* Washington, D.C.: U.S. Government Printing Office, 165–73.

Brown, Barry S., D. R. Jansen, and G. J. Benn. 1975. Changes in attitudes toward methadone. *Archives of General Psychiatry* 32:214–18.

Brown, Barry S., Nicholas J. Kozel, Marilyn B. Meyers, and Robert L. DuPont. 1973. Use of alcohol by addict and nonaddict populations. *American Journal of Psychiatry* 130:599–601.

Brown, Barry S., and Raymond F. Thompson. 1973. Impact of straight and formerly addicted counselors on client functioning. *Proceedings of the Fifth*

*National Conference on Methadone Treatment*. Vol. 1. New York: National Association for the Prevention of Addiction to Narcotics, 228–34.

———. 1975–76. The effectiveness of formerly addicted and nonaddicted counselors on client functioning. *Drug Forum* 5:123–29.

Brown, Barry S., John K. Watters, Austin S. Iglehart, and Carl Akins. 1982–83. Methadone maintenance dosage levels and program retention. *American Journal of Drug and Alcohol Abuse* 9:129–39.

Burt Associates. 1977. *Drug treatment in New York City and Washington, DC: Followup studies*. Rockville, Md.: National Institute on Drug Abuse.

Butynski, William, and Diane Canova. 1988. *An Analysis of State Alcohol and Drug Abuse: Profile Data*. Washington, D.C.: National Association of State Alcohol and Drug Abuse Directors.

Campbell, Donald T., and Julian C. Stanley. 1963. *Experimental and quasi-experimental designs for research*. Chicago, Ill.: Rand McNally College Publishing Company.

Caplovitz, David. 1976. *The working addict*. New York: City College of New York.

Carroll, Jerome F. X., and Bernard S. Sobel. 1986. Integrating mental health personnel and practices into a therapeutic community. In George De Leon and James T. Ziegenfuss, Jr., eds., *Therapeutic Communities for Addictions: Readings in theory, research and practice*. Springfield, Ill.: Charles C. Thomas, 209–26.

Chambers, Carl D. 1974. Some epidemiological considerations of onset of opiate use in the United States. In Eric Josephson and Eleanor E. Carroll, eds., *Drug use: Epidemiological and sociological approaches*. Washington, D.C.: Hemisphere Publishing Corp., 65–82.

Chambers, Carl D., and Arthur D. Moffett. 1969. *Drug addiction in the Commonwealth of Kentucky*. Lexington, Ky.: National Institute of Mental Health Clinical Research Center.

Chick, J., N. Kreitman, and Martin Plant. 1981. Saving face? Survey respondents who claim their last week's drink was atypical. *Drug and Alcohol Dependence* 7:625–72.

Clark, William, and Lorraine Midanik. 1982. Alcohol use and alcohol problems among U.S. adults: Results of the 1979 national survey. *Alcohol and Health*, Monograph 1. Rockville, Md.: National Institute on Drug Abuse, 3–52. DHHS Publication No. ADM 82-1190.

Clayton, Richard R. 1985. Cocaine use in the United States: In a blizzard or just being snowed? In Nicholas J. Kozel and Edgar H. Adams, eds., *Cocaine use in America: Epidemiological and clinical perspectives*. Research Monograph 61. Rockville, Md.: National Institute on Drug Abuse, 8–34. DHHS Publication No. ADM 85-1414.

———. 1987. The nature and extent of drug abuse. *Drug Abuse and Drug Abuse Research: The Second Triennial Report to Congress from the Secretary, Department of Health and Human Services*. Rockville, Md.: National Institute on Drug Abuse, 13–31. DHHS Publication No. ADM 87-1486.

Cole, Steven G., and Lawrence R. James. 1975. A revised treatment typology based on the DARP. *American Journal of Drug and Alcohol Abuse* 2:37–49.

Collins, James J., and Margaret Allison. 1983. Legal coercion and retention in drug abuse treatment. *Hospital and Community Psychiatry* 34:1145–49.

Collins, James J., Henrick J. Harwood, Mary Ellen Marsden, Robert L. Hubbard, Susan L. Bailey, J. Valley Rachal, and Elizabeth R. Cavanaugh. 1987. *Crime control and economic benefits of drug abuse treatment.* Summary report for the National Institute of Justice. Research Triangle Park, N.C.: Research Triangle Institute.

Collins, James J., Robert L. Hubbard, Elizabeth R. Cavanaugh, and J. Valley Rachal. 1983. *Criminal behavior before and during drug treatment: 1979–1981 admission cohorts.* RTI/1901/01-03S. Research Triangle Park, N.C.: Research Triangle Institute.

Collins, James J., Robert L. Hubbard, and J. Valley Rachal. 1985. Expensive drug use and illegal income: A test of explanatory hypotheses. *Criminology: An Interdisciplinary Journal* 23:743–64.

Collins, James J., Robert L. Hubbard, J. Valley Rachal, and Elizabeth Cavanaugh. 1988. Effects of legal coercion on drug abuse treatment. In M.D. Anglin, ed., *Compulsory treatment of opiate dependence.* New York: Haworth Press.

Collins, James J., Robert L. Hubbard, J. Valley Rachal, Elizabeth R. Cavanaugh, and S. Gail Craddock. 1982. *Criminal justice clients in drug treatment.* RTI/1901/01-02S. Research Triangle Park, N.C.: Research Triangle Institute.

Collins, James J., J. Valley Rachal, Robert L. Hubbard, Elizabeth R. Cavanaugh, S. Gail Craddock, and Patricia L. Kristiansen. 1982. *Criminality in a drug treatment sample: Measurement issues and initial findings.* RTI/1901/01-07S. Research Triangle Park, N.C.: Research Triangle Institute.

Cook, C. C. H. 1988. The Minnesota model in the management of drug and alcohol dependency: Miracle, method, or myth? Part I. The philosophy and the programme. *British Journal of Addiction* 83:625–34.

Cook, Thomas D., and Donald T. Campbell. 1979. *Quasi-experimentation: Design and analysis issues for field settings.* Chicago, Ill.: Rand McNally.

Cooper, James R., Fred Altman, Barry S. Brown, and Dorynne Czechowicz, eds. 1983. *Research on the treatment of narcotic addiction: State of the art.* Research Monograph Series. Rockville, Md.: National Institute on Drug Abuse. DHHS Publication No. ADM 83-1281.

Corty, Eric, and John C. Ball. 1987. Admissions to methadone maintenance: Comparisons between programs and implications for treatment. *Journal of Substance Abuse Treatment* 4:181–87.

Coulson, Grant. 1975–76. Considerations for improving the effectiveness of the therapeutic community approach in the rehabilitation of drug abusers. *Drug Forum* 5:95–113.

Courtwright, David T. 1982. *Dark Paradise.* Cambridge, Mass.: Harvard University Press.

Cox, Thomas J., and Bill Longwell. 1974. Reliability of interview data concerning current heroin use from heroin addicts on methadone. *International Journal of the Addictions* 9:161–65.

Craddock, S. Gail, Robert M. Bray, and Robert L. Hubbard. 1985. *Drug use before and during drug abuse treatment: 1979–1981 TOPS admission cohorts.* Treatment Research Monograph. Rockville, Md.: National Institute on Drug Abuse. DHHS Publication No. ADM 85-1387.

Cronkite, Ruth C., and Rudolf H. Moos. 1980. Determinants of the posttreatment functioning of alcoholic patients: A conceptual framework. *Journal of Consulting and Clinical Psychology* 48:305–16.

Cushman, Paul. 1977. Ten years of methadone maintenance treatment: Some clinical observations. *American Journal of Drug and Alcohol Abuse* 4:543–53.

Cuskey, Walter R., J. Ipsen, and T. Premkumar. 1973. An inquiry in the nature of changes in behavior among drug users in treatment. In *Second Report of the National Commission on Marihuana and Drug Abuse.* Appendix. Washington, D.C.: U.S. Government Printing Office.

D'Amanda, Christopher D. 1983. Program policies and procedures associated with treatment outcome. In James R. Cooper, Fred Altman, Barry S. Brown, and Dorynne Czechowicz, eds., *Research on the treatment of narcotic addiction: State of the art.* Treatment Research Monograph. Washington, D.C.: U.S. Government Printing Office, 637–79. DHHS Publication No. ADM 83-1281.

D'Aunno, Thomas, and Richard H. Price. 1985. Organizational adaptation to changing environments: Community mental health and drug abuse services. *American Behavioral Scientist* 28:669–83.

Day, Noel A., Amanda Houston-Hamilton, James Deslondes, and Mary Nelson. 1988. Potential for HIV dissemination by a cohort of black intravenous drug users. *Journal of Psychoactive Drugs* 20:179–226.

Deitch, David A., and Joan E. Zweben. 1976. The impact of social change on treating adolescents in therapeutic communities. *Journal of Psychedelic Drugs* 8:199–208.

DeLeon, George. 1974. Phoenix House: Psychopathological signs among male and female drug-free residents. *Addictive Diseases* 1:135–51.

———. 1984. *The therapeutic community: Study of effectiveness—social and psychological adjustment of 400 dropouts and 100 graduates from the Phoenix House Therapeutic Community.* Services Research Monograph. Rockville, Md.: National Institute on Drug Abuse. DHHS Publication No. ADM 84-1286.

———. 1985. The therapeutic community: Status and evolution. *International Journal of the Addictions* 20:823–44.

———. 1986. The therapeutic community: Looking ahead. In George DeLeon and James T. Ziegenfuss, Jr., eds., *Therapeutic communities for addictions: Readings in theory, research and practice.* Springfield, Ill.: Charles C. Thomas, 185–89.

DeLeon, George, and George M. Beschner, eds. 1976. *The therapeutic community. Proceedings of Therapeutic Communities of America Planning Conference.* Services Research Report. Rockville, Md.: National Institute on Drug Abuse. DHEW Publication No. ADM 77-464.

DeLeon, George, and Mitchell Rosenthal. 1979. Therapeutic communities. In Robert L. DuPont, Avram Goldstein, and John O'Donnell, eds., *Handbook on drug abuse.* Washington, D.C.: U.S. Government Printing Office, 39–47.

Densen-Gerber, Judianne. 1972. *We mainline dreams: The Odyssey House story.* Garden City, N.Y.: Doubleday.

DesJarlais, Don C., and Samuel R. Friedman. 1988. The psychology of preventing AIDS among intravenous drug users: A social learning conceptualization. *American Psychologist* 43:865-70.

DesJarlais, Don C., and Gopal S. Uppal. 1980. Heroin activity in New York City, 1970-1978. *American Journal of Drug and Alcohol Abuse* 7:335-46.

Dole, Vincent P., and Herman Joseph. 1978. Long-term outcome of patients treated with methadone maintenance. *Annals of the New York Academy of Sciences* 311:181-89.

Dole, Vincent P., Francis Foldes, Harold Trigg, J. Waymond Robinson, and Saul Blatman. 1971. Methadone poisoning. *New York State Journal of Medicine* 71:541-43.

Dole, Vincent P., and Marie E. Nyswander. 1965. A medical treatment for diacetyl-morphine (heroin) addiction. *Journal of the American Medical Association* 193:80-84.

Dole, Vincent P., Marie E. Nyswander, and Alan Warner. 1968. Successful treatment of 750 criminal addicts. *Journal of the American Medical Association* 206:2708-11.

Dorus, Walter, and Edward C. Senay. 1980. Depression, demographic dimensions, and drug abuse. *American Journal of Psychiatry* 137:699-704.

Duncan, David F. 1975. The acquisition, maintenance and treatment of polydrug dependence: A public health model. *Journal of Psychedelic Drugs* 7:209-13.

Dunham, R. G., and A. L. Mauss. 1982. Reluctant referrals: The effectiveness of legal coercion in outpatient treatment for problem drinkers. *Journal of Drug Issues* 12:5-20.

DuPont, Robert L. 1972. Heroin addiction treatment and crime reduction. *American Journal of Psychiatry* 128:856-60.

Eckerman, William C., J. Valley Rachal, Robert L. Hubbard, and W. Kenneth Poole. 1976. Methodological issues in identifying drug users. In *Drug use and crime: Report of the Panel on Drug Use and Criminal Behavior.* Appendix. Research Triangle Park, N.C.: Research Triangle Institute.

Espada, Frank. 1979. The drug abuse industry and the minority communities: Time for change. In Robert L. DuPont, Avram Goldstein, and John O'Donnell, eds., *Handbook on drug abuse.* Washington, D.C.: U.S. Government Printing Office, 293-300.

Finnegan, Loretta P. 1979. Women in treatment. In Robert L. DuPont, Avram Goldstein, and John O'Donnell, eds., *Handbook on drug abuse.* Washington, D.C.: U.S. Government Printing Office, 121-31.

Finney, John W., and Rudolf H. Moos. 1986. Matching patients with treatments: Conceptual and methodological issues. *Journal of Studies on Alcohol* 47:122-34.

Finney, John W., Rudolf H. Moos, and C. R. Mewborn. 1980. Posttreatment experiences and treatment outcome of alcoholic patients six months and two years after hospitalization. *Journal of Consulting and Clinical Psychology* 48:17-29.

Frederick, C. J., H. L. P. Resnick, and B. J. Wittlin. 1973. Self-destructive aspects of hard core addiction. *Archives of General Psychiatry* 28:579–85.

Friedman, Alfred S., and George M. Beschner, eds. 1985. *Treatment services for adolescent substance abusers.* Treatment Research Monograph. Rockville, Md.: National Institute on Drug Abuse. DHHS Publication No. ADM 85-1342.

Friedman, S. B., G. L. Horvat, and R. B. Levinson. 1982. The Narcotic Addict Rehabilitation Act: Its impact on federal prisons. *Contemporary Drug Problems* 11:101–10.

Gandossy, Robert P., Jay R. Williams, Jo Cohen, and Henrick J. Harwood. 1980. *Drugs and crime. A survey and analysis of the literature.* Washington, D.C.: U.S. Government Printing Office.

Gawin, Frank H., and Everett H. Ellinwood, Jr. 1988. Medical progress. Cocaine and other stimulants: Action, abuse, and treatment. *The New England Journal of Medicine* 318:1173–82.

Gawin, Frank H., and Herbert D. Kleber. 1985. Cocaine use in a treatment population: Patterns and diagnostic distinctions. In Nicholas J. Kozel and Edgar H. Adams, eds., *Cocaine use in America: Epidemiological and clinical perspectives.* Research Monograph 61. Rockville, Md.: National Institute on Drug Abuse, 182–92. DHHS Publication No. ADM 85-1414.

———. 1986. Abstinence symptomatology and psychiatric diagnosis in cocaine abusers. *Archives of General Psychiatry* 43:107–13.

Gearing, Frances R. 1972. Methadone maintenance: Six years later. *Contemporary Drug Problems* 1:191–206.

Ginzburg, Harold M. 1984. Intravenous drug users and the Acquired Immune Deficiency Syndrome. *Public Health Reports* 99:206–12.

Glaser, Frederick B. 1974. Some historical aspects of the drug-free therapeutic community. *American Journal of Drug and Alcohol Abuse* 1:37–52.

———. 1980. Anybody got a match? Treatment research and the matching hypothesis. In G. Edwards and M. Grant, eds., *Alcoholism treatment in transition.* Baltimore, Md.: University Park Press, 178–96.

Glasscote, Raymond M., James N. Sussex, Jerome H. Jaffe, John C. Ball, and Leon Brill. 1972. *The Treatment of Drug Abuse.* Washington, D.C.: American Psychiatric Association.

Gold, Ron, and Lois R. Chatham. 1973. *Characteristics of NARA patients in aftercare during June 1971.* Washington, D.C.: National Institute of Mental Health.

Goldstein, Avram, and Barbara A. Judson. 1983. Critique of William A. Hargreaves. Methadone dose and duration for maintenance treatment. In James R. Cooper, Fred Altman, Barry S. Brown, and Dorynne Czechowicz, eds., *Research on the treatment of narcotic addiction: State of the art.* Treatment Research Monograph. Washington, D.C.: U.S. Government Printing Office, 80–91. DHHS Publication No. ADM 83-1281.

Gordis, Enoch. 1988. Methadone maintenance and patients in alcoholism treatment. *Alcohol Alert.* Rockville, Md.: National Institute on Alcoholism and Alcohol Abuse, August.

Gorsuch, R. L., M. Abbamonte, and Saul B. Sells. 1976. Evaluation of treatments for drug users in the DARP: 1971–1972 admissions. In Saul B. Sells and D. Dwayne Simpson, eds., *The effectiveness of drug abuse treatment.* Vol. 4. *Evaluation of treatment outcomes for the 1971–1972 admission cohort.* Cambridge, Mass.: Ballinger, 10–251.

Graff, Harold, and John C. Ball. 1976. The methadone clinic: Function and philosophy. *International Journal of Social Psychiatry* 22:140–46.

Greenberg, Karen M., and Barry S. Brown. 1984. Agency director/staff views of the changing nature of drug abuse and drug abuse treatment. *Clinical Research Notes.* Rockville, Md.: National Institute on Drug Abuse, 10–12, February.

Hall, Sharon M. 1983. Methadone treatment: A review of the research findings. In James R. Cooper, Fred Altman, Barry S. Brown, and Dorynne Czechowicz, eds., *Research on the treatment of narcotic addiction: State of the art.* Treatment Research Monograph. Washington, D.C.: U.S. Government Printing Office, 575–632. DHHS Publication No. ADM 83-1281.

———. 1984. Clinical trials in drug treatment: Methodology. In Frank M. Tims and Jaqueline P. Ludford, eds., *Drug abuse treatment evaluation: Strategies, progress, and prospects.* Research Monograph 51. Rockville, Md.: National Institute on Drug Abuse.

Hargreaves, William A. 1983. Methadone dosage and duration for maintenance treatment. In James R. Cooper, Fred Altman, Barry S. Brown, and Dorynne Czechowicz, eds., *Research on the treatment of narcotic addiction: State of the art.* Treatment Research Monograph. Washington, D.C.: U.S. Government Printing Office, 19–79. DHHS Publication No. ADM 83-1281.

Harrell, Frank. 1980. The LOGIST procedure. In *SAS supplementary library user's guide.* 1980 ed. Cary, N.C.: SAS Institute.

Harris, Rachal, Margaret W. Lynn, and Kathleen I. Hunter. 1979. Suicide attempts among drug abusers. *Suicide and Life Threatening Behavior* 9:25–32.

Harwood, Henrick J., James J. Collins, Robert L. Hubbard, Mary Ellen Marsden, and J. Valley Rachal. 1987. The costs of crime and benefits of drug abuse treatment: A cost benefit analysis. Report submitted to the National Institute of Justice. Research Triangle Park, N.C.: Research Triangle Institute.

Harwood, Henrick J., Robert L. Hubbard, James J. Collins, and J. Valley Rachal. 1988. The costs of crime and the benefits of drug abuse treatment: A cost-benefit analysis using TOPS data. In Carl G. Leukefeld and Frank M. Tims, eds., *Compulsory treatment of drug abuse: Research and clinical practice.* Research Monograph Series 86. Rockville, Md.: National Institute on Drug Abuse.

Harwood, Henrick J., Diane M. Napolitano, Patricia L. Kristiansen, and James J. Collins. 1984. *Economic costs to society of alcohol and drug abuse and mental illness: 1980.* RTI/2734/00-01FR. Research Triangle Park, N.C.: Research Triangle Institute.

Harwood, Henrick J., J. Valley Rachal, and Elizabeth Cavanaugh. 1985. Length of stay in treatment for alcohol abuse and alcoholism: National estimates for short term hospitals, 1983. Report submitted to National Institute on Alcohol Abuse and Alcoholism. Research Triangle Park, N.C.: Research Triangle Institute.

Havassy, Barbara E., and Sharon Hall. 1981. Efficacy of urine monitoring in methadone maintenance. *American Journal of Psychiatry* 138:1497–1500.

Havassy, Barbara E., and William A. Hargreaves. 1979. Self-regulation of dose in methadone maintenance with contingent privileges. *Journal of Addictive Behaviors* 4:31–38.

Havassy, Barbara E., and Jeanne M. Tschann. 1983. Client initiative, inertia, and demographics: More powerful than treatment interventions in methadone maintenance. *International Journal of the Addictions* 18:617–31.

Helfrich, Antoinette Anker, Thomas J. Crowley, Carol A. Atkinson, and Robin Dee Post. 1983. A clinical profile of 136 cocaine abusers. In Louis S. Harris, ed., *Problems of drug dependence 1982*. Research Monograph 43. Rockville, Md.: National Institute on Drug Abuse, 343–50.

Holder, Harold D. 1985. *Alcoholism treatment and health care utilization and costs: Potential for "affected" reductions.* Chapel Hill, N.C.: The Human Ecology Institute.

Holland, Sherry. 1982a. *Evaluating community-based treatment programs: A model for strengthening inferences about effectiveness.* Chicago: Gateway Houses.

———. 1982b. *Residential drug-free programs for substance abusers: The effect of planned duration on treatment.* Chicago: Gateway Houses.

———. 1986. Measuring process in drug abuse treatment research. In George DeLeon and James T. Ziegenfuss, Jr., eds., *Therapeutic communities for addictions: Readings in theory, research and practice.* Springfield, Ill.: Charles C. Thomas, 169–81.

Hubbard, Robert L. 1976. A preliminary comparison of self-reported job history with social security administration records. *Proceedings of the American Statistical Association, 1975.* Washington, D.C.: American Statistical Association, 484–87.

Hubbard, Robert L., Robert M. Bray, Elizabeth R. Cavanaugh, S. Gail Craddock, J. Valley Rachal, James J. Collins, and Margaret Allison. 1986. *Drug abuse treatment client characteristics and pretreatment behavior in 1979–1981 TOPS admission cohorts.* Treatment Research Monograph. Rockville, Md.: National Institute on Drug Abuse. DHHS Publication No. ADM 86-1480.

Hubbard, Robert L., Robert M. Bray, S. Gail Craddock, Elizabeth R. Cavanaugh, William E. Schlenger, and J. Valley Rachal. 1986. *Issues in the assessment of multiple drug use among drug treatment clients.* Research Monograph Series 68. Rockville, Md.: National Institute on Drug Abuse. DHHS Publication No. ADM 86-1453.

Hubbard, Robert L., Elizabeth R. Cavanaugh, J. Valley Rachal, and Harold M. Ginzburg. 1985. Characteristics, behaviors, and outcomes for youth in the TOPS. In Alfred S. Friedman and George Beschner, eds., *Treatment services for adolescent substance abusers.* Research Monograph Series. Rockville, Md.: National Institute on Drug Abuse. DHHS Publication No. ADM 85-1342.

Hubbard, Robert L., James J. Collins, Margaret Allison, Elizabeth R. Cavanaugh, and J. Valley Rachal. 1982. Validity of self reports of illegal activities and arrests by drug treatment clients. *Proceedings of the American*

*Statistical Association Meeting, 1981.* Washington, D.C.: American Statistical Association, 329–34.

Hubbard, Robert L., James J. Collins, J. Valley Rachal, and Elizabeth R. Cavanaugh. 1988. The criminal justice client in drug abuse treatment. In Carl G. Leukefeld and Frank M. Tims, eds., *Compulsory treatment of drug abuse: Research and clinical practice.* Research Monograph Series 86. Rockville, Md.: National Institute on Drug Abuse. DHHS Publication No. ADM 88-1578.

Hubbard, Robert L., William C. Eckerman, and J. Valley Rachal. 1977. Methods of validating self-reports of drug use: A critical review. *Proceedings of the American Statistical Association, 1976.* Washington, D.C.: American Statistical Association, 406–9.

Hubbard, Robert L., William C. Eckerman, J. Valley Rachal, and Jay R. Williams. 1978. Factors affecting the validity of self-reports of drug use: An overview. *Proceedings of the American Statistical Association, 1977.* Washington, D.C.: American Statistical Association, 360–65.

Hubbard, Robert L., Henrick J. Harwood, and Alvin M. Cruze. 1977. *Impacts of drug use, drug treatment and vocational services on employment related behavior of drug abusers and addicts.* Research Triangle Park, N.C.: Research Triangle Institute.

Hubbard, Robert L., Milas G. Kirkpatrick, Albert Williams, and J. Valley Rachal. 1981. Variations in response rates among types of programs in a national longitudinal study of drug treatment programs. In *Proceedings of the American Statistical Association, 1980.* Section on Survey Research Methods. Washington, D.C.: American Statistical Association.

Hubbard, Robert L., and Mary Ellen Marsden. 1986. Relapse to use of heroin, cocaine and other drugs in the first year after treatment. In Frank M. Tims and Carl G. Leukefeld, eds., *Relapse and Recovery in Drug Abuse.* Research Monograph 72. Rockville, Md.: National Institute on Drug Abuse, 157–66. DHHS Publication No. ADM 86-1473.

Hubbard, Robert L., Mary Ellen Marsden, and Margaret Allison. 1984. *Reliability and validity of TOPS data.* RTI/1901/01-15S. Research Triangle Park, N.C.: Research Triangle Institute.

Hubbard, Robert L., Mary Ellen Marsden, Elizabeth R. Cavanaugh, J. Valley Rachal, and Harold M. Ginzburg. 1987. Drug use after drug abuse treatment. Report submitted to the National Institute on Drug Abuse. Research Triangle Park, N.C.: Research Triangle Institute.

———. 1988. Role of drug abuse treatment in limiting the spread of AIDS. *Reviews of Infectious Diseases* 10:377–84.

Hubbard, Robert L., J. Valley Rachal, S. Gail Craddock, and Elizabeth R. Cavanaugh. 1984. Treatment Outcome Prospective Study (TOPS): Client characteristics and behaviors before, during, and after treatment. In Frank M. Tims and Jacqueline P. Ludford, eds., *Drug abuse treatment evaluation: Strategies, progress, and prospects.* Research Monograph 51. Rockville, Md.: National Institute on Drug Abuse, 42–68. DHHS Publication No. ADM 84-1329.

Hunt, Dana E., Douglas S. Lipton, and Barry Spunt. 1982. Patterns of criminal activity among methadone clients and current narcotics users not in treatment. Paper presented at the American Society of Criminology Annual Meeting, Toronto, Canada, November.

Hunt, Dana E., David L. Strug, Douglas S. Goldsmith, Douglas S. Lipton, Kenneth Robertson, and Linda Truitt. 1986. Alcohol use and abuse: Heavy drinking among methadone clients. *American Journal of Drug and Alcohol Abuse* 12:147–64.

Hunt, Dana E., David L. Strug, Douglas S. Goldsmith, Douglas S. Lipton, Barry Spunt, Linda Truitt, and Kenneth A. Robertson. 1984. An instant shot of 'Aah': Cocaine use among methadone clients. *Journal of Psychoactive Drugs* 16:217–27.

Hunt, Leon Gibson. 1978. Incidence of first use of nonopiate drugs: Inferences from current data. In Donald R. Wesson, Albert S. Carlin, Kenneth M. Adams, and George M. Beschner, eds., *Polydrug abuse: The results of a national collaborative study.* New York: Academic Press, 183–210.

Inciardi, James A. 1977. *Methadone diversion: Experiences and issues.* Services Research Monograph. Rockville, Md.: National Institute on Drug Abuse. DHEW Publication No. ADM 77-488.

Jackson, George W., and Alex Richman. 1973. Alcohol use among narcotics addicts. *Alcohol Health and Research World,* 1(1):25–28.

Jaffe, Jerome H. 1979. The swinging pendulum: The treatment of drug users in America. In Robert L. DuPont, Avram Goldstein, and John O'Donnell, eds., *Handbook on drug abuse.* Rockville, Md.: National Institute on Drug Abuse, 3–16.

———. 1984. Evaluating drug abuse treatment: A comment on the state of the art. In Frank M. Tims and Jacqueline P. Ludford, eds., *Drug abuse treatment evaluation: Strategies, progress, and prospects.* Research Monograph 51. Rockville, Md.: National Institute on Drug Abuse.

———. 1987. Footnotes in the evolution of the American National Response: Some little known aspects of the first American Strategy for Drug Abuse and Drug Traffick Prevention. The Inaugural Thomas Okey Memorial Lecture. *British Journal of Addiction* 82:587–600.

Joe, George W., and Michael G. Gent. 1978. *Drug treatment histories for a sample of drug users in DARP.* IBR Report No. 78-634. Fort Worth: Texas Christian University, Institute of Behavioral Research.

Johnson, Bruce D., Paul J. Goldstein, Edward Preble, James Schmeidler, Douglas S. Lipton, Barry Spunt, and Thomas Miller. 1985. *Taking care of business: The economics of crime by heroin abusers.* Lexington, Mass.: Lexington Books.

Johnson, Gregory. 1976. Conversion as a cure: The therapeutic community and the professional ex-addict. *Contemporary Drug Problems* 5:32–50.

Johnston, Lloyd D., Patrick M. O'Malley, and Jerald G. Bachman. 1988. *Illicit drug use, smoking, and drinking by America's high school students, college students, and young adults, 1979–1987.* Rockville, Md.: National Institute on Drug Abuse.

Jones, Kenneth R., and Thomas R. Vischi. 1979. Impact of alcohol, drug abuse, and mental health treatment on medical care utilization. *Medical Care* 17:1–82.

Joseph, Herman, and Phillip Appel. 1985. Alcoholism and methadone treatment: Consequences for the patient and program. *American Journal of Drug and Alcohol Abuse* 11:37–53.

Judson, Barbara A., Serapio Ortiz, Linda Crouse, Thomas M. Carney, and Avram Goldstein. 1980. A follow-up study of heroin addicts five years after first admission to a methadone treatment program. *Drug and Alcohol Dependence* 6:295–313.

Kajdan, Robert A., and Edward C. Senay. 1976. Modified therapeutic communities for youth. *Journal of Psychedelic Drugs* 8:209–14.

Kleber, Herbert D. 1984. Is there a need for "professional psychotherapy" in methadone programs. *Journal of Substance Abuse Treatment* 1:73–76.

Kleber, Herbert D., and Frank H. Gawin. 1984. The spectrum of cocaine abuse and its treatment. *Journal of Clinical Psychiatry* 45:18–23.

Kleber, Herbert D., and Frank Slobetz. 1979. Outpatient drug free treatment. In Robert L. DuPont, Avram Goldstein, and John O'Donnell, eds., *Handbook on drug abuse.* Washington, D.C.: U.S. Government Printing Office, 31–38.

Kleinman, Paula H., Eric D. Wish, Sherry Deren, and Gregory A. Rainone. 1986. Multiple drug use: Asymptomatic behavior. *Journal of Psychoactive Drugs* 18:77–86.

Kosten, Thomas R., Frank H. Gawin, Bruce J. Rounsaville, and Herbert D. Kleber. 1986. Cocaine abuse among opioid addicts: Demographic and diagnostic factors in treatment. *American Journal of Drug and Alcohol Abuse* 12:1–16.

Kosten, Thomas R., Bruce J. Rounsaville, and Herbert D. Kleber. 1987a. Multidimensionality and prediction of treatment outcome in opioid addicts: 2.5-year follow-up. *Comprehensive Psychiatry* 28:3–13.

———. 1987b. A 2.5-year follow-up of cocaine use among treated opioid addicts. Have our treatments helped? *Archives of General Psychiatry* 44:281–84.

———. 1988. Antecedents and consequences of cocaine abuse among opioid addicts: A 2.5-year follow-up. *The Journal of Nervous and Mental Diseases* 176:176–81.

Labouvie, Eric W. 1978. Experimental sequential strategies for the exploration on ontogenetic and social-historical changes. *Human Development* 21:161–69.

Lau, John P., and John Benvenuto. 1978. Three estimates of prevalence of nonopiate drug abuse. In Donald R. Wesson, Albert S. Carlin, Kenneth M. Adams, and George Beschner, eds., *Polydrug abuse: The results of a national collaborative study.* New York: Academic Press, 211–18.

Laundergan, Jay C. 1982. *Easy does it: Alcoholism treatment outcomes, Hazelden and the Minnesota Model.* Duluth, Minn.: Hazelden Foundation.

Leukefeld, Carl G., and Frank M. Tims, eds. 1988. *Compulsory treatment of drug abuse: Research and clinical practice.* Research Monograph Series 86. Rockville, Md.: National Institute on Drug Abuse. DHHS Publication No. ADM 88-1578.

Longwell, Bill, John Miller, and Andrew W. Nichols. 1978. Counselor effectiveness in a methadone maintenance program. *International Journal of the Addictions* 13:307–15.

LoSciuto, Leonard A., Leona S. Aiken, and Mary Ann Ausetts. 1979. *Professional and paraprofessional drug abuse counselors: Three reports.* Services Research Monograph. Rockville, Md.: National Institute on Drug Abuse. DHEW Publication No. ADM 79-858.

Lowinson, Joyce H., and Robert B. Millman. 1979. Clinical aspects of methadone maintenance treatment. In Robert L. DuPont, Avram Goldstein, and John O'Donnell, eds., *Handbook on drug abuse.* Washington, D.C.: U.S. Government Printing Office, 49–56.

Luetgert, Mary J., and Ann H. Armstrong. 1973. Methodological issues in drug usage surveys: Anonymity, recency, and frequency. *International Journal of the Addictions* 8:683–89.

Lukoff, Irving F., and Paula H. Kleinman. 1977. The addict life cycle and problems in treatment evaluation. In A. Schecter and S. J. Mule, eds., *Rehabilitation aspects of drug dependence.* Cleveland, Ohio: CRC Press.

McAuliffe, William E., and James M. N. Ch'ien. 1986. Recovery training and self-help: A relapse-prevention program for treated opiate addicts. *Journal of Substance Abuse Treatment* 3:9–20.

McAuliffe, William E., James M. N. Ch'ien, Elaine Launer, Rob Friedman, and Barry Feldman. 1985. The Harvard Group Aftercare Program: Preliminary evaluation results and implementation issues. In Rebecca S. Ashery, ed., *Progress in the development of cost-effective treatment for drug abusers.* Research Monograph Series 58. Rockville, Md.: National Institute on Drug Abuse. DHHS Publication No. ADM 85-1401.

McGlothlin, William H., and M. Douglas Anglin. 1981. Shutting off methadone: Costs and benefits. *Archives of General Psychiatry* 38:885–92.

McGlothlin, William H., M. Douglas Anglin, and Bruce D. Wilson. 1977. A followup of admissions to the California Civil Addict program. *American Journal of Drug and Alcohol Abuse* 4:197–99.

McLellan, A. Thomas, A. R. Childress, J. Griffith, and George E. Woody. 1984. The psychiatrically severe drug abuse patient: Methadone maintenance or therapeutic community? *American Journal of Drug and Alcohol Abuse* 10:77–95.

McLellan, A. Thomas, Lester Luborsky, John Cacciola, Jeffrey Griffith, Peggy McGahan, and Charles P. O'Brien. 1985. *Guide to the addiction severity index: Background, administration, and field testing results.* Treatment Research Report. Rockville, Md.: National Institute on Drug Abuse.

McLellan, A. Thomas, Lester Luborsky, Charles P. O'Brien, Harriet L. Barr, and Fredrich Evans. 1986. Alcohol and drug abuse treatment in three different populations: Is it predictable? *American Journal of Drug and Alcohol Abuse* 12:101–20.

McLellan, A. Thomas, Lester Luborsky, Charles P. O'Brien, George E. Woody, and Keith A. Druley. 1982. Is treatment for substance abuse effective? *Journal of American Medical Association* 247:1423–28.

McLellan, A. Thomas, George E. Woody, Lester Luborsky, and Leslie Goehl. 1988. Is the counselor an "active ingredient" in substance abuse rehabilitation? An examination of treatment success among four counselors. *The Journal of Nervous and Mental Diseases* 176:423–30.

McLellan, A. Thomas, George E. Woody, Lester Luborsky, Charles P.

O'Brien, and Keith A. Druley. 1983. Increased effectiveness of substance abuse treatment: A prospective study of patient-treatment "matching." *Journal of Nervous and Mental Disease* 171:597–605.

Maddux, James F. 1988. Clinical experience with civil commitment. In Carl G. Leukefeld and Frank M. Tims, eds., *Compulsory treatment of drug abuse: Research and clinical practice*. Research Monograph Series 86. Rockville, Md.: National Institute on Drug Abuse. DHHS Publication No. ADM 88-1578.

Maddux, James F., and David P. Desmond. 1975. Reliability and validity of information from chronic heroin users. *Journal of Psychiatric Research* 12:87–95.

Maddux, James F., and Boyce Elliott, III. 1975. Problem drinkers among patients on methadone. *American Journal of Drug and Alcohol Abuse* 2:245–54.

Magruder-Habib, Kathy, Robert L. Hubbard, and Harold M. Ginzburg. 1988. *Effects of drug abuse treatment on symptoms of depression and suicide*. Research Triangle Park, N.C.: Research Triangle Institute.

Mandell, W., P. G. Goldschmidt, and P. Grover. 1973. *Interdrug—An evaluation of treatment programs for drug abusers*. Baltimore, Md.: The Johns Hopkins University School of Hygiene and Public Health.

Marsden, Mary Ellen, and James J. Collins. 1987. *Drug use and predatory crime in the year after drug abuse treatment*. Research Triangle Park, N.C.: Research Triangle Institute.

Marsden, Mary Ellen, Robert L. Hubbard, and Susan L. Bailey. 1988. *Treatment histories of drug abusers*. Research Triangle Park, N.C.: Research Triangle Institute.

Marsden, Mary Ellen, Robert L. Hubbard, and William E. Schlenger. 1984. Alcohol use by TOPS drug treatment clients. Report submitted to the National Institute on Drug Abuse. Research Triangle Park, N.C.: Research Triangle Institute.

Marsden, Mary Ellen, Robert L. Hubbard, and William E. Schlenger. 1987. *Changes in alcohol use during and after drug abuse treatment*. Research Triangle Park, N.C.: Research Triangle Institute.

Metzger, David S., and Jerome J. Platt. 1987. Methadone dose levels and client characteristics in heroin addicts. *The International Journal of the Addictions* 22:187–94.

Meyer, Roger. 1983. Introduction: Factors affecting the outcome of methadone treatment. In James R. Cooper, Fred Altman, Barry S. Brown, and Dorynne Czechowicz, eds., *Research on the treatment of narcotic addiction: State of the art*. Treatment Research Monograph. Washington, D.C.: U.S. Government Printing Office, 495–99. DHHS Publication No. ADM 83-1281.

Mezochow, John, Sheldon Miller, Frank Seixas, and Richard J. Frances. 1987. The impact of cost containment on alcohol and drug treatment. *Hospital and Community Psychiatry* 38:506–10.

Midanik, Lorraine. 1981. Alcohol use and depressive symptoms. In Draft report on the 1979 national survey. Berkeley: University of California, School of Public Health, Social Research Group.

Milby, Jesse B. 1988. Methadone maintenance to abstinence. How many make it? *The Journal of Nervous and Mental Diseases* 176:409–22.

Miles, C. P. 1977. Conditions predisposing to suicide: A review. *Journal of Nervous and Mental Disease* 164:231–46.

Moore, Mark H. 1977. *Buy and Bust.* Lexington, Mass.: Lexington Books, D. C. Heath and Co.

Mulford, Harold A., and Donald E. Miller. 1960. Drinking in Iowa. II. The extent of drinking and selected sociocultural categories. *Quarterly Journal of Studies on Alcohol* 21:26–39.

Musto, David F. 1987. The American disease: Origins of narcotic control. New York: Oxford University Press.

Musto, David F., and Manuel R. Ramos. 1981. A follow-up study of the New Haven morphine maintenance clinic of 1920. *New England Journal of Medicine* 304:1071–77, 1098–99.

Myers, Jerome K., Myrna M. Weissman, Gary L. Tischler, Charles E. Holzer, Phillip J. Leaf, Helen Orvaschel, James C. Anthony, Jeffrey H. Boyd, Jack D. Burke, Jr., Morton Kramer, and Roger Stoltzman. 1984. Six-month prevalence in psychiatric disorders in three communities. *Archives of General Psychiatry* 41:959–70.

Nash, George. 1974. The sociology of Phoenix House—A therapeutic community for the resocialization of narcotic addicts. In George DeLeon, ed., *Phoenix House: Studies in a therapeutic community (1968–1973).* New York: MSS Information Corporation.

———. 1976. An analysis of twelve studies of the impact of drug abuse treatment upon criminality. In *Drug use and crime: Report of the Panel on Drug Use and Criminal Behavior.* Appendix. Research Triangle Park, N.C.: Research Triangle Institute.

———. 1978. Predicting success and failure in drug abuse treatment: Some unpleasant realities. Paper presented at the Conference on the Utilization of Research in Drug Policy Making, Washington, D.C., May.

Nathan, Peter E. 1983. Failures in prevention: Why we can't prevent the devastating effect of alcoholism and drug abuse. *American Psychologist* 459–67.

National Institute on Drug Abuse [NIDA]. 1982. *Data from the Client Oriented Data Acquisition Process (CODAP): Trend report. January 1978–September 1981.* NIDA Statistical Series E, no. 24. Washington, D.C.: U.S. Government Printing Office. DHHS Publication No. ADM 82-1214.

———. 1983. *Data from the National Drug and Alcoholism Treatment Utilization Survey (NDATUS): Main findings for drug abuse treatment units, September 1982.* NIDA Statistical Series F, no. 10. Washington, D.C.: U.S. Government Printing Office. DHHS Publication No. ADM 83-1284.

———. 1987. *National Household Survey on Drug Abuse 1985 population estimates.* Rockville, Md.: U.S. Government Printing Office. DHHS Publication No. ADM 87-1539.

———. 1988a. *Demographic characteristics and patterns of drug use of clients admitted to drug abuse treatment programs in selected states.* Rockville, Md.: U.S. Government Printing Office.

———. 1988b. *National Household Survey on Drug Abuse: Main findings 1985.* Rockville, Md.: National Institute on Drug Abuse. DHHS Publication No. ADM 88-1586.

Newman, Robert G. 1977. *Methadone treatment in narcotics addiction.* New York: Academic Press.

————. 1987. Methadone treatment: Defining and evaluating success. *New England Journal of Medicine* 317:447–50.

Newman, Robert G., and Walden B. Whitehill. 1979. Double-blind comparison of methadone and placebo maintenance treatments of narcotic addicts in Hong Kong. *The Lancet*. Saturday, 8 September, 485–489.

New York City Department of Health AIDS Surveillance. 1986. The AIDS epidemic in New York City, 1981–1984. *American Journal of Epidemiology* 123:1013–25.

Novick, David M., Emil F. Pascarelli, Herman Joseph, Edwin A. Salsitz, Beverly L. Richman, Don C. DesJarlais, Mary Anderson, Vincent P. Dole, and Marie E. Nyswander. 1988. Methadone maintenance patients in general medical practice: A preliminary report. *Journal of American Medical Association* 259:3299–302.

Nurco, David N., John W. Shaffer, Thomas E. Hanlon, T. W. Kinlock, K. R. Duszynski, and P. Stephenson. 1988. Relationships between client/counselor congruence and treatment outcome among narcotic addicts. *Comprehensive Psychiatry* 29:48–54.

O'Brien, William B., and D. Vincent Biase. 1984. The therapeutic community: A current perspective. *Journal of Psychoactive Drugs* 16:9–21.

Obuchowsky, Marta, and Joan E. Zweben. 1987. Bridging the gap: The methadone client in 12-step programs. *Journal of Psychoactive Drugs* 19:301–2.

O'Donnell, John A. 1969. *Narcotics addicts in Kentucky*. PHS Publication No. 1881. Washington, D.C.: U.S. Government Printing Office.

————. 1975. Locating subjects and obtaining cooperation. In *Prospective cohort study of drug abusers admitted to treatment: Developing a research protocol*. Final report submitted to NIDA. Research Triangle Park, N.C.: Research Triangle Institute.

Ogborne, Alan C., and Christopher Melotte. 1977. An evaluation of a therapeutic community for former drug users. *British Journal of Addiction* 72:75–82.

Osborn, June E. 1986. The AIDS epidemic: An overview of the science. *Issues in Science and Technology* 2:40–55.

Panel on Drug Use and Criminal Behavior. 1976. *Drug use and crime*. NTIS No. PB 259-167/5. Research Triangle Park, N.C.: Research Triangle Institute.

Parry, Hugh J., Mitchell B. Balter, and Ira H. Cisin. 1971. Primary levels of underreporting psychological drug use. *Public Opinion Quarterly* 34:582–92.

Patch, Vernon D., Anthony E. Raynes, and Alan Fisch. 1973. Methadone maintenance and crime reduction in Boston—Variables compounded. Paper presented at the Annual Meeting of the American Psychiatric Association.

Peterson, M. A., and Harriet B. Braiker. 1980. *Doing crime: A survey of California prison inmates*. Santa Monica, Calif.: Rand Corporation.

Polich, J. Michael, David J. Armor, and Harriet B. Braiker. 1981. *The course of alcoholism*. New York: Wiley.

Polich, J. Michael, Phyllis L. Ellickson, Peter Reuter, and James P. Kahan. 1984. *Strategies for controlling adolescent drug use*. R-3076-CHF. Santa Monica, Calif.: Rand.

President's Commission on Mental Health. 1978. *Report to the President*. Vol. 2. Appendix. Washington, D.C.: U.S. Government Printing Office.

Purcell, Archie T., Jill Anderson, Elizabeth R. Cavanaugh, and Robert L. Hubbard. 1983. *Treatment Outcome Prospective Study followup field and methodology report: 1979 and 1980 TOPS admission cohorts.* Research Triangle Park, N.C.: Research Triangle Institute.

Quinones, Mark A., Kathleen M. Doyle, Amiram Sheffet, and Donald B. Louria. 1979. Evaluation of drug abuse rehabilitation efforts: A review. *American Journal of Public Health* 69:1164–69.

Rachal, J. Valley, L. Lynn Guess, Robert L. Hubbard, Stephen A. Maisto, Elizabeth R. Cavanaugh, Richard Waddell, and Charles H. Benrud. 1980. *Adolescent drinking behavior.* Vol. 1. *The extent and nature of adolescent alcohol and drug use: The 1974 and 1978 national sample studies.* NTIS No. PB 81-199267. Research Triangle Park, N.C.: Research Triangle Institute.

Rachal, J. Valley, Jay R. Williams, Mary Lee Brehm, Betty Cavanaugh, R. Paul Moore, and William C. Eckerman. 1975. *A national study of adolescent drinking behavior, attitudes and correlates.* NTIS No. PB 246-002. Research Triangle Park, N.C.: Research Triangle Institute.

Rawson, Richard A., Arnold M. Washton, Richard B. Resnick, and Forest S. Tennant, Jr. 1981. Clonidine hydrochloride detoxification from methadone treatment: The value of naltrexone aftercare. In Louis S. Harris, ed., *Problems of Drug Dependence 1980.* Research Monograph 34. Rockville, Md.: National Institute on Drug Abuse, 101–8. DHHS Publication No. ADM 81-1058.

Reuter, Peter. 1984. The (continued) vitality of mythical numbers. *The Public Interest* 75:135–47.

Riordan, Charles E., Marjorie Mezritz, Frank Slobetz, and Herbert D. Kleber. 1976. Successful detoxification from methadone maintenance: Followup study of 38 patients. *Journal of the American Medical Association* 235:2604–7.

Robins, Lee N. 1974. A followup study of Vietnam veteran's drug use. *Journal of Drug Issues* 4:61–63.

Rosenbaum, Marcia, and Sheigla Murphy. 1987. Not the picture of health: Women on methadone. *Journal of Psychoactive Drugs* 19:217–26.

Rosenbaum, Marcia, Sheigla Murphy, and Jerome Beck. 1987. Money for methadone: Preliminary findings from a study of Alameda County's new maintenance policy. *Journal of Psychoactive Drugs* 19:13–19.

Roszell, Douglas K., Donald A. Calsyn, and Edmund F. Chaney. 1986. Alcohol use and psychopathology in opioid addicts on methadone maintenance. *American Journal of Drug and Alcohol Abuse* 12:269–78.

Rounsaville, Bruce J., Zelig S. Dolinsky, Thomas F. Babor, and Roger E. Meyer. 1987. Psychopathology as a predictor of treatment outcome in alcoholics. *Archives of General Psychiatry* 44:505–13.

Rounsaville, Bruce J., and Herbert D. Kleber. 1985. Untreated opiate addicts. *Archives of General Psychiatry* 42:1072–77.

———. 1986. Psychiatric disorders in white addicts: Preliminary findings on the course and interaction with program types. In R. Meyer, ed., *Psychopathy and addictive disorders.* New York: Guilford.

Rounsaville, Bruce J., Thomas R. Kosten, and Herbert D. Kleber. 1987. The antecedents and benefits of achieving abstinence in opioid addicts: A

2.5-year follow-up study. *American Journal of Drug and Alcohol Abuse* 13:213–29.

Rounsaville, Bruce J., Thomas R. Kosten, Janet B. W. Williams, and Robert L. Spitzer. 1987. A field trial of DSM-III-R psychoactive substance dependence disorders. *American Journal of Psychiatry* 144:351–55.

Rounsaville, Bruce J., Robert L. Spitzer, Janet B. W. Williams. 1986. Proposed changes in DSM-III substance use disorders: Description and rationale. *American Journal of Psychiatry* 143:463–68.

Safer, Jeanne M., and Harry Sands. 1979. *A comparison of mental health treatment center and drug abuse treatment center approaches to non-opiate drug abuse.* Services Research Report. Rockville, Md.: National Institute on Drug Abuse. DHEW Publication No. ADM 79-879.

Sandorf, Marilyn K., M. Lee Brehm, J. Valley Rachal, and Elizabeth R. Cavanaugh. 1978. *Comparison of mental health treatment and drug abuse treatment response to nonopiate drug abuse.* RTI/1325/01-01F. Research Triangle Park, N.C.: Research Triangle Institute.

Sansone, J. 1980. Retention patterns in a therapeutic community for the treatment of drug abuse. *International Journal of the Addictions* 15:711–36.

Savage, L. James, and D. Dwayne Simpson. 1978. Illicit drug use and return to treatment: National followup study of admissions to drug abuse treatments in the DARP during 1969–1971. *American Journal of Drug and Alcohol Abuse* 5:23–28.

Schaie, K. Warner. 1965. A general model for the study of developmental problems. *Psychological Bulletin* 64:92–107.

———. 1977. Quasi-experimental research designs. In J. F. Birren and K. W. Schaie, eds., *Handbook of the psychology of aging.* New York: Van Nostrand.

Schlenger, William E., Mary Ellen Marsden, J. Valley Rachal, Elizabeth R. Cavanaugh, and Robert L. Hubbard. 1984. *Alcohol use among drug treatment clients before and during drug abuse treatment.* RTI/1901/01-13S. Research Triangle Park, N.C.: Research Triangle Institute.

Schnoll, Sidney H., Judy Karrigan, Sarah B. Kitchen, Amin Daghestani, and Thomas Hansen. 1985. Characteristics of cocaine abusers presenting in treatment. In Nicholas J. Kozel and Edgar H. Adams, eds., *Cocaine use in America: Epidemiological and clinical perspectives.* Research Monograph 61. Rockville, Md.: National Institute on Drug Abuse, 171–81.

Schut, Jacob, Karen File, and Theodora Wohlmuth. 1973. Alcohol use by narcotic addicts in methadone maintenance treatment. *Quarterly Journal of Studies on Alcohol* 34:1356–59.

Scitovsky, Ann, and Dorothy Rice. 1987. Estimates of the direct and indirect costs of Acquired Immunodeficiency Syndrome in the United States, 1985, 1986, 1990. *Public Health Reports* 102:5–17.

Sells, Saul B. 1979. Treatment effectiveness. In Robert L. DuPont, Avram Goldstein, and John O'Donnell, eds., *Handbook on drug abuse.* Rockville, Md.: National Institute on Drug Abuse, 105–18.

Sells, Saul B., ed. 1974. *Effectiveness of drug abuse treatment.* Vols. 1 and 2. Cambridge, Mass.: Ballinger.

Sells, Saul B., Robert G. Demaree, and C. W. Hornick. 1979. *Comparative effectiveness of drug abuse treatment modalities.* Services Research Administrative Report. Rockville, Md.: National Institute on Drug Abuse.

Sells, Saul B., and D. Dwayne Simpson. 1977. *Evaluation of treatment for youth in the Drug Abuse Reporting Programs (DARP).* Fort Worth: Texas Christian University, Institute of Behavioral Research. IBR Report No. 77-9.

Sells, Saul B., and D. Dwayne Simpson. 1979. Evaluation of treatment outcome for youths in the drug abuse reporting program (DARP): A followup study. In G. M. Beschner and A. S. Friedman, eds., *Youth drug abuse: Problems, issues, and treatment.* Lexington, Mass.: D. C. Heath.

Sells, Saul B., and D. Dwayne Simpson, eds. 1976. *Effectiveness of drug abuse treatment.* Vols. 3–5. Cambridge, Mass.: Ballinger.

Semlitz, Linda, and Mark S. Gold. 1985. Adolescent cocaine abuse. In Louis S. Harris, ed., *Problems of Drug Dependence 1984.* Research Monograph 55. Rockville, Md.: National Institute on Drug Abuse, 271–75.

Siegel, Ronald K. 1985. Treatment of cocaine abuse: Historical and contemporary perspectives. *Journal of Psychoactive Drugs* 17:1–9.

Siguel, Eduardo N. 1977. Characteristics of clients admitted to treatment for cocaine abuse. In Robert C. Petersen and Richard C. Stillman, eds., *Cocaine: 1977.* Research Monograph 13. Rockville, Md.: National Institute on Drug Abuse, 201–10.

Siguel, Eduardo N., and William H. Spillane. 1978. The effect of prior treatment on treatment success. *International Journal of the Addictions* 13:797–805.

Simpson, D. Dwayne. 1974. Patterns of multiple drug abuse. In S. B. Sells, ed., *Effectiveness of drug abuse treatment.* Vol. 2. Cambridge, Mass.: Ballinger, 175–88.

———. 1979. The relation of time spent in drug abuse treatment to posttreatment outcome. *American Journal of Psychiatry* 136:1449–53.

———. 1980. *Followup outcomes and length of time in treatment for drug abuse.* IBR Report 80-9. Fort Worth: Texas Christian University, Institute of Behavioral Research.

———. 1981a. Employment by opioid addicts during a four year followup after drug abuse treatment. *Journal of Drug Issues* 11:435–49.

———. 1981b. Treatment for drug abuse: Followup outcomes and length of time spent. *Archives of General Psychiatry* 38:875–80.

———. 1984. National Treatment System Evaluation based on the Drug Abuse Reporting Program (DARP) followup research. In Frank M. Tims and Jacqueline P. Ludford, eds., *Drug abuse treatment evaluation: Strategies, progress and prospects.* Research Monograph 51. Rockville, Md.: National Institute on Drug Abuse. DHHS Publication No. ADM 84–1329.

Simpson, D. Dwayne, George W. Joe, Wayne E. K. Lehman, and Saul B. Sells. 1986. Addiction careers: Etiology, treatment, and 12-year follow-up outcomes. *Journal of Drug Issues* 16:107–22.

Simpson, D. Dwayne, and Michael R. Lloyd. 1977. *Alcohol and illicit drug use: National followup study of admissions to drug abuse treatments in the DARP during 1969–1971.* Services Research Report. Rockville, Md.: National Institute on Drug Abuse. DHEW Publication No. ADM 77-496.

———. 1981. Alcohol use following treatment for drug addiction: A four year follow-up. *Journal of Studies on Alcohol* 42:323–35.

Simpson, D. Dwayne, Michael R. Lloyd, and Michael J. Gent. 1976. *Reliability and validity of data: National followup study of admissions to drug abuse treatments in the DARP during 1969–1972.* IBR Report 76-18. Fort Worth: Texas Christian University, Institute of Behavioral Research.

Simpson, D. Dwayne, and L. James Savage. 1978. *Outcomes and return to treatment during a three year followup: National followup study of admissions to drug abuse treatments in the DARP during 1969–1972.* IBR Report 78-2. Fort Worth: Texas Christian University, Institute of Behavioral Research.

———. 1980. Drug abuse treatment readmissions and outcomes. *Archives of General Psychiatry* 37:896–901.

Simpson, D. Dwayne, L. James Savage, and George W. Joe. 1980. Treatment histories of clients treated for drug abuse. *American Journal of Drug and Alcohol Abuse* 7:127–40.

Simpson, D. Dwayne, L. James Savage, George W. Joe, Robert G. Demaree, and Saul B. Sells. 1976. *DARP Data Book: Statistics on characteristics of drug users in treatment during 1969–1974.* IBR Report 76-4. Fort Worth: Texas Christian University, Institute of Behavioral Research.

Simpson, D. Dwayne, L. James Savage, Michael R. Lloyd, and Saul B. Sells. 1978. Evaluation of drug abuse treatments based on first year followup. Services Research Monograph Series. Rockville, Md.: National Institute on Drug Abuse. DHEW Publication No. ADM 78-701.

Simpson, D. Dwayne, and Saul B. Sells. 1974. Patterns of multiple drug abuse: 1969–1971. *International Journal of the Addictions* 9:301–4.

———. 1982. Effectiveness of treatment for drug abuse: An overview of the DARP research program. *Advances in Alcohol and Substance Abuse* 2:7–29.

Singer, Burton. 1986. Self-selection and performance-based ratings: A case study in program evaluation. In H. Wainer, ed., *Drawing inferences from self-selected samples.* New York: Springer-Verlag.

Skinner, Harvey A., and Adele E. Goldberg. 1986. Evidence for a drug dependence syndrome among narcotic users. *British Journal of Addiction* 81:479–84.

Smart, Reginald G. 1976. Outcome studies of therapeutic community and halfway house treatment for addicts. *International Journal of the Addictions* 11:143–59.

Smith, David E. 1986. Cocaine-alcohol abuse: Epidemiological, diagnostic and treatment considerations. *Journal of Psychoactive Drugs* 18:117–29.

Sorensen, James L., Alphonso Acampora, Mella Trier, and Mark Gold. 1987. From maintenance to abstinence in a therapeutic community: Follow-up outcomes. *Journal of Psychoactive Drugs* 19:345–51.

Spencer, Bruce D. 1989. On the accuracy of estimates of numbers of intravenous drug users. In Charles F. Turner, Heather G. Miller, and Lincoln E. Moses, eds., *AIDS: Sexual behavior and intravenous drug use.* Washington, D.C.: National Academy Press.

Spiegel, Douglas K. 1974. Drug use by sex, age, and race. In Saul B. Sells, ed., *Effectiveness of drug abuse treatment: Research on patients, treatments, and outcomes.* Vol. 2. Cambridge, Mass.: Ballinger, 21–29.

Stephens, Richard C. 1972. The truthfulness of addict respondents in research projects. *International Journal of the Addictions* 7:549–58.

Stimmel, Barry, Murry Cohen, Victor Sturiano, Raymond Hanbury, David

Korts, and George Jackson. 1983. Is treatment for alcoholism effective in persons on methadone maintenance? *American Journal of Psychiatry* 140:862–66.

Strategy Council on Drug Abuse. 1979. *Federal strategy for drug abuse and drug traffic prevention.* Washington, D.C.: U.S. Government Printing Office.

Strug, David L., Dana E. Hunt, Douglas S. Goldsmith, Douglas S. Lipton, and Barry Spunt. 1985. Patterns of cocaine use among methadone clients. *International Journal of the Addictions* 20:1163–75.

Tims, Frank M. 1981. *Effectiveness of Drug Abuse Treatment Programs.* National Institute on Drug Abuse Treatment Research Report. Washington, D.C.: Superintendent of Documents. DHHS Publication No. ADM 84-1143.

———. 1984. Introduction. In Frank M. Tims and Jacqueline P. Ludford, eds., *Drug abuse treatment evaluation: Strategies, progress, and prospects.* Research Monograph 51. Rockville, Md.: National Institute on Drug Abuse.

Tims, Frank M., and Carl G. Leukefeld, eds. 1986. *Relapse and recovery in drug abuse.* Research Monograph 72. Rockville, Md.: National Institute on Drug Abuse.

Tims, Frank M., and Jacqueline P. Ludford, eds. 1984. *Drug abuse treatment evaluation: Strategies, progress, and prospects.* Research Monograph 51. Rockville, Md.: National Institute on Drug Abuse.

Turner, Charles F., Heather G. Miller, and Lincoln E. Moses, eds. 1989. *AIDS: Sexual behavior and intravenous drug use.* Washington, D.C.: National Academy Press.

Uhde, Thomas W., D. Eugene Redmond, Jr., and Herbert D. Kleber. 1982. Psychosis in the opioid addicted patient: Assessment and treatment. *Journal of Clinical Psychiatry* 43:240–47.

U.S. Bureau of the Census. 1979. *Characteristics of the population below the poverty level: 1977.* Current Population Reports, Series P-60, no. 119. Washington, D.C.: U.S. Government Printing Office.

U.S. Department of Health and Human Services. 1980. Alcohol, Drug Abuse, and Mental Health Administration and Food and Drug Administration. Methadone for treating narcotic addicts: Joint revision of conditions for use. *Federal Register* 45(184), pt. 3, September 19.

U.S. Department of Justice, Bureau of Justice Statistics. 1983a. *Justice Expenditures and Employment in the U.S., 1979.* Washington, D.C.: Bureau of Justice Statistics.

———. 1983b. *Sourcebook of Criminal Justice Statistics.* Washington, D.C.: Bureau of Justice Statistics.

———. 1984. *The Economic Cost of Crime to Victims.* Washington, D.C.: Bureau of Justice Statistics.

U.S. Department of the Treasury, Internal Revenue Service. 1983. *Income Tax Compliance Research.* Washington, D.C.: Internal Revenue Service.

U.S. General Accounting Office. 1980. *Action needed to improve management and effectiveness of drug abuse treatment.* Washington, D.C.: U.S. Department of Commerce. NTIS PB80-167299.

U.S. General Accounting Office. 1985. *Reported federal drug abuse expenditures— fiscal years 1981 to 1985.* Washington, D.C.: Government Printing Office.

U.S. General Accounting Office. 1988. *Controlling drug abuse: A status report.* Washington, D.C.: Government Printing Office.

Vaillant, George E. 1966. A 12-year follow-up of New York narcotic addicts. III. Some social and psychiatric characteristics. *Archives of General Psychiatry* 15:559–609.

———. 1983. *The natural history of alcoholism.* Cambridge, Mass.: Harvard University Press.

Voss, Harwin L., and Richard C. Stephens. 1973. Criminal history of narcotic addicts. *Drug Forum* 2:1–202.

Washton, Arnold M., Mark S. Gold, and A. Carter Pottash. 1985. The 800-COCAINE helpline: Survey of 500 callers. In Louis S. Harris, ed., *Problems of Drug Dependence 1984.* Research Monograph 55. Rockville, Md.: National Institute on Drug Abuse, 224–30.

Washton, Arnold M., and Andrew Tatarsky. 1984. Adverse effects of cocaine abuse. In Louis B. Harris, ed., *Problems of drug dependence 1983.* Research Monograph 49. Rockville, Md.: National Institute on Drug Abuse, 247–54.

Watkins, J. D. [Chairman]. 1988. *Report of the Presidential Commission on the Human Immunodeficiency Virus Epidemic.* Washington, D.C.: U.S. Government Printing Office.

Weissman, Myrna M., Jerome K. Myers, and P. S. Harding. 1978. Psychiatric disorders in a U.S. urban community: 1975–1976. *American Journal of Psychiatry* 135:462.

Weissman, Myrna M., Frank Slobetz, B. Prusoff, M. Mezritz, and P. Howard. 1976. Clinical depression among narcotic addicts maintained on methadone in the community. *American Journal of Psychiatry* 133:1434–38.

Wesson, Donald R., Albert S. Carlin, Kenneth M. Adams, and George M. Beschner, eds. 1978. *Polydrug abuse: The results of a national collaborative study.* New York: Academic Press.

Wesson, Donald R., David E. Smith, Steven E. Lerner, and Vernon R. Kettner. 1974. Treatment of polydrug users in San Francisco. *American Journal of Drug and Alcohol Abuse* 1:159–79.

Wexler, Harry K. 1986. Therapeutic communities within prisons. In George De Leon and James T. Ziegenfuss, Jr., eds., *Therapeutic communities for addictions: Readings in theory, research and practice.* Springfield, Ill.: Charles C. Thomas, 227–37.

Wexler, Harry K., and Ronald Williams. 1986. The stay'n out therapeutic community: Prison treatment for substance abusers. *Journal of Psychoactive Drugs* 18:221–30.

Wheeler, Barbara L., D. Vincent Biase, and Arthur P. Sullivan. 1986. Changes in self-concept during therapeutic community treatment: A comparison of male and female drug abusers. *Journal of Drug Education* 16:191–96.

Williams, Jay R. 1975. *Prospective cohort study of drug abusers admitted to treatment: Developing a research protocol.* RTI/1146/01–01F. Research Triangle Park, N.C.: Research Triangle Institute.

Wilson, G. Terence. 1987. Cognitive processes in addiction. *British Journal of Addiction* 82:343–52.

Winston, Arnold, George Jackson, K. Suljaga, M. Kaswan, and Mary Lou Skovron. 1986. Identification and treatment of alcoholics who use opiates. *Mount Sinai Journal of Medicine* 53:90–93.

Woody, George E. 1983. Treatment characteristics associated with outcome. In James R. Cooper, Fred Altman, Barry S. Brown, and Dorynne Czechowicz, eds., *Research on the treatment of narcotic addiction: State of the art.* Treatment Research Monograph. Washington, D.C.: U.S. Government Printing Office, 541–64. DHHS Publication No. ADM 83-1281.

Woody, George E., and Jack Blaine. 1979. Depression in narcotic addicts: Quite possibly more than a chance association. In Robert L. DuPont, Avram Goldstein, and John O'Donnell, eds., *Handbook on drug abuse.* Rockville, Md.: National Institute on Drug Abuse, 277–85.

Yablonsky, Lewis. 1965. *The tunnel back: Synanon.* New York: Macmillan.

Zuckerman, M., S. Sola, J. W. Masterson, and J. V. Angelone. 1975. MMPI patterns in drug abusers before and after treatment in therapeutic communities. *Journal of Consulting Clinical Psychology* 43:286–96.

Zweben, Joan E. 1986. Treating cocaine dependence: New challenges for the therapeutic community. *Journal of Psychoactive Drugs* 18:239–45.

Zweben, Joan E., and David E. Smith. 1986. Changing attitudes and policies toward alcohol use in the therapeutic community. *Journal of Psychoactive Drugs* 18:253–60.

# Index

Abstinence, ix, 10, 45, 63, 69, 124, 148, 150, 163. *See also* Methadone-to-abstinence

Abstinence rates, 100–101; and heroin use, 103, 125; and cocaine use, 108–10, 125; and psychotherapeutic drug use, 114–15, 125; and marijuana use, 117, 125, 140, 150; and criminal activity, 128, 150; and alcohol use, 140, 150; and depressive symptoms, 145

Acquired Immune Deficiency Syndrome (AIDS): and drug abuse treatment, xiv, 2–3, 11, 43, 99, 100, 167, 177; and health care costs, 1, 3, 11, 166; and intravenous drug use, 2–3, 11, 98, 99, 100, 122–24, 125, 162, 171; prevention of, 11, 153, 162, 163, 167–68; and cocaine use, 111

Addiction Severity Index, 169

Admission cohorts, in TOPS research, xi, 8, 17–19, 41; interviews of, 36–37; and trends in client populations, 72, 91–92, 97; and changes in intravenous drug use, 123–24

Admissions, prior, 75–76, 77, 146; and decrease in heroin use, 104, 105; and posttreatment cocaine use, 110; and posttreatment employment, 137; and posttreatment suicidal symptoms, 145

Aftercare services, 54, 63, 68, 69–70, 172–73, 175, 177

Age, of clients, 21, 28, 72–73; and posttreatment psychotherapeutic drug use, 115; and posttreatment marijuana use, 116–19; and treatment histories, 147, 148; and client readmission, 149–50

Alcoholics Anonymous, 5, 55, 175

Alcohol use, 28, 30–31, 86–87, 92, 93; and treatment programs, 5, 10, 11, 13, 99, 138–42, 150–51, 164–65, 175; patterns of, 35–36; as primary form of drug abuse, 79–81; and length of client treatment, 96, 97

Amphetamines, 1, 3, 111, 112, 113; as primary drug of abuse, 79–81

Analyses: analysis framework, 33–35; descriptive analysis, 36–37; explanatory analyses, 37–40. *See also* Data, for TOPS research: analyses of; Regression analyses, in TOPS research

Anti-Drug Abuse Act of 1988, 163, 169, 176

Barbiturates, 1, 3, 22, 111, 112, 113

Behavior, of clients: changes in, 9, 10, 11, 12, 13, 15, 18, 22, 26–27, 36–37; analyses of, 33–40. *See also* Alcohol use; Criminal activity; Depression; Drug use; Employment

Beth Israel Hospital, 4, 44

Block grants, xiv, 12, 71

Bureau of Prisons, 55, 64

California Civil Addict Program, 99, 102, 105

Client Oriented Data Acquisition Process (CODAP), 18, 21–22, 32, 102, 106

Client populations, 42, 72, 90–94, 97, 171, 173; and effectiveness rates, 110

Clients: interviews of, xi, 18–19, 21, 29–30, 36–37, 40–41; psychological problems of, 9, 22, 173–74, 175; during the 1970s, 71; admission characteristics of, 75–78; drug-related problems of, 88–89, 92, 93; and length of treatment, 94–97; treatment histories of, 146–48, 169; readmissions of, 148–50; retention of, 171–72, 176. *See also* Behavior, of clients; Criminal justice system, referrals by; Sociodemographic characteristics, of clients

Client survey data, 24–33; points of interview, 25–27; content, 27–28; reliability and validity, 30–33

Client/Treatment Study phase, 15, 18, 21–22

Clinical/Medical Record Review Form, 25, 32

Cocaine use, 43, 99, 106–11, 113, 125, 167, 173; and treatment programs, 1, 2, 3, 107, 124, 164, 175; as primary form of drug abuse, 79–80, 106, 108

Cohorts, in TOPS research, 17–18. *See also* Admission cohorts, in TOPS research

Comprehensive Employment and Training Act (CETA), 55, 64

Cost-effectiveness, of drug abuse treatment, 5, 33, 41, 152, 159–62, 166, 177

Cost-of-illness framework, 153, 166

Costs, of drug abuse: crime-related, 1, 152–54, 155–58, 161–62, 166; for treat-